G

His

Melvin Banks

Marshall Pickering

An Imprint of HarperCollins*Publishers*

Marshall Pickering is an Imprint of
HarperCollins*Religious*
Part of HarperCollins*Publishers*
77–85 Fulham Palace Road
London W6 8JB

First published in Great Britain
in 1999 by Marshall Pickering

1   3   5   7   9   10   8   6   4   2

Copyright © 1999 Melvin Banks

Melvin Banks asserts the moral right to be
identified as the author of this work

A catalogue record for this book is
available from the British Library

ISBN 0 551 03206 5

Printed and bound in Great Britain by
Caledonian International Book Manufacturing Ltd, Glasgow

CONDITIONS OF SALE
This book is sold subject to the condition that it
shall not, by way of trade or otherwise, be lent, re-sold,
hired out or otherwise circulated without the publisher's
prior consent in any form of binding or cover other
than that in which it is published and without a
similar condition including this condition being
imposed on the subsequent purchaser.

All rights reserved. No part of this publication may be
reproduced, stored in a retrieval system, or transmitted,
in any form or by any means, electronic, mechanical,
photocopying, recording or otherwise, without the prior
permission of the publishers.

Contents

I dedicate this book to the anointed ministers Pastor Herbert and Mrs Mary Harrison. As my pastors they first revealed to me the living God in action on a local church level, in the Bethshan Church, Newcastle upon Tyne. Wonderful soul-winners, their lives inspire me and – by God's Word the Bible which they taught me – cause me every day to see 'God in action'.

MIRACLES ON THE STREETS

Dusk was falling as I journeyed along the quiet lanes of Lincolnshire. It was March, and spread all around me were the familiar ploughed fields and rows of turnips. Familiar, too, was the smell of manure in the air.

It was 12 years since I had left the county where God had given birth to my ministry. Now, having preached around the world and affected hundreds of thousands of people, I was back for my first major crusade there.

I say major, but I was really expecting something low key and quiet. Each year, out of 100 missions around the world, I try to go to two or three rural areas; and rural Lincolnshire is very quiet. Once, the whole of the county had been the same – I remember preaching to 16 people in the city of Lincoln itself 25 years ago. But the years of pioneering work I had done during the sixties and seventies had paid off, and all over the county, strong churches had been built up. The prayers of God's people, continuing crusading and good pastoral leadership had brought this healthy state to so many churches.

But some areas had not been reached by the gospel and this was one of them. Despite that, the elderly pastor who had arranged the meetings had made a point of not inviting any other churches – only a handful of his own church members and, he hoped, flocks of non-Christians. I admired his faith, but could not help wondering if the old pastor was stretching things too far, relying on a completely alien, uncommitted, unchurched community to fill the large school hall every night. Oh well, I thought, it would be nice to have a change from the usual hectic pace. I could use a little peace and tranquillity, and might get another chapter of my current book written. How wrong could I be?

It was dark by the time I reached the small village high street. Dim street lamps revealed the old war memorial just ahead, set back from the road and surrounded with spring flowers. Across the road stood a group of teenagers, and I wound the window down and called out, 'Which way to the school hall where the miracles are going to happen?'

One of them wandered across, looking puzzled. Then he replied, 'Oh, that's right. I read about that and folk have been talking about it around here. Is it true? Does it really happen?'

'Well, come and see! God can do anything, you know!' He looked surprised, but grinned and gave me directions to the school.

A few hundred yards on I found the school and swung into the car park. There was one other car there, waiting with its lights on. As I got out, one of its doors opened and a voice called out, 'What time is it opening?'

'It starts in an hour and a half,' I replied. 'You're early, but it won't be long.'

Then I heard two pairs of feet crunching through the darkness. What? More people early? This was amazing for Lincolnshire, where even the committed had difficulty getting to church on time.

Soon, the large hall was filling up. One of the country pastors had wondered how many we would get; he was amazed when he saw that there was standing room only. Many found Jesus; many were healed. But that first evening was just a foretaste of what was to come.

There was a cold, crisp, Lincolnshire wind blowing when I stepped out of the car for the second meeting the following afternoon. But there was nothing cold about the interest. I found the hall full from wall to wall – every inch of space filled. People overflowed into the porch, many had to listen to the service from the streets outside. It was tantamount to a revival.

Some of those in wheelchairs could not get in, so I went out to pray for them as the service began, so that they would not have to wait all the way through it in the bitter wind. A woman instantly threw down her crutches and walked from her wheelchair. Another man could move his paralysed legs. Revival had begun in the streets outside! People came to the windows of their houses; passers-by stopped in the street to watch. And as I moved into the building, one blind person after another saw; the deaf heard; the lame walked. What a meeting! What a welcome home! Altogether, 50 were converted that day.

One of my allies was the *Lincolnshire Echo*, which took a sceptical, anti-Christian stance from the first. No mention of this being a worldwide ministry, begun in their county, which had returned to bring benefit to their people. They were just interested in a critical story and, though they reported some of the healings, that was what they printed. But the effect was to prompt more people to attend the meetings, not fewer, and soon the hall was packed for each meeting.

I arrived early for one afternoon service. It was fortunate, for as I walked through the village, a lady shouted, 'You'd better hurry up: folk are queuing up and hammering on the door of the hall. It's cold out here, isn't it?'

I ran the rest of the way and when I got there, what should I see but the doors of the hall wide open and, already, people unable to get in. *And there were still two hours to go before the start of the meeting.* People were sitting on tables, windowsills, even the stage, and were also crammed into the side rooms and kitchens. It took me 10 minutes to squeeze in myself. I made for the stage and called for calm.

By the time the service began, there were more people outside the hall than inside. A note was passed to me on the stage – it was from Lilian, who had not been able to get inside herself. 'Can you come and pray for sick outside. Many wheelchairs, many cannot get in. Very cold outside.'

It is a good job I am a small man, because the only way I could get out was by being lifted bodily over the heads of the crowd in the building. As soon as I got outside I began laying hands on people. And straight away amazing things happened, which staggered even Lilian and me. People left wheelchairs, sticks were thrown away, people shouted out that their pain was gone ... I had seen such miracles in Britain before inside a hall, but here it was all happening out in the streets, on the pavements of that Lincoln suburb. Neighbours came to their doors or craned out of windows, crowds came out of the shops, people from a local factory peered over the wall, and the press came and had a field day.

Among those facing me on that bitterly cold Lincolnshire street was Mrs Beryl Smith. This short, well-built lady sat gracefully in her wheelchair. She looked so red faced, deathly, icily cold, through waiting for so long. Like the others in the line on the pavement, she had never met me before. But she had heard of strange movings of God in this Lincolnshire village, and was so desperate that she had waited patiently for a long time, wondering if her time for healing prayer would ever come. She laughs sometimes and tells me now, 'I never did get healed in your meeting, Melvin Banks, because I never even got in!' Which is very true – God *has* got a sense of humour. As Woody Allen says, 'If you want to make God laugh, tell him your future plans!'

I asked this total stranger, 'What is wrong with you my dear?'

She replied hoarsely, 'I have motor neurone disease, it is incurable, I have less than two years to live, I cannot walk at all.'

I knew about this dreadful sickness, that wears a person down from a perfectly healthy specimen into a complete vegetable, killing all the muscles and nerves and sapping away the total strength of the body, till every faculty is dying and the victim cannot move at all. Beryl was on the way to this, time was short, no medic could help her.

I replied, 'Let's look to Jesus Christ. *By His stripes* (Christ's suffering wounds, his blood) *we are healed...*'

5

I kept saying it, '...by His stripes ... by His stripes ... you are healed...'

Suddenly she felt warm liquid burning fire go through her body. 'I want to stand!' she cried, and soon, with not even a small aid, she stood. In seconds her ankle bones and leg muscles received a divine quickening, she stepped forward, then another step, one more, then to the astonishment of the now crowded street, the glistening eyes of the reporters, the shouts of amazement from bystanders, she waltzed around the gutter, danced, stepped up and down like a happy goose. The street was staggered. Had England ever seen miracles on its streets?

This was revival breaking out among the people. It was shocking, amazing, incredible; the wheelchair was folded up, Beryl walked away and has gone on walking with doctors confirming her wondrous cure from MND. She goes on well today, and writes to me, '...not in your meeting, Jesus healed me on the streets of Lincoln!' I join in the fun. God does humble us, God does have the last laugh on us!

Soon, the news spread and the crowds grew bigger and the traffic blocked up. People clapped at each miracle and there was laughter, joy and excitement – all praise to God in the open air. What an afternoon! They will never be forgotten, the wonders, the blessings, the miracles of that day. And God did it all openly, before all people.

When I left the county a few days later, I was thrilled that the work of my youth had not been wasted. How wonderful to see the growth which had taken place in the county over the years, in churches which I had planted 25 years earlier. And how wonderful to have my ministry affirmed in such a way.

God had shown that His power was too great to be contained. His Spirit moved out into the streets in an act of spontaneity. He is a God of liberty, always able to surprise us and do a new thing to show the world His love, His wonders, His goodness. I love Job's words:

> Behold God exalteth by His power. Who teacheth like Him? Remember that thou magnify His marvels, which men behold that every man may see it.
>
> JOB 36:22,24,25

2

SHEER POWER

It was a normal March day, the long winter almost over. A glint of sun blazed through the gap in the curtains in the Browns' homestead, so much so that Paula asked Carl to open the window a little so she could feel the quick wisps of fresh sea air. It felt so good. 'If only I could be mobile enough myself to get out there. I could run along that promenade today,' she mused silently. How often had that thought gone through her over the past few years? Even locking that window would have taken ages. The children were so good to do all that they did to help Mum: they were 'little angels', as she had said so often.

Making her way round the furniture, she stopped for a little breather, then to gather her senses, for mobility and dizziness are two factors one fights for and against in this disease. The children shouted a hasty 'bye-bye' and then, with a heavy slam of the door, they were out to school. A jumper lay in the passageway, a coat half hung on its hook, a hanky at the bottom of the stairs, papers strewn in the dining room corner, dishes to wash up. Paula stared around ... a cobweb up there that totally frustrated her. 'If only...' those words haunted her. A fit woman would just leap up, or stand on the chair, or get the brush and flick it down, but to her that was an impossible act. It made her breathe more heavily just to think of doing such an impossible thing.

How despairing she was, how she valued good health in others. It must be wonderful just to get up and walk out, down to Weston seafront, breathe in the Channel's breezes, hear the seagulls wavering above, her hair blowing in the gusts, and to hop down the old Victorian pier, watch her friends the fishermen, with their long rods and lines picking up the pike and carp, perhaps take a steamer down the Channel to Wales, or Lundy Island. 'Oh I wish...'

Then a squeak of the door, a call, it was John come in, he had been out on an early morning call to mend a TV and was full of the joys of spring. How patient he was, she mused, such a good husband. She staggered up and zigzagged slowly, careered along the furniture. 'Ouch!' she moaned, as her shin caught an armchair end. She loved to sit and have breakfast, but the job this morning must have been a smaller repair than expected, for she had nothing ready for him yet. 'I'll cut some bread from the fresh loaf Carl brought in early, darling. I'll do the toast right away for you.'

John seemed excited. 'I had another job to do but will go out in five minutes,' he commented. 'I had to pop in and tell you.'

'Tell me what, love? No wonder you're early, what's all the excitement?'

John, normally a subdued, thoughtful, not rash character, seemed unduly thrilled and 'full of it' that bright morning. 'It's like this darling. I was down at Mrs Moody's, you know, doing her set, when she told me she was going to some big faith healer, who was coming to town...'

'A *faith healer*!' Paula exclaimed. 'What's that?'

'Well, you know, them people who are supposed to have some sort of ... well, you know, a gift, they can make people better?' John, trying to theologize what he did not understand.

'They really make people better?' Paula asked in surprise.

'They have that reputation, and this is supposed to be a good one, they say it really works for lots of people...'

'What are you thinking, that I should go?'

'Why miss such a chance? There's nothing to lose, I mean I could take you down, then come back for you later.'

'You mean you'd drop me there all on my own, I'd have to see this chap by myself?'

'There would be others there; it's not my cup of tea, it's this weekend, and a lot of jobs come in Saturdays usually – you know that, I must be on call, and in any case this ... er hum ... faith healer won't be long, I expect. You pay him and he sees to you and you're off, maybe half an hour and it's all over!'

'I hope not,' Paula commented, 'I'm not going to be finished off!' They both laughed, the smell of coffee by now was filling the kitchen air.

'Let's have a cuppa and then ring up the number. I got it here on this leaflet, and we can book seats. What do you say, old girl?'

'I don't know if I have much faith, but I'll give it a go...' Paula added. More laughter, coffee, a phone call, and all was set up for the visit, to what the local papers had billed as 'MR MIRACLE'S VISIT TO WESTON'.

When the Saturday evening arrived, Paula sat nervously. John had had such a spate of 'call-outs' that he had hardly been in all day. 'Where is he?' she said to herself, looking up at the clock. It was almost half past seven, this meeting was due to start at that time. She had learnt by Jim's call that you were not 'in and out' as John had thought, but there was a 'proper church service' and the Reverend who had come with this 'special gift' then saw you and prayed over you. 'I hate going in late,' she spat out frustratedly. Then the grind of van wheels on the tarmac, hurried footsteps, and in came John. 'Sorry I'm late, love, complicated valve job ... I'm ready, I'll take you straight down, it's only five minutes.'

'I'm going to be late, everyone will look at me struggling in there, we shall know a lot of people.' Paula was now wanting to put the trip off, nerves were getting the better of her. 'I can't go now ... I'll go tomorrow...'

John blurted, 'It'll have to be now, I have a long job in the repair shop tomorrow, it's too complicated to uproot myself. Go now ... I can drop you off on the way to Mrs Smart's up Nailsea Hill...' That look of determination from John, always quiet but insistent.

'Just for you then ... but don't be late picking me up.'

The van had to steer delicately between all the cars in the car park. 'A lot of bloomin' people here,' John commented. 'I'll try to get you as close to the front entrance as I can, love.' Paula sat, as John sheepishly went into the public hall and in a few seconds came out with a very well-dressed gentleman, looking very cheery and polite, as he opened her door of the van. 'Any way we can help, don't worry about being late, we are just singing some hymns.' He chatted away, as they slowly paced into the public hall.

'It was very warm inside, that's what hit me first,' remembers Paula. 'My knees felt doubly weak, probably with apprehension of what was required of me to be "faith healed".' But she was welcomed by a number of people, who came and shook her hand. She was told to relax and sit, not try and stand for each song. John whispered to the 'steward' on the doors that he had to 'go to work', they shook hands, John waved through the glass doors to Paula, and was off.

Later he admitted, 'I was a real atheist, this was only a last resort, a church service would embarrass me, I did not believe in anything.' Paula was taken aback by the carefree attitude of the 'pastor', Clem Spicer, as he jokingly and amusingly led the service, and his son, Lawson, very young looking and boyish, sang to the congregation in very modern idiom, jumping about sometimes. Paula thought, 'Is this the modern church? I'm quite enjoying this, this is different...'

It went on for a long time. Only her dead muscles and sitting on a plastic oval seat made her fidget a bit, but there was so much joy around her, even shouting, which was strange. At the collection, 'Empty your wallets and purses!' Clem said, then added, 'if you're writing out a cheque, make it a big one!' But even this made Paula think there was sincerity in their voices, it was all so hearty, happy and genuine.

Then this balding, 50-year-old, rather gentle, laid-back 'Reverend' stepped up. He wore a dog collar, but up to now had left everything to Clem and Lawson, the 'laymen'. He spoke very quietly, confidently, and with purpose, Paula noted.

After such a long service (over 70 minutes) she

thought, 'Now for a long sermon.' But Mr Banks told how he was going to be the 'shortest preacher you've ever heard', then went on to tell a story about a vicar he knew, whose sermons got so long that they nicknamed him not Reverend but Neverend!

'I was thankful for this admission,' Paula said. 'I was in quite some pain, could not move hardly a muscle, felt so weak, and was wondering when John would turn up!

'In 18 minutes Melvin Banks was over,' she said. He had spoken on a subject hitherto totally foreign to her, 'How to be saved and know it'. Saved from what? she thought. 'Only my sickness is all I need to be free of.' But then he spoke rapidly about sin, it was so gripping that 'I felt I was the biggest sinner on the face of the earth. There was no escape from the preacher. I thought he was speaking only to me, not to all the others in that place also.

'He didn't look very much, smartly dressed, but so unassuming, but now he got going, it seemed like hours he spoke,' Paula told us later. 'I saw all my sins come up before me. Then he quickly packed up, urging us to repent, which he called "apologizing to God, sorrow for sin" – to pack up the old life and not go back to it! I felt that I had all the sins of the world on my shoulders, we were soon bowing our heads in prayer, I never learnt about such things before, and never realized there was a real place, that is a conscious state of hell and suffering after this life, for unbelieving people. I was overwhelmed!

'The minister became subdued, leading us in praying, urging us to "weep rivers of tears till we come into God's kingdom ... cry to God till the old life dies in you ... start again ... be born again ... others stepped out but God will step in ... from an undergoer you can become an *overcomer* ... tomorrow is the first day of the rest of your life ... tomorrow has never happened before ... start a brand new, fantastic life with Jesus Christ ..." I felt I *must*, I could not raise my dead hands like other people around me, but I prayed some words (I did not know how you prayed till that moment) that the preachers gave us. I felt a warm glow, it brought tears to my eyes, someone else seemed to be inside of me. I was bolstered, uplifted, clean, glowing, it was wonderful, all my blues, depressions, darknesses, forebodings seemed to be instantly forgotten...

'I couldn't move with my immobility and sickness, tears streamed down my face, mascara darkened my cheeks, I could hardly lift a hand to wipe away the tears. Yet I did not seem to mind, I was oblivious to everything, I was lost in wonder. The love, the praises of God around me, just shook me. It was like heaven looking back. Someone – a lady – put her arm around me, whispered more prayers in my ears, said some kind words, told me more about Christ. I cannot remember it all, I was so out of this world! But soon Reverend Banks was lifting many people up at the front, and was putting his hands on their heads. One man gave his stick over to a helper and ran up the aisle – this quite shocked me. Then a deaf woman showed her hearing aids and was speaking and hearing all sorts of sentences. A little child was helped to walk, it went on and on.

'I said to the lady, "Shall I try and get up to him?" She then waved out and intimated I needed help, and to save me the struggle, Mr Banks walked right over to my place. He gently took my very icy cold hand. I was warm, burning inside, but due to my sickness of multiple sclerosis, was dead outside. He whispered some Scripture, he did not raise his voice like he had in the preaching. He was very still, he kept saying some Bible words, I was to learn later came from Isaiah – "by His stripes we are healed ... by His stripes we are healed ... healed ... healed..." I felt such a heat go through my body, it shook me from top to toe.

'I felt a little strange, it was uncanny, out-of-this-world, divine, my muscles suddenly loosened, strength came into my legs, the wobbliness seemed to vanish. As Melvin asked me to stand, I felt almost like Superman. "Move quickly, move quickly," he urged, "God's power is here, healing forces are released, you will never, never be the same again ... look up your salvation draweth near..." I bounced literally out of my seat, I felt brand new now, outside as well as within. It was wonderful, even some of my shyness was going, I felt bolder, I was up and running, right down the middle aisle, I ran and ran, I did not want to rest, all my MS, this dreadful sickness seemed to have gone.

'Round and round I went, I had to stop to get my breath, everyone was cheering, some knew me in our small seaside town, handshakes came, shouts of "thanks be to God" and "It's Jesus". I was full with a bubbling joy. The excitement in the audience was amazing, suddenly after some time, I was just walking back and forth, strong, my old normal self, confident, happy, I could hardly believe it, it was like a most wonderful dream, my nightmares had come to an end.

'Then suddenly who should I see above the faces around me ... but John, walking through the open doors of the venue. His look was startling, a member of Rev. Banks' team was with him. I ran into his arms – he was astonished! It was a long while before we finally left the hall, drove back in the van. I opened the door when we got into the drive, stepped out myself, with John following tongue-tied behind me, and beaming, as I pranced into the house, unlocking the back door myself, and I did a dance round the front room. The children came down the stairs and stopped in their tracks, and watched me as if I was an extra-terrestrial being from an outer galaxy. What a night, what a new world, what new health!

'We soon found our way along to the new church started in the town. Looking back, as we have grown in trust with our Saviour, as we have learned so much more about Him, it's like it happened an hour ago, God is fresh, good, glorious. *God in action*!'

THE SHEER POWER OF GOD

Ingersoll, the noted atheist of the last century, used to say, 'Show me the miracles, power, signs, and wonders of the Bible and I will believe in Christianity.'

G. K. Chesterton wrote, 'We are daily gorged with miracles, the whole of life is full of miracles if we can but see them.'

Even the agnostic sceptic George Bernard Shaw said, 'We must not reject something because there is no explanation normally for it. There are miracles we cannot explain.'

Rubenstein, the amazing pianist, commented, 'When I go to church, I like to visit a place of worship where they challenge me with the supernatural.'

3

Voices from Heaven

A reporter asked me, 'Have you ever seen God?' He was persistent. 'You say you have heard His voice many times. This is strange, even Billy Graham, or the Pope, the Archbishop of Canterbury or the Cardinal of all England, have all agreed they have never seen God, they have never heard a voice from God. How is it you have seen Him and you have heard Him?'

I replied quietly, 'Every time a dying child is brought before me for a miracle of healing and the laying on of hands for prayer ... every time a poor, diseased, sickly lady in a wheelchair is pushed before me for healing ... As I look into their faces I see the face of God. And every time I hear a pain-filled, crippled, hurting baby cry out, or a bowed-down, arthritic sufferer call, "Help me, help me," I hear the voice of God.'

There was no reply from the sceptic!

A fine, godly pastor, hearing of this incident, tackled me over supper late one night. 'That could be construed to be modernistic, Melvin, that we are *all* the children of God, to say you see and hear God in these people.'

Then his wife spoke up before I could digest the last of my green salad, 'Not at all, the preacher is right, I will read to you from Matthew [*The Message* translation]: "The King will say, 'Enter Thou blessed of my Father ... and why? I was hungry and you fed me, I was thirsty and you gave me to drink, I was homeless and you gave me a room, I was shivering and you gave me clothes, I was sick and you stopped to visit, I was in prison and you came to me' ... What are you talking about? When did we see you hungry, sick ... thirsty? Then the King said to them, 'I'm telling you the solemn truth, whenever you do any of these things to someone ... that was me ... you did it to me!'"'

The very wise minister (I know no one in Europe who knows the Bible better than he) gulped a few times, sat up straight and replied, 'I can't argue with that!' We could add in Malcolm Muggeridge's words:

I was
Hurt in battle, you bound up my wounds.
Searching for kindness, you held out your hand.
When I was Negro, or Chinese, or white, and
Mocked and insulted, you carried my cross.

When I was old, you bothered to smile.
When I was restless, you listened and cared.

You saw me covered with spittle and blood,
You knew my features, though grimy with sweat.

When I was laughed at, you stood by my side.
When I was happy, you shared in my joy.

When I was naked, you gave me your coat.

When I was weary, you helped me find rest.
When I was anxious, you calmed all my fears.

When I was little, you taught me to read.
When I was lonely, you gave me your love.

When God is working through us there is a joy, a generosity in us. That is why today you must – as I seek to every day – *bless someone* for you may never bless them again, *touch someone's life* for you may never touch them again in this life. *Give to someone* for you may never give to them again, *encourage someone who is down*, for you may not uplift them again in this life.

GOD IS SPEAKING

His voice is never far from me, He is always acting for me. It's amazing.

I was on a European speaking tour, it was a tight schedule – I spoke in three nations in 48 hours, in one programme, in Austria, Germany and Switzerland. The interpreter, also my chauffeur, told me one night was kept free, due to the long travelling in between. He told me, 'I phone someone I never met before, a number given me, they begged me to take you to this mountain retreat in Wuitenberg, South Germany!' It was a most magnificent conference centre, in stunning countryside.

When I arrived and was resting, the hostess asked to see me. They were a strict evangelical group, they had not known anything of the latter-day moving of the Holy Spirit. Devout, sweet, faithful people, but this leader especially was hungry for more and more of God. She had been praying to Jesus to send someone 'who moves in miracle power, who knows God always answers prayer, to come soon and encourage us'.

I did not get my night off! She got a glorious new release and filling with the Holy Spirit. I was asked to speak, and soon with no mention of opportunity for healing, one after another folk came up for laying on of hands, and a miracle! These people were all from staunch evangelical backgrounds where this ministry was normally very much resisted. There are many more churches in Germany and Switzerland like this than in the UK.

So God broke through on my day off! God is always in action. From this came an invitation to hold the first ever renewal and Holy Spirit healing conference in that country, and in that centre with a long history of traditional evangelical Protestant structure. God has moved through that region since, and through that centre, amazingly touching many today across Germany.

- God's plans are miraculous
- God's actions are always perfect
- God's voice is always so clear

God is calling us to:

- Love as He loves
- Help as He helps
- Give as He gives
- Serve as He serves

Deep faith in action is love. Love in action is service. With Jesus everything is possible because God is love.

Gandhi said, 'If Christians had lived their Christianity in action as Christ, there would be no Hindus left in India!'

Total lack of surrender is our failure. We cannot meet the King of the ages on our own terms, but by surrender. He must conquer us first. A French admiral defeated by Lord Nelson in a naval combat came aboard to meet Nelson. He offered his hand in respect, but was refused, and was told, 'Your sword first, Sir, then your hand.'

As Malcolm Muggeridge put it, 'As far as I am concerned it's Christ or nothing!'

A. W. Tozer wrote, 'The living Holy Spirit does invade our human will, and seeks to bring it gently to a joyous union with the will of God.'

THIS IS THE CRUNCH

The quest of God is to bring us to heel, to win our hearts.

Hudson Taylor never looked very much, skinny, always melancholy, bouts of the blues, yet he went to China as the first successful missionary, and the mighty revival there today is no doubt due in a vital part to him, and his faithful workers' hard sowing and pioneering at the beginning. He made his surrender with these words: 'God was looking for someone small enough to use and found me.'

A 'surrendered man', or as McCheyne called him, 'A *holy* man is an awesome weapon in the hands of Almighty God.'

If you are willing to give up earthly dreams and live for the kingdom, *God can use you*. A badge on a girl's lapel in Bond Street, London, read, 'Look after your-self!' But God says, 'I will look after your interests, if you first will take care of mine.' That's *surrender*!

The African martyr of the 1980s, Festo Kingere, put it, 'The man without Christ is a man without a centre.'

'Through the Word we are put together and shaped up for the tasks God has for us' (2 Timothy 3:17 *The Message*).

'Good character will shine through their actions, adding lustre to the teaching of our Saviour' (Titus 2:10 *The Message*).

4

RESCUING THOUSANDS

I often say when appealing to people at the close of a service to seek and find God, 'Don't come out to the front unless you are prepared to leave your sins on your seat!' Martin Luther did it even more theologically when he said, 'The truest repentance is to do it no more.' God is calling for action *from us*, if He is to act *for* us. Many do not know they need rescuing, both from themselves and from their sins into a sparkling, brand-new life.

The story is told of a group of sailors marooned on a life raft off Brazil. After a few days without water they were on the verge of death, and were rescued by a passing ship in the nick of time. When they were safely on board, their rescuers asked them why they were so thirsty, to which they replied that they had no water.

'No water? You had only to reach over the side of your raft for an endless supply of water.' They had been passing through the freshwater stream that pushes right out into the Atlantic from the mighty Amazon River. The shortage was illusory. All they had needed to do was drink!

So many in the world are like that, suffering an illusory shortage of the Holy Spirit. But He is there, all around, waiting to be invited and released. How tragic that people can perish while their salvation surrounds them.

A man in Doncaster came to St Mary's Church when I was there. The crowds were densely packed, on a cold

February night; so many people came that long queues formed around the block and we could not get another soul in. Many sick were locked outside, and this man was one of them. He was on crutches and in pain, but as the power swept through the building and the area, it hit him in the legs. He suddenly dropped his crutches and literally flew up the street running like a two-year-old, *pain free*! There was as much excitement and commotion outside as inside the actual meeting. God was rescuing people who never hitherto had met Him. Miracle after miracle happened.

Another man who had actually got into the service walked so slowly in, it took him ages to get into the meeting. It was so hot and stifling within, but bitterly cold outside, and his very chronic heart condition was troubling him – he walked, almost crawled like a snail, puffing and panting each few feet, but God moved on him, God rescued him: he ran from the service, and later returned, telling the host of the meeting he had run to see what time the bus was so that he could stay till the last minute. He now so loved God's Word and his heart was and still is perfect! God rescued him.

How can God do these things? Where is He? How does He work in such strange ways?

A heckler on Tower Hill once asked Lord Donald Soper, the open-air preacher, what shape the soul is. 'Oblong,' he replied – and he was right, for that is the shape of a human body.

'Where is the soul in the body?' came the next question.

'Where the music is in the organ,' replied Lord Soper. That is marvellously true. You could dismantle the organ, but you would never find its music. 'Soul' is the life of the body.

Jesus was physically raised from the dead, and we are told that the Spirit who raised up Jesus will also quicken our mortal bodies.

A PHYSICAL TRANSFORMATION

Archbishop William Temple once said that Christianity is the most *materialistic* of all religions. The reason for that is simple: unlike all the others, Christianity is genuinely concerned with our bodies. It is not a religion which separates soul from body. From the moment of man's creation, when he *became* a living soul (not *received* a soul), the religion of the Bible is concerned with the physical as well as the spiritual.

Yes, God rescues the *whole man*: your healing, your sick mind or diseased body is very important to Him, just as is your soul and spirit.

A young minister just rang me days ago: he had fallen, torn ligaments and tendons, would not be walking for a long time, then only with difficulty. He had a secular job while preaching evenings and Sundays to a small, growing church. He also had a family and mortgage that depended on him. He rang in much distress. He was losing work, money was low, he had to struggle to church, he was in pain, off work for months, could be in deep debt possibly affecting his house, repossession being not a remote possibility!

I prayed over the phone early that Sunday morning, 'I will send you a prayer cloth, lay it on your body.' (These handkerchiefs, like the one used in Acts 19:2–12 by Paul, are our practice also.) We pray for the person and send these cloths all over the world. It is laid upon the person as they pray and read the Scripture and in deep devotion seek the Lord. Many are the astonishing reports of medically sound, confirmed healings from this.

Five days later I was holding a packed service in a revival in Reading, Berkshire, when a call came to my 'digs' from this young pastor speaking in a very excitable, thrilled voice: 'I'm healed Brother, I'm off my crutches, it's wonderful, I'll be back at work in days ... it's wonderful ... glorious ...'

I replied, 'The GOD who rescued you, who did this marvellous act, is the mighty, the wonderful one!' He agreed and talked so much I could not get him off the phone! God is interested in *every bit of us*! All our lives, all our problems, all our heartstrings, all our desires.

We need to turn to the Cross as a start on this journey

Our thoughts have strayed from the Cross. In the words of Oliver Cromwell, when faced with a strong Scots army on his right flank, coming to the aid of Charles I, 'I beseech you, think it possible that you may be mistaken.' They failed to listen to him, and not one Scottish soldier returned! Next time they sent an army they made sure they were on Cromwell's side!

Think on this – you could be wrong the way you're going, the Scripture says. 'There is a way that seemeth right unto a man, but the ways thereof are the ways of death.' As the Methodist Church uses the word in their

sacraments – as they invite communicants to partici-
pate – 'Let all who love the Lord come here'! Come
back on to the narrow road to God and purpose, and
faith, glory and heaven in the end.

Sir James Simpson, who discovered and patented the
use of chloroform, corrected a fellow doctor when he
commented that this was a great discovery: 'No it was
not, my greatest discovery was that Jesus Christ is my
saviour!'

To find a real, deep, abiding presence and walk with
Him is life's most distinguished experience. A. J. Cronin
told in one of his tales of a nurse who walked miles to
nurse poor people who could not pay her. One day a
colleague exclaimed, 'Why don't you charge them? God
knows, you deserve it!'

The nurse replied, 'That's true, but if God knows I'm
worth it, that's all that matters.' God knows and wants
you. You are all that matters to Him. He has paid the
price to rescue you; don't drift so deep that you get
away from the simple truth: 'Jesus loves me, this I
know, for the Bible tells me so.'

A person I knew was about to cross a bridge across
one of our widest rivers – a turbulent river, in very high
winds and a wild storm. It forced authorities to close
the world's longest suspension bridge. When it finally
opened, a long string of cars crossed over.

Ann and her family drove up to the booth to pay the
toll, but the attendant said, 'You don't need to pay. The
guy in front of you paid your toll for you.' As they
watched the tail-lights of the mini-van in front of them
disappear, they knew they had no chance to thank the
generous driver. He paid the toll.

Moore wrote:

> All my iniquities on Him were laid.
> He nailed them all to the tree;
> Jesus the debt of my sin fully paid.
> He paid the ransom for me.

Our salvation is free because *Christ paid an enormous price*. Jesus gave His all for me – how can I give Him less? 'You were ... redeemed ... with the precious blood of Christ' (1 Peter 1:18–19).

A few years ago all America waited anxiously. Many prayed. Captain Scott O'Grady's F-16 had been shot down as he was flying over Serbia. Had he been killed or captured? Was he seriously injured? The hours ticked by. Five days passed. On the sixth day another pilot picked up a faint message from O'Grady's radio. He was alive, managing somehow to hide from hostile soldiers.

Immediately all the resources needed for a daring rescue operation were set in motion. O'Grady was snatched up to safety by a helicopter – and the US rejoiced. *Newsweek* magazine reported that the weapons and machinery used for the rescue of that one pilot were valued at $6 billion. We can't estimate the value of one human soul. If all the stars in all the galaxies were changed into platinum, that incalculable sum could not begin to purchase our salvation!

> Jesus sought me when a stranger,
> Wandering from the fold of God;
> He to rescue me from danger
> Interposed His precious blood.

William Booth, the founder and commanding general of the Salvation Army, was unable to sleep one night. His son Bramwell, who lived next door, saw that the light was on in his father's home. Thinking something might be wrong, he went to his parents' house. He found his father pacing back and forth with a wet towel wrapped around his head. 'Father,' he asked, 'shouldn't you be asleep?'

'No,' William replied, 'I am thinking.' Seeing the puzzled look that crossed his son's face, he put his hands on Bramwell's shoulders and solemnly said, 'I am thinking about people's sins. What will they do with their sins?' 'I, even I, am He who blots out your transgressions for My own sake; and I will not remember your sins' (Isaiah 43:25).

Search me, O God, and know my heart today;
Try me, O Saviour, know my thoughts, I pray.
See if there be some wicked way in me;
Cleanse me from every sin and set me free.

The road to worship begins at the Cross

Cleanse your hands, you sinners; and purify your hearts, you double-minded.

JAMES 4:8

Put to death ... fornication, uncleanness, passion, evil desire, and covetousness.

COLOSSIANS 3:5

NO PLACE TO HIDE

The story is told of two hunters who came across a bear so big that they dropped their rifles and ran for cover. One man climbed a tree while the other hid in a nearby cave. The bear sat down between the tree and the cave. Suddenly, the hunter in the cave came rushing out, almost ran into the waiting bear, hesitated, and dashed back in. The same thing happened a second time. When he emerged the third time, his friend frantically called out, 'Woody, are you crazy? Stay in the cave till he leaves!'

'Can't,' panted Woody. 'There's another bear in there!'

Take Christ as your Saviour, then you'll have a place to hide. Jesus said, 'I have come into this world, that those who do not see may see' (John 9:39). When you trust God's Son, darkness gives way to light.

Anna Mae Pennica was born with cataracts that left her blind. But in October 1981, Dr Thomas Pettit of the Jules Stein Eye Institute in Los Angeles removed the cataract from Anna Mae's left eye – and for the first time she could see! She even passed a driving test.

But there is a sad postscript to this surgical triumph. The technique for correcting Mrs Pennica's eye condition had been in use since the 1940s. She could have been enjoying 40 years of sight, but instead had remained blind needlessly.

What a greater tragedy it is to stumble through this world with sightless souls and be lost in impenetrable night forever!

Sper wrote:

If God is calling you today
To trust in Christ His Son,
Respond to Him in simple faith –
Salvation's work is done.

SALVATION IS A GIFT TO BE RECEIVED – NOT A GOAL TO BE ACHIEVED

Darcie Claesson was watching TV with her three-year-old daughter Emily one day when a news clip came on about a famous person who had died. Emily's immediate reaction was, 'Is he going to heaven?' When her mum explained that he would go to heaven if he had asked Jesus to be his Saviour, Emily proceeded to ask the same question about every family member she could think of.

Not to be left out, Emily added, 'You know what, Mom? I talked to Jesus on the phone the other day, and I asked Him to come into my heart.'

'That's great!' Darcie said. 'But how did you know His number?'

Emily's reply was simple, yet profound. 'He called me!' she declared.

Whom He called, these He also justified – Romans 8:30.

Little Thomas in Reading was brought to my crusade there 17 years ago. He was three years old and had never walked, the family did not attend any church. They had never been to a revival or evangelist's meeting prior to this. A leaflet in the door, then news from neighbours of the crowds flocking to the Assembly of God Church in Earley suburb attracted them. News of people being miraculously healed made them inquisitive. 'Let's give it a try, take Thomas along for a prayer,' they said.

The little fellow, fair hair, sweet, boyish smile, attracted the attention of the densely packed service. I prayed in the mighty, all-prevailing, all-powerful, awesome name of Jesus Christ. 'My God shall supply all your needs through Christ Jesus.' I cried to God, tears came to my cheeks. 'O Jesus the loving Son of God, have mercy on this child, cause the limbs to expand, let the dead nerves grow, put new nerves into his legs, create, move, set free, heal by a magnificent miracle...'

I suddenly said, my lips moved upon by the Spirit of God – I was surprised myself by what came out – for I said, 'Take him home and Thomas will walk in about three weeks, when the nerves have grown up in his legs...' The mother looked at me quite shocked!

I was in another city preaching, had even forgotten my prayer – in between I had visited at least five other towns, and prayed for about 3,000 other people – when a letter came in the mail. It was opened by my wife in the office and then handed to me. 'Do you know about this case?' Lilian enquired. I picked up the front page newscutting from the city paper – 'CHILD WALKS FOR FIRST TIME – A MIRACLE MOTHER SAYS'. Thomas was indeed walking, and there Jesus was front page news again. The three-year-old was shown in a large photo, running down the garden path. *Jesus rescued this family*.

Mr Lawrence had severe spine trouble. He was a roofing contractor, fell and hurt his spine: the doctors said, 'It is incurable and can only deteriorate.' His job, finances, future were on the line. He heard right down in Berkshire that I was preaching in Sheffield City Hall. He drove in great pain 150 miles, and was miraculously healed. I told him, again not knowing what I was saying, that he would minister to others and his spine be fit and healed, so he could dedicate his life to blessing others. He went home, still in pain, but in five days he was well. The doctors were astounded, he went on in his job and prospered. Eighteen years afterwards he was called to the ministry, and he is now a Pentecostal pastor with a thriving congregation in the south of England! God rescued him, and every word God gives comes true, every salvation and healing Christ grants lasts!

IT'S ALL THROUGH THE CROSS

Perfectionists are not comfortable people to be with, because they are a constant rebuke to our imperfections. Henry Royce, co-founder of Rolls-Royce, was a perfectionist, which explains why his cars became a by-word for engineering accuracy. The story is told that one day he was walking around the factory and saw a man turning a piece on a lathe. After a while he put the piece on the pile of finished work, muttering, 'That'll do.' Henry Royce heard the remark, and dismissed the man on the spot. For him, the *name* of Rolls-Royce was at stake.

For God, the name of God is at stake, too. He cannot accept anything short of perfection and His was a perfect, efficacious, acceptable sacrifice on Calvary. *A real Lord, a real salvation*!

A small child was promised by his mum a horse for his birthday, and as the days got closer to the event, he got more and more excited. Then his mum realized she could not keep a live horse in the garden. So she tried to persuade him to have a rocking horse, but no, he argued, he wanted a real horse, not a wooden horse. He exclaimed, 'I want a horse made of *horse*!'

Thank God we have a *real* Redeemer, a *real* Lord and Saviour, a *real* sacrifice was made on our behalf.

I used to sing in the Salvation Army as a boy:

There was none other good enough to pay the price of sin,
He only could unlock the gate of heaven and let us in...

When my son used to play with his Meccano set, he would bolt together a few metal strips, pulleys and things. If I asked him what he was making, he said, 'It's a crane.' Now it did not yet look like a crane to my eyes. Frankly, it looked like a random assembly of nuts and bolts and strips of metal. But for him it was a crane, from the start – because in his mind was a picture of the finished work. He saw the perfect article, he saw a magnificent construction. God brought us the finished work of Calvary, a marvellous Redemption, a great salvation. 'And it is marvellous in our eyes.'

There is a painting by Holman Hunt, the Pre-Raphaelite artist who painted *The Light of the World*, which is called *The Scape-goat*. It is not well known, because it is in a private art gallery in Manchester. He regarded it as his major work – indeed, he spent two years on the shores of the Dead Sea painting it.

It is a meticulously accurate painting of an animal, a goat, which is dying under the weight of some enormous, unseen burden. The title explains the picture: Holman Hunt painted a goat, but in a way he was painting Christ; the very eyes are filled with sadness. He is the perfect 'scape-goat' to whom the Old Testament animal testified in advance.

So the Cross is a complete and satisfactory way of dealing with man's sin without affronting the principle of justice. But its effectiveness requires faith on our part. When the sinner believes that Jesus died for him, in that moment his sins are forgiven and he has a place in heaven.

But that is not all. That is simply the beginning of a new kind of life – a life lived out every day in the light of the Cross. The secret of that life is not just to say, 'He died for me,' but to add, 'and I died with Him.'

Christ is meant to be my substitute not only in death but in life. So that the life I now live is no longer mine, but the life of Christ, who died for me and now lives in me. I died with him on the Cross, and His risen life is mine as well.

To me there are five 'meanings', basing them on the five letters of the word 'Cross'.

1. In relation to the devil, the Cross was a *Conquest*.
2. In relation to the world, the Cross was a *Reconciliation*.
3. In relation to God, the Cross was an *Offering*.
4. In relation to the law, the Cross was a *Satisfaction*.
5. In relation to the sinner, the Cross was a *Substitution*.

A famous British Prime Minister fought an election campaign many years ago on the slogan – 'UP AND UP, AND UP, ON AND ON AND ON!' It was very successful, and he was elected with a large majority. Unfortunately he could not keep his promises, and finished a failure. But God never fails, has never lost a case, is undefeated, invincible. By His Cross He has conquered, He will take you on and on, and up and up!

The Cross is the attraction! He has rescued thousands recently. Through His blood and sacrifice we are running through a troop and leaping over a wall. We are more than conquerors, there is a shout in the camp of victory. *God is in action*.

> We are on our way, the deliverance has come,
> Reach out and make your connection,
> Reach out and touch His hand,
> God is marching us to the sunset not to the dawn!

5

GOD'S PERFECT PLAN FOR YOU

In Stoke-on-Trent, Staffordshire, years ago I heard of a man, very illiterate, who had been living a very bad sort of life, but one day received Jesus as his Saviour at a Gospel meeting and showed he was truly converted. His way of life was radically changed – his morals, his heavy drinking curbed, his cursing and blaspheming all gave way to wholesome living and speaking, and kindly behaviour instead of selfish, crude manipulations.

One Sunday morning he came home from the church service very miserable. 'What's the matter with you?' his wife asked, 'I thought you said you'd got saved?'

'I am, but I'm so miserable today because everyone in the church had red jerseys on but me.'

'Oh,' replied his wife, 'that's easy, I'll knit you one.' So she sat down and knitted him one that very week (it was cheaper in those days than buying). The next Sunday he went to the meeting proudly wearing his new red jersey, but later came home miserable again.

'What's the matter with you now?' asked his puzzled wife.

'Well, you see,' he said, 'everyone else had some lovely white letters on their red jerseys, but I had none!'

'What can we do about that?' pondered his wife. 'What are we going to put on it?' The poor woman could not read either, so she didn't know what to do. As she sat down at her window, she noticed some words across the street, on a banner outside a store. So she decided to copy these words although she did not understand what they said.

The next Sunday morning he came home radiant. 'Do you know, my dear,' he said, 'everybody said that I had the best jersey in the church.' Do you know what was written on it? 'UNDER NEW MANAGEMENT'! Are you under His control, are you under His perfect plan, are you under New Management? Is Jesus Christ King in practice as well as in theory? Is the kingdom of your personality His? Has He had a coronation day in your heart?

'Thine is the kingdom,' some say, yet add, 'but my non-Christian girlfriend I will not give up!'

You say, 'Yours is the power,' yet you add, 'but my money, home, possessions come first in my thinking.' You say, 'Thine is the glory,' yet add on a P.S. – 'It's my life, I will not have it interfered with, I will run it myself!' So instead of God's plan and purpose for your life, it's 'My home, my business, my time, my godless friends, my money, my pleasure, my way! I'll do it my way...' And you wonder why there is no pattern, no fulfilment, no blessing, no peace, no fullness of joy?

GOD HAS A GIFT FOR YOUR LIFE!

What keeps God's active Spirit and power constantly at work in this ministry I exercise? Many ask how this can be. Why are there so many miracles of healing?

- Why, as recently in Wigan, are three cancer cases all cleared as cured after prayer?

- Why in Swansea do ambulances from hospitals bring dozens of sick?
- Why, as in a Lancashire town, are 100 new people added to one church after a revival?
- Why is so much local revival linked with evangelists' meetings?

How can God's perfect plan work out for you? Your church? Your area or city or town?

The building of the Panama Canal was a formidable task because of the difficult terrain through which it had to pass. Matters were made worse by the mosquitoes which infested the area. This great project could not have been accomplished without the remarkable courage and determination of the men who worked on it. They tackled the job with great spirit. For example, each workman had a plan of the completed canal next to his bunk so that he had a visible goal towards which to strive. The men were also inspired by what became known as 'The Panama Song':

> If you have rivers they say are uncrossable
> Or mountains you cannot tunnel through,
> We are specialists in the wholly impossible,
> Doing the thing that nobody can do.

They had a great plan, and they worked against every hindrance and obstacle until it was realized.

George Tomlinson, a young cotton weaver, believed that God was calling him to train for the ministry. He started getting up at 1.30 every morning to study before putting in 10 hours of hard work at the mill. He was very disappointed when he was not accepted for the ministry, but he did not become bitter. Instead he looked for other ways in which to serve his fellow man. He entered politics and eventually became the Secretary of State for Education. He applied his Christian values to his work in this office and thus wielded a great influence for good. He had discovered God's plan for his life, and it was not quite what he had expected it to be.

I vividly remember the day when I arrived in the tiny Lincolnshire town of Horncastle. I had come to fill in for a minister who had been unable to make it to a healing crusade which he was to have led. This was the first crusade I had ever been involved in, and I was literally trembling with fear as I walked down the main street of the town. But during the two weeks of the campaign over 100 people were saved. I was merely a substitute for someone else; I had no idea that the crusade would be so blessed by God! Ever since that time I have been caught up in a worldwide gospel mission. God had a plan for me, even though I could not see it clearly at the beginning.

Have you found God's plan for your life? He has promised to guide us so that we fulfil His purposes for us. He has said, 'I will instruct you and teach you in the way you should go; I will counsel you and watch over you' (Psalm 32:8). 'I know the plans I have for you ... plans to prosper you and not to harm you, plans to give you hope and a future' (Jeremiah 29:11).

A traveller once asked someone for directions. 'How far away am I from my destination?' he asked.

'Thousands of miles!' was the reply.

'But I know it's just a few miles away,' said the puzzled traveller.

'Yes, that's right, but you're going in the wrong direction. If you carry on that way you'll have to go all around the world to get to your destination!'

Perhaps your back is turned towards God's plan for your life. If so, it will take you a very long time to find it!

Two men were looking at a painting of a harbour scene in the National Gallery. Pointing to the fishermen who were idly sitting or strolling about, one of the men remarked, 'This picture should be called *The Micawbers*! Look at them – they're all just waiting for something to turn up!'

'But don't you see the mended nets and the boats which are all ready to set sail?' said the other man. 'The fishermen have got everything ready, and they are now waiting for the tide to turn.' We sometimes need to do what those fishermen did. There are times when there is nothing more for us to do: we have prepared ourselves and have done everything we can, and all we can now do is to wait for the turn of the tide. We must wait for God to speak and to show His plan to us. He will always reveal Himself in the end to the seeking heart.

God often reveals His plan to us in the dark and difficult times in our lives. At a time of great need in his life Isaiah saw the Lord 'seated on a throne, high and exalted' (Isaiah 6:1). A live coal touched his lips and he received his calling. Thus he found out God's purpose for his life.

During a visit to Belgium the late Dr Don Gray Barnhouse went into a shop to buy some lace for his wife. He asked to see a sample, expecting that the lace would simply be placed on the counter so that he could look at it. But no, when one is buying expensive lace it is placed on a large black cushion. Only when it is on such a background can its intricate beauty be clearly seen. In a similar way, God's wonderful plans for us are often placed against a dark backdrop so that we may perceive them clearly.

Colin Urquhart calls some believers 'billiard-ball Christians', because they get knocked about, rolling from here to there with no co-ordination, plan or purpose. God doesn't want His people to be like that. He has redeemed us; we are worth a great deal to Him, and He has plans for us. We can have full confidence in Him. His Word says, 'So do not throw away your confidence; it will be richly rewarded' (Hebrews 10:35).

I love to see confidence in Christians, because it can enable them to achieve great things for God. If ever I am tempted to doubt that someone can ever do anything much for the Lord, I think about a story I once heard about Sir Arthur Conan Doyle, the creator of Sherlock Holmes. He was once chatting with a young actor who was at that time earning just a few shillings a week playing a part in one of Sir Arthur's plays. The actor was a nobody, but with tongue in cheek he suggested that the famous Sir Arthur and he should pool their incomes and share the total equally for the rest of their days. Of course, Sir Arthur didn't take him seriously. After all, he had no time to waste on a cocksure, cheeky little whippersnapper ... *whose name happened to be Charlie Chaplin*!

Confidence in Christ is something like that. We may seem insignificant, but if we trust Him He can use us mightily. Of course, our confidence in Jesus should not make us cocky, boastful, brash or disrespectful. Instead we should be *humbly* confident. We must yield to whatever God reveals to us, even if we don't like all that He says to us.

A while ago I read in a magazine that when two mountain goats meet in a very narrow defile or on a rocky ledge, where there is no room to pass and where to go back might be difficult or even fatal, one of the goats lies down while the other walks over it. Sadly, human beings often fail to display this sort of good sense. They refuse to swallow their pride and give way. As a result they cause a great deal of trouble for themselves.

We need to submit to God; we need to lie down and let Him walk over us. If we do that He will reward us and bless us. His plan for our lives will unfold and He will show us the way to peace, power, fruitfulness, joy, success and prosperity. He will show us the way forward: 'He will guard the feet of His saints' (1 Samuel 2:9).

All that God requires of us is submission and obedience. His Word says, 'Be careful to do what the Lord your God has commanded you; do not turn aside to the right or to the left. Walk in all the way that the Lord your God has commanded you, so that you may live long and prosper' (Deuteronomy 5:32–33). God's plan is yours for the asking. He will not fail you.

For you are not a mere number but a real person. You have a place in the heart and mind of Jesus. That place in the Saviour's heart can be as real for you today as it was for those for whom He cared personally when He walked upon earth in the flesh.

Give Him your heart and He will give you His heart.

FIRST STEP TO GOD'S PLAN – PUT THE KING IN THE MIDDLE

A Christian farmer was marking his sheep with his mark of ownership. A fellow Christian visiting the farm watched him doing this. Over a cup of tea afterwards the farmer said, 'Christ's sheep are marked too, you know – on the ear and on the foot.'

'Why do you say that?' asked his friend.

'Because Jesus said, "My sheep listen to my voice; I know them, and they follow me"' (John 10:27).

It is sadly the case that not all of Christ's sheep really listen to Him or really follow Him with true devotion. They cannot truly say that He is at the centre of their lives.

Luke records that when Jesus appeared to the disciples after His resurrection, He 'stood among them' (Luke 24:36), in the central place in the midst of them. When He was a boy His parents found Him in the Temple in Jerusalem, 'sitting among the teachers, listening to them and asking them questions' (Luke 2:46). He had the central place even among the theologians. Wouldn't it be wonderful if that were the case today!

Two boys were having difficulty putting together a jigsaw puzzle which was meant to depict a royal procession. One looked hard at the picture on the box and said, 'I see what we've been doing wrong! We must put the King in the middle.' They did so, and then instead of a puzzle they had a picture. Likewise, we must put

Christ, our King, in the middle of our lives – we must put Him first and let Him control us. He must be the influence which dominates our lifestyle.

Even those who are working hard for the Lord sometimes fail to put Him at the centre of things. It is possible for us to become so engrossed in our work for the Lord that we forget the Lord of our work! We need to have a clear vision of Christ before us at all times. We need to see Him crucified, raised from the dead and ascended to the right hand of God. If you have lost that vision, do whatever you have to do to recapture it. Do not succumb to the negative pessimism which infiltrates the Church today, but instead be restored to the sparkling purity and joy of the gospel!

It was C. H. Spurgeon who, after a morning service one day, was confronted by a lady who said to him, 'Mr Spurgeon, that was a wonderful sermon you preached this morning.'

'Yes ma'am,' he said, 'the devil told me that 10 minutes ago.' Let us go from our services crying 'What a wonderful Lord!' not 'What a great, powerful preacher he is!' or 'Let's follow this big man!' or 'Go and see this special man or woman!' The spiritual temperature rises and the Church becomes irresistible when Christ is in the middle. His is the first and central place.

SECOND STEP TO GOD'S PLAN –
HAVE CONFIDENCE

'No confidence – that's my problem, Mr Banks!' said the man, tears welling up in his eyes. 'I don't have so much as a pennyworth of confidence in myself!' People have often told me that sort of thing. And yet many times in the Bible we read of people who had no confidence in themselves being anointed with a God-given confidence. This was true of Elijah, Jonah, Isaiah, Peter, John Mark and many others.

Under the law of the Roman Empire a soldier who deserted his legion had to have the little finger of his right hand chopped off. As a young man, John Mark went on a missionary journey with the Apostle Paul but deserted him in his hour of need. Later he returned to Paul's side and became a faithful missionary, even writing one of the four Gospels. There is a story dating from the early Church that he cut his own little finger off as a permanent reminder to himself never to lose confidence again. Tradition suggests that he was known in the Church as *Kolobo-Dactylus*, which means 'Maimed-in-the-Finger'.

I was recently trying to help someone who had a desperate feeling of being inferior. There is no doubt that many people are not getting the best out of life because they feel like this. They are afraid of themselves and afraid of other people and of what they think about them. But God answered all our quibbling about our own worth when He allowed His Son, Jesus Christ, to die on the Cross. We were worth so much to God that He was willing to sacrifice even His Son in order to buy us back from sin and death.

We need to remember that the initiative is always with God. When Adam and Eve, having eaten the fruit of the tree of the knowledge of good and evil, were hiding from God in the garden, He came looking for them, calling, 'Where are you?' This clearly shows that God is forever approaching man. Of course, the climax of His seeking after man was Jesus' coming into the world. And it was to timid men, who were constantly worried about their lives and their relationships, that He said, 'You did not choose me, but I chose you' (John 15:16).

This is the only solid basis for our hope. Remember that it is the same for everyone. You are not worth something to God because you serve His Church or because you are good or clever or because you give money or say your prayers. You are worth something because He has chosen you and you belong to Him.

Perhaps you have let this fear about yourself, this awful feeling of inferiority, burden your personality. Perhaps you have got to the stage where the only happiness that you have is to be miserable. You need at this very moment an injection of the confidence that only Jesus Christ can give through His Spirit. You need it, and He will give it to you. God's Word tells us that he 'is able to do immeasurably more than all we ask or imagine, according to His power that is at work within us' (Ephesians 3:20).

Years ago Dr W. E. Sangster published a book entitled *He is Able*. Its theme was the power and gracious willingness of Christ our Lord to help us with life's everyday problems. Some of the chapter headings were as follows: 'When worn with sickness – He is able!'; 'When in loneliness – He is able!'; 'When evil thoughts molest – He is able!'; 'When I find it hard to pray – He is able!' In all of life's circumstances – in every problem we meet, no matter how difficult the task, no matter

how heavy the burden, no matter how sharp the pain –
Christ is able and willing to help us.

You see, Christian confidence and hope is not a
matter of having the right kind of temperament. It is a
question of entrusting yourself to God. He is able to
keep all that we have entrusted to Him (2 Timothy
1:12). He is able to build us up (Acts 20:32). He is able
to make all grace abound towards us (2 Corinthians
9:8). He is able to keep us from falling (Jude 24). And
He is able to help us when we are tempted (Hebrews
2:18). He is able! What confidence and hope and
promises of grace are to be found in these passages! No
matter what the problem, need, pain or loss you face
today, take heart, for Christ your Lord has the power to
help and comfort and sustain you. The Apostle John
says, 'This is the assurance (confidence) that we have in
approaching God: that if we ask anything according to
His will, He hears us' (1 John 5:14).

Stop rushing about, stop doing things, and really
pause for a few minutes and consider the fact that Jesus
loves you in spite of everything you have been and have
not been. There will never come a time when His love
for you will break down.

–6–

OPEN DOORS TO MIRACLE
AFTER MIRACLE

Wise King Solomon said, 'A man's gift maketh room for him and bringeth him before ... men.'

And D. H. Lawrence said, 'Their time, their thrills are mine.'

As the years have slipped by, and as the gift of healing has become more accepted in the Church and in the outside world, I have been amazed and humbled by the many doors which God has opened to me. For instance, I have recently spent seven weeks in Australia, New Zealand and the Pacific. During that time I took part in almost 70 television and radio programmes – including the popular *Good Morning Australia* breakfast show – and was the subject of some 30 newspaper articles, reports and interviews. Through this means the gospel of Christ was brought to some 4 million people. Every year I am given the opportunity to confront millions of people in the UK and overseas with the marvels of God.

A typical challenge these days is to heal people 'on air'. One particular radio station in the Pacific has done this four times now. On the first three occasions they brought along four or five sick people, and as I prayed, God healed them one by one, live. Almost all of them went away well.

The last time, the radio people must have been thinking, 'We must stop him somehow.' They reasoned that if I healed even one out of a group of sick people I had 'won' somehow. So to reduce the odds they presented me with just one badly crippled woman. I had some idea of what they were up to, and had spent many hours in prayer, quietness and solitude before going to the studio. I said to the Lord: 'You cannot fail, whether it's one person or 50. You love every one of the sick. Touch this badly crippled lady.'

The red light in the studio came on, and after some music and a few questions, the poor woman was wheeled in. I prayed, and before long she was rejoicing and dancing round the studio. The media folk were more flabbergasted than before!

But I am constantly being astonished by the opportunities God gives me, the doors He opens...

I preached at a Hindu temple

During a crusade in a big tent in Wellingborough, busloads of Hindus came from miles around. It started with Patel, a little Hindu girl who had been brought by some Asian friends in a car from Leicester. She was six and had never walked in her life. A family friend had chanced to see a poster about the crusade, and though they knew nothing about the healing power of the Holy Spirit and had never been to a Christian meeting before, they came.

At the end of the meeting I laid hands on Patel, a poor, sickly child, and I felt great love and compassion filling my heart. Within five minutes of prayer, even these normally quiet and subdued Asians were jumping and shouting and hugging each other as little Patel trotted up the aisle, her thin, weak legs getting stronger by the minute.

This let the lid off the kettle, as they say, and soon minibuses and large coaches were coming from all over, full of Asian folk with sick friends and relatives. One big coachful arrived from Leicester an hour and a half before the service. Never before had there been such a movement among Asians in the South Midlands, never before such openness to the gospel.

As a result, I was approached by a prominent Asian businessman in Leicester, a strong Hindu, and asked if I would visit their temple and pray for the sick. I wrote back saying that my healing ministry could not be separated from the gospel of Jesus, the Saviour of all, 'for there is none other name under heaven given amongst men, whereby we must be saved'.

I expected no reply, but soon received an excited phone call. 'I have talked to our leaders. They are happy for you to come. You can preach what you want, we don't mind. We need God's power through you.'

How could I resist such an opportunity (even though none of the local Christians seemed to appreciate it as such)? I found no back-up from the churches in the area, despite this being an unheard-of invitation. One church leader, whom I knew well as being keen on mission, sending missionaries out to India and Pakistan, nevertheless failed to offer any help. That was his Bible study night, he explained!

Undaunted, Lilian and I pressed ahead and arrived at the businessman's house in a wealthy Leicester suburb, where we were to spend the night before the mission. That evening, over a hot curried chicken with rice,

I learnt many things about hospitality I have never forgotten and I was able to talk to our hosts about Jesus. We slept well, and spent the morning praying hard for the two services which were to take place in the afternoon and evening.

I was not speaking in the Hindu shrine itself, but in a community hall which was part of the temple complex. When we arrived half an hour before the first service, the street was already full of people in turbans, women in saris, little children, mothers carrying sick infants. I was shown into the hall by courteous guides and soon the place was full with some 700 people, interested, hungry, curious. I spoke through a young woman interpreter for about 45 minutes about Christ, the only mediator between man and God; how He shed His blood to forgive us our sins for ever; how He died; how He rose again on the third day – hallelujah!

At the end, there was hardly one person who did not raise their hand and pray the sinner's prayer. Many could not do it with a dry eye. And scores were healed, the blind saw, cripples walked, little babies were made well again.

The evening service was equally well attended, and afterwards Lilian and I walked out tired, sad that the local churches had missed the chance to jump in with support and follow-up ... but thrilled at the great work God had begun among the Hindus that night.

THE POOR RICH MAN

In Zurich, Switzerland, I had the opportunity to talk to a multi-millionaire. There were plenty of 'doors' for

God to open that night, for it took me a full half hour to get around the Dobermans, through all the electronic doors, past all the security checks and under the secret cameras which surrounded his securely guarded house. And this was just one of the houses he had scattered around the major cities of Europe.

I finally passed the test and, leaving my shoes at the door, walked across magnificent Persian carpets into his presence. He shook my hand warmly and we sat down, he with a whisky, me with an orange juice. I caught myself marvelling at how I, a simple, unworthy preacher, could be brought by God into contact with such a rich, powerful man. He told me about the futility of his life, his emptiness, his forlornness. He told me how he felt no security, no peace – indeed, how poor his life was.

I in turn told him about the thrills and joys of knowing Jesus. I told him what God could do for him. It was perhaps the first, perhaps the only, chance he had to hear the glories of salvation offered to him through our blessed Lord.

Sadly, he turned down the chance. I have been able to witness our Lord heal many life-threatening diseases, but on that occasion was unable to heal him of his riches. He clung instead to his sinful pleasures, unwilling to give up his idols and seek first God's kingdom.

£3,000 FOR A HEALING

Also in Switzerland there lived a millionairess, who contacted me a few years ago, asking me to go and pray for her. In return, I was offered a plane ticket, a hotel room for the night, a chauffeur to pick me up from the airport – and £3,000. I was pioneering new churches on a shoestring budget and really needed all the money I could get.

I had no thought of personal gain, but getting the money for the work of the gospel was a great temptation. And yet there came a clear leading in my conscience that it was not right. I spoke to the woman and prayed for her on the phone that she would be healed, but never accepted her generous offer. The gifts of God are free. Indeed, they are without price. I was poorer financially for that decision, but richer in every other way. *And* the woman's condition improved from that night on.

The drug-addicts' church

It was a small congregation in the community centre of an old German town. That morning I had preached at a huge Pentecostal meeting of some 300–400 people, but here, just 30 miles away on a crisp January afternoon, were some 40 young married couples and their children. Their pastor told me the story of this remarkable group.

Less than a year earlier, nearly everyone there had been a hardened drug addict. Most were well educated and many had once held good jobs. But then they had opted out, started living together, got interested in eastern religions and become hooked on cocaine, barbiturates, even glue. Some, though, had wanted to kick the habit, and one day three of them decided: 'Right, let's try this guy Jesus. We see His figure (the crucifix) outside the churches.' And so, unprompted, they began to pray, 'O Jesus, fellow, if you're there somewhere in the cosmos, help us...'

They wept, they cried, they called, until, one after another, they felt a Presence, a Power, an assurance. Peace came to them, all at once, and they began to weep in earnest, and laugh and jump around the room. Later they found an old Bible and began to realize what had happened to them. And fortunately a young Scandinavian preacher was in Germany at the time and bumped into them 'by accident'. He was able to give them the basic Bible teaching they needed.

And now here I was a year later, standing before the fruits of that first conversion. The news of their miraculous change had spread quickly and others in their alternative community came forward to be delivered. Those not married were wed, families came back together, love grew, eastern religions were abandoned, drugs were given up. When I arrived there was a lot of noise – chairs scraping, children running about, doors banging. But as soon as they settled down, all opened their Bibles and fixed their eyes on me. Speaking through an interpreter, I gave the longest sermon I have ever preached – nearly two hours on the truths of the Christian faith. And almost the only sound was the rustle as they turned the pages of their Bibles.

When it was over it was quite late and I was due at another church that evening. But it was a long time before I could tear myself away. They hugged me, they crowded round, asked questions – even produced an 'English tea' with lovely German gateaux. Later we were able to arrange for a fine, pioneering German speaker from Switzerland to go and minister to them. I have been back there many times, each time with a sense of privilege at being able to visit such a remarkable, growing church.

MIRACLES IN A CREMATORIUM

A well-known TV celebrity once contacted me and asked if I could conduct his mother's funeral. A few years earlier I had seen him healed of a dreadful hernia at one of my meetings. I accepted, but with trepidation, for in nearly 25 years of ministry up to that time I had only conducted about three funerals. I don't know, it seemed that everyone in our churches lived for ever. I heard that people came to our church because they could be sure of staying healthy and living a good long time!

When I turned up at the crematorium, I found the place packed with a large crowd of familiar figures from the showbiz world. The TV celebrity was well respected and many actors, musicians and performers had come on his account. I had one of the most marvellous opportunities to present the Good News about Jesus Christ to people who were in the main far from God, lost in their careers, fame, riches and ambition. For half an hour I preached that all ought to repent; I warned of hell; and I urged them to make a real commitment of their lives, in the belief that the Holy Spirit would regenerate them. In the quiet closing moments, one hand after another was raised to ask for peace and salvation through the shed blood of Christ.

Afterwards, at the funeral lunch, a number came up to me and told how they had been touched in their hearts by the Spirit of God. One famous star said the last time he had been to a Christian service was during a visit by Billy Graham to London. He had not responded at the time and had never thought he would have the chance to make his peace with God. Now he felt his life had changed. It was a sad day for my friend in a way, but also a wonderful day of comfort, hope and power.

Preaching in a Muslim's night-club

My local organizer was getting desperate, trying to find a church in Gloucester for our meetings. Despite a good press, a good record of conversions, and a good name in the city, he could get no interest from the churches there. He looked for a vacant hall. Still no success.

One day, one of my friends was talking to a Muslim who owned a night-club.

'What a shame you cannot find a place,' said the Muslim. 'Why not come here?'

Surely, we thought, people would not come to such a sordid place for healing. But they did. We had three services there on a day in the middle of the week and 400 people turned up. One hundred and thirty were saved, and one man literally leapt from a wheelchair and ran around the club. God worked in a Muslim's night-club, and put the churches to shame.

God ... which doeth great things past finding out,
yea, marvellous wonders without number.

JOEL 9:2–10

The Hunchback of Macclesfield

It was in a big tent in Macclesfield. When we saw the hunchback's condition, our hearts were touched not only with compassion, but also with admiration. What faith! What a miracle would be needed, though, to cure such a lump. Yet, as we prayed, the crowd fell silent with speculation and wonder. Then came gasps, cries, tears and sobbing, as the coat fell limp where the tailor had built the material up to accommodate the hump. Soon the yard or so of extra material lay like an empty sack, flopping about on the man's back. The cheering did not abate for some minutes, and we all went home in wonder, fear, love and praise. No wonder a thousand people made a decision for Christ during those revival meetings.

The cured lady who complained

The lady who came back after a healing service in the Midlands had been so stone deaf she had not been able to hear a car revving up next to her. She had been cut off from the rest of the world by a wall of silence. One night I heard her loud voice complaining to the local pastor, big, jovial, blunt Geordie, Bob Smith. A minute later there came a knock at the door of the vestry, where I was deep in Bible study. Bob came in.

'We have a problem here, Melvin.'

'My whole ministry is made up of people's problems,' I replied. 'What's new about this one?'

'Oh, this one's different. This lady (I peered around him and spotted her standing outside the door) – this lady got healed the other night. She'd been stone deaf, never heard since her childhood 60 years ago. And now she can't sleep!'

'Why is that?' I asked, bewildered.

'Because she hears so well now, she is kept awake by the clock ticking in the bedroom *of the house next door.*'

You can't win, can you! (We suggested she moved her bed to the opposite wall of her room, or asked her neighbour to move his clock downstairs.)

Seeing after seventy years

One thrilling story relates to a Lancashire lady, who was touched during my Accrington healing mission two years ago. When ITV Granada talked to her, broadcast to a vast audience just after the main news, she was walking in her garden, talking to the interviewer, learning to appreciate the sights she could now see for the first time in her life. Through the laying on of hands and through prayer, God touched her, and slowly a lifetime of darkness slipped away.

I remember the night she was healed. As I prayed with our local Assemblies of God pastor beside me, she said she saw strips of light. I wondered for a moment what she meant, then realized that behind my back the street lamps were shining through the long strip windows of the church. This was how her sight began, and it grew in clarity over the months which followed. It was a true miracle, touching the hearts of the general public in the North of England.

THE FISH AND CHIP SHOP INCIDENT

The meeting in the Birmingham suburb was crowded with reporters and photographers. As I moved down the long line of sick and incurable people, they followed me, pouncing on anyone who felt any sense of power, any feeling of improvement or pain receding or sight coming.

'Did you know Mr Banks before?' 'Have you ever met him?' 'Is this your first visit to a crusade?' 'How do you feel?' Thus it went on, and when a man walked the length of the church without his two sticks, this really got them going!

But then I came to someone in a wheelchair – a poor, pain-riddled, paralysed person. I spoke gently to her, and began to pray. But no response. No feeling of the power from God flowing through me and into her. It was like the sea in a storm dashing against a great quayside and splashing back again with no effect. I struggled, I sweated, I prayed with compassion and earnestness for a full 10 minutes, but not a twinkle of feeling, no response, no healing, no life, nothing happening in her at all. The reporters hung on every prayer, but as I got weaker and more discouraged, they got more deflated. With a final word or two of love and faith, I tried to encourage her and then moved on to someone else.

The evening ended, and on the whole it had been a successful night. Most folk seemed to have been healed and even the reporters were thrilled. But as I drove to my digs in the city, I could not forget that one lady in the wheelchair. If only she had walked...

The Bible says, the wind bloweth where it listeth: who can understand the mysterious movings of God? I felt a failure because of that dear lady not being healed, but God knew best.

At about the same time as I was driving home dejectedly, the lady's husband was lifting his wife into the front seat of their car as usual. They drove home, but on the way he stopped at a fish and chip shop to pick up some supper. When he returned to the car with the food, he found the car door open and his wife gone. What could have happened? Had she been kidnapped?

Then he looked up the street and there, under a lamp, he saw her – walking by herself along the pavement towards their home! He had to lean against the car to steady himself. Then he jumped into the car to catch her up.

The next night she came back to the crusade to give her testimony – with no reporters present this time. She told how, as she sat in the car outside the shop, she had felt this mighty, loosening warmth spreading through her body. She felt the urge to try to move her legs and when she did so, she felt no pain. So she shuffled them a little, opened the car door and climbed out by herself. Almost immediately she could stand up and then *she felt she just wanted to walk home*. She felt so confident and strong. And she has remained well ever since.

THE GOAL THAT WAS DIVINE

He was a million-pound footballer, amongst the first. His name was famous, with headlines on sports pages of all the big dailies. He was raved over. But his knee and cartilage had been knocked out of place; his leg was in a very bad condition from a nasty clash in the midst of a vital match which had left him missing a good part of the rest of the season.

One of my meetings had been recommended to him in passing. He was not 'the religious sort', but needed to try anything. He came and was astonished (I heard later) by what he had witnessed in the service that night: sick people being healed, he could hardly believe his eyes. Then his turn came. He said he 'turned queer' as I prayed, as if under a dose of anaesthetic, although it was 'warm, sweet and a nice feeling', an experience he had never 'touched before'.

To cut a long story short, he was playing the next Saturday, amazing physiotherapists, trainers and his manager and staff. *And* the Sunday papers featured his terrific goal in that match. One paper in its headline on the sports page put it like this: 'THAT GOAL WAS JUST *DIVINE*'. They did not know where he had been, or that it was true in more ways than one!

That famous player has never forgotten that prayer of faith which changed his life.

FAMOUS OPERA SINGER GETS A NEW SONG

Just before the service, after our prayer-time together with the elders and staff, I was told that one of Europe's most famous opera singers was present with us. She had flown from the continent to be there, having heard of the marvellous miracles in our services. She had lost her voice and had not been able to sing for a year, cancelling her engagements around the world. She is renowned in the international operatic world. Following the song service, worship, and the preaching of the Word of God, a great long queue of sick people formed for the laying on of hands and prayer, as is customary in our meetings.

When the lady reached me, the lady stewardess and healing-line worker explained she could not speak or sing. I asked her to nod her head in answer to my questions. I asked her if she would give her life to Jesus. The worker explained that the woman was a Roman Catholic, but she agreed she had neglected religion and did not know Jesus as her Saviour. She agreed to come to Christ!

I asked her if she would sing regularly for Jesus now. She nodded. I prayed. She gulped, she spoke faintly. 'I can swallow properly, I can speak. I can speak!' she shouted. I asked her to sing for Jesus *now*. She got a hymn book and sang beautifully and clearly, filling the auditorium with her rich voice, '*The old rugged cross...*'

On a hill far away, stood an old rugged cross
The emblem of suffering and shame...
I will cling to the old rugged cross
till my trophies at last I lay down...

She is still singing for Jesus around the world and has not yet laid her trophies down in heaven. She was singing recently in the New York Opera House and also Covent Garden. But she sings for Jesus regularly in churches and functions in between.

God gave her a new heart, a new voice, a new song to sing to the world.

'I WAS GOING TO PUT MY HEAD IN THE GAS OVEN UNTIL THAT NIGHT MY CHILD WAS HEALED'

So said the tall, dark 25-year-old mother of a little brain-damaged child on Britain's west coast. I had been holding a mission there, and we had dealt with hundreds of poor, sick people during a week-long, fatiguing mission. This mother held the limp, weak, almost lifeless body in her arms tight across her chest.

'There is no hope unless he gets a miracle today. We need a miracle,' she sobbed. The child, if it lived long enough I was told, would never sit up, never communicate, never recognize anyone!

I prayed. The father stood halfway up the crowded aisle, watching, half unsure, feeling forlorn and helpless. I prayed on a *strong prayer* ... the mother wept louder, a lady worker put her arm around her. I went on praying down the line. About 15 minutes later there was near hysteria in one corner, shouting, laughing, clapping. I gazed over and we heard the child had opened its eyes and was looking around, seemingly trying to communicate.

I was back in that area one year later, and little Chris was walking, running up and down the aisle of the church, now begging to say some words, communicating, healthy, noisy, strong; the child the best surgeons, specialists and doctors said would not live and if he lived he would not sit up, would be a cabbage in his short life here – that little fellow certainly shot up enough steam in that service to make everyone know he was very much *alive ... and would be for a long time to come*. Faithful Christians know that family follows the Master who is the great miracle-worker today – Jesus Christ of Nazareth.

'I MUST LEAVE MY LOVER AND GO HOME TO MY CHILD AND HUSBAND'

These were the words of a young woman in the counselling area, following a night of revival in South Shields on the north-east coast of Britain. I had preached the gospel to the packed chapel and made my customary appeal, that sacred moment when we ask people who feel deeply convicted in their hearts, who are willing to repent (to turn away from their sins with sorrow) and commit themselves to Jesus Christ, to make Him their Saviour and Lord, to ask him to come and save them although unworthy. Many came. The whole front of the chapel altar and around the pulpit was filled.

Some 15 miles away in County Durham, a little boy was being put to bed. He knelt to say his prayers, his father – apprehensive and doubtful – let him pray. The six-year-old prayed: '*Lord, send Mummy home tomorrow, you can do it God, please talk to Mummy tonight and tell her to come home tomorrow, Amen!*'

His Dad tucked him into bed and said, 'Goodnight, Son.' Hiding a tear, the little fellow said perkily, 'Goodnight, Dad, don't worry. Mum will be home tomorrow because I asked God!' The father slipped out of the room not knowing what to say.

Meanwhile, two and a half hours later, as I made that appeal in South Shields, among those who came forward was *that mother*. She had left her husband, home and little boy for a lover, months before. Now drawn by the crusade, she was weeping before God. All came out as she shared it with two of my team. She found God to be real, forgiveness to be certain, and the Holy Spirit to be her purifier.

Soon she made that confession, and we heard later that she had packed her bags, left the man she was living with *and the next day returned home to her husband and child*. They are happily married today and living wholesome, clean lives. What special joy I find in seeing this happen often – the miracle of a restored, reconciled family – one of life's *greatest miracles*! God is at work today.

£10,000 STOLEN MONEY RETURNED

The minister ushered the small but well-built lady into the vestry. I never see ladies alone for counselling, but had made an allowance on this one occasion due to the requests of the pastor. The meeting was just over, we had seen every miracle in the book in this small Welsh town. The place had been packed so much I thought folk were going to faint. No doubt the blind woman who had received her sight a few days before and had been featured in the paper that night had even further expanded the already congested conditions.

I was really thinking of these practical problems, of how we could manage when no hall was available to us in the town, when the little lady began with a soft Welsh voice, 'Thank you for seeing me, Reverend Banks, I do have a great problem...' I had heard it all before, but everyone thinks they are the only people who have done such wrong, made such mistakes or lowered themselves in such a way, so I let her go on.

'It's like this, I have had such a responsible position in the firm...' She told me how she had been a trusted employee for many decades, handling large sums of cash. She had finally fallen to temptation, though it would be almost impossible for the firm to find out how much and what had been stolen. Ten thousand pounds had been involved (that would be worth more like £100,000 today). She could not be caught out.

But in my meeting that night her conscience had been so awakened and pricked and wounded that she could never find peace until this had been sorted out. She felt terrible. The Holy Spirit had done His work – the spirit of honesty and power and fear of God had moved her spirit for good. It was quite clear God had done something very direct and deep in her heart, for she had no ulterior motive and was quite beyond any police action.

Her whole story convinced and stunned me. God had ministered a very heavy conviction of sin and clearly pointed her to the need for restitution, as Zacchaeus had done in Luke 19:8 when he repaid back all he stole and four times as much. I administered both comfort and peace, and followed on with the efforts to urge her to follow this conviction through. I gave her the assurance the church would stand by her, believers would secretly pray, and if it meant prison they would visit her. No shame would stand in the way of us showing loving kindness, helpfulness to her family, and being true friends, brothers and sisters all the way.

She left that vestry at peace. Later she was to see God answer prayer with mercy shown by the employers. She paid back all she stole; she was not taken to court or sacked. She lost some wages in that she was demoted to a lower position in the firm, but she still works there, is admired by her bosses, and is now a born-again believer of good reputation.

A MINISTER'S WIFE RAISED FROM HER DEATHBED

'Over a decade ago I had meningitis. I had got a bit better but was very thin and weak but I knew something was wrong inside, that I was not as I should be. Eventually I was diagnosed as having ESR blood cancer, a very serious – a 30 count – very poor, it was critical. I was a minister's wife, it did not worry me about dying but I did not want to leave my husband and two children who were still very small yet! I wanted to be alive for them.

'I asked the hospital if they would release me to go over the ferry from the Isle of Wight, where we lived at that time, to the Melvin Banks crusade in Portsmouth. I had to be carried onto the boat, I was so weak, I felt that I was dying and wondered whether I would make it to the meeting.

'I knew God could heal me, I was unconscious most of the journey on the ferry boat across to the mainland and did not come to until in the auditorium in the city of Portsmouth. The meeting was packed out, I could hardly cope, all these people, I just wilted in my heart. There was this little man buzzing about. I asked who it was. They said that's the evangelist Melvin Banks. I had heard about him and the marvellous gift of healing but he looked so ordinary, moving amongst the people, mixing, just like anyone else ... It was so noisy, I felt only God could help me ... the meeting was so long, I got down to the front, I thought, "After all this effort and I feel so ill I am going to make an effort to get something from God." A lady near me said, "I am going for a blessing to get my corns healed." I thought, if an old lady can believe for a few corns to go, what can He do for me if I trust Him through His servant?

'Then just in front of me was this poor little lady; she was so crippled, so bad and sick, my heart went out to her. I forgot myself. Melvin called her out ... so wonderful, just amazing ... she was so sick, then in moments her body straightened before our eyes, her sickness vanished, her limbs became upright, all pain and suffering vanished. Then Melvin asked me what was wrong ... I couldn't speak and tell him what was wrong with me, I was choked with emotion. Then what the Bible calls the gift of the Word of Knowledge came to him, he said, "It's in your chest, isn't it?" I nodded, agreeing. He asked me to breathe in deeply, but I just felt I couldn't. It was difficult to get breath enough to keep alive, let alone to breathe and breathe as Melvin suggested, the pain was terrible. I tried, I made every effort; I thought it would kill me, but as I did so I felt amazing, thrilling me through and through: it was easing. I can only describe it like ten pints of new blood and ten times more fresh, new energy pumped into me! The power, the relief, the joy, the healing, the hope I received was marvellous.

'I went out of that great auditorium feeling as if I had never had anything ever wrong with me. It was gone midnight when we eventually got back across the water to the Isle of Wight and home. The next day I knew I was cured, no one had to lift me, help me, carry me any more. I had energy out of this world. I praised God like I had never done before...'

That lady, fit and well today, continues as a minister's wife in Shropshire.

THE FIRE FALLS AND THE DEBT VANISHES!

'I do want you to come to my town,' Ben, the Scottish minister, declared. He was pastor to a rising church in the Lincolnshire fen country. 'But to tell you the truth, the debt on our new building is so huge it will take us years to pay it off and to be able to afford any major evangelistic effort.'

'I believe God has spoken to me about moving this great country area and market town,' I said. 'God can help us with all the money we need. I am sure about that.'

Ben looked at me. 'Well, the church is looking up, excited with the new building. But we lack new life coming in: we lie on this huge council estate, and no one attends from the local area.' 'We must do something ... but it's that debt – if only we did not have that debt...' he murmured thoughtfully.

'Let's believe that the money will come in from the offerings for all advertising,' I said. 'Let us put people first, and their needs; that has always been my motto. God cannot let us down. I will sell my little car and give you the money if necessary.'

Ben was amazed. 'Now I don't think we expect that,' he said, a little embarrassed. 'Somehow we will find a little cash for the advertising, and then believe God for the rest through the offerings.' So we shook hands and what, unknown to us, was to become an historic event, was set in motion.

In that crusade a chauffeur to the Royal family was converted; a paralysed girl ran from her wheelchair and was featured on the front page of the local newspaper; hundreds came to Christ. The crusade was extended and every inch of the building became congested with the crowds. The vast working-class housing estate, normally seeing few ever attending any church, saw many whole families converted to Christ, and the church became a centre for family worship for years afterwards.

Five hundred registered a commitment for Jesus during those days of power and blessing. Today there are two thriving Full Gospel churches in the town. Much has happened over the years, but God has worked and developed believers into two fellowships that are making separate but distinct impacts on the area.

But the notable *after-thought of God*, when he had worked so many miracles of regeneration and healing on this Lincolnshire town, was that not only were all financial needs met for the existing bills (the advertising of the crusade, heating, lighting of the church, etc.), but He added on a remarkable bonus! A telephone call came from the pastor to my office some weeks after the crusade had ended, thanking me and full of appreciation for the many new people crowding into his church now, and the marvellous testimonies of changed lives. And then he added, 'By the way, a strange thing has happened. Some gifts came this week from new friends of the church and this has cleared every penny of the huge debt. Instead of being saddled with this for 25 years, we have it cleared completely. It's amazing! I don't know how to say thank you!' *When the fire fell on this town, it burned up the debt. God in action indeed!*

A PUB IS CONVERTED!

It was in the same marvellous meeting that I was introduced to one of the 60 converts that night. The chief counselling steward introduced me to a tall thin lady.

'I have a problem.' I was so used to nearly everyone I met saying that, it did not take me aback. I only had to guess what it was, a family problem, cash problem, sickness problem, a son or daughter problem, or a score of other needs that people share with me. No, this was to be different to anything I had ever heard before.

'I own a pub.' It was me who was aghast now. 'It is a good hostelry; we have nice customers, a good business. My husband died some years ago and I run it myself. But I do not know what to do now I have received Christ. What do you advise?'

I looked at her, thrilled with the grace of God to reach down to this needy lady. And yet, she was human like anyone else, was she not?

'Pray every day. A new world of guidance will open to you, your conscience will work, God will speak to you. You will know what to do.'

I never saw that lady again till six months later. I was speaking at a crowded meeting in a school hall near Bodmin, north Cornwall; she had travelled some miles to be with us. She told me afterwards she had brought five people with her, some of her customers. She had put up Bible texts and also crusade posters about my meetings all around the pub; more of her customers were due to attend the next night. They now nicknamed her 'the preacher'. She had much opposition, but had been able to help a lot of her 'congregation'. She had prayed for folk and even led people to Jesus in the pub. It was getting a nickname as 'the soul-saving centre'. But opposition was mounting, plus the long hours she had to work, which was a hindrance to her getting Christian fellowship.

I saw her two years later while preaching near St Austell. She had by then sold her pub and was running a little shop near the seaside, going on and growing with God and still telling others of the miracle Christ ... and still winning the lost. But in that area of north Cornwall, the pub is still known as the 'soul-saving centre'!

When I return home exhausted from one of these long, exciting miracle tours – after seeing God in action in so many ways – I walk wearily up the garden path, through the front door and greet my family for perhaps the first time in weeks or months, then these miracles revive me. The memory of them soon transforms and refreshes me, and reminds me constantly of the goodness and unfailing promises of God.

I like to feel that my travels – and the miracles achieved in them – have made things easier for others.

There is a story of a young boy walking home one day with an old man. In those days the paths at the side of the roads were just cinder tracks, and a new load of sharp ashes had been spread during the day.

'Let's walk on the road,' suggested the boy after a while, tired of stumbling through the cinders.

'No,' the old man smiled. 'We'll walk on the path. If we don't tread it smooth, the folk who come after us will have to do it.'

If my travels have done that, in any small way, then I could hope for nothing better.

7

A Powerhouse for Society

When God acts so convincingly, the Church and the world marvels at this 'God who makes things work', as Zachariah the prophet put it. Not human ingenuity, but the sheer dynamic of God: we are seeing a sense of divine majesty being recaptured.

Campbell McAlpine used to say, 'I see a church more governed by psychology than theology!' The world looking at the Church cannot see the theology of power.

'Not in word only but with demonstration of the Spirit and power'

When a terrible disaster hit the national headlines in the UK a few years ago, the death of so many young people one Wednesday morning through a crazed demonic gunman, the sensational *Daily Mirror* headline read: 'THE DAY GOD SLEPT IN'.

But God never slumbers nor sleeps. His eye is on the sparrow. 'His eye goes out throughout the whole earth.' God lived and lives: 'The eyes of the Lord move throughout the earth to strengthen those whose hearts are fully committed to him' (2 Chronicles 16:9 NIV).

The people have got discouraged, many reached a low point. In spite of all the razzmatazz in the Church, the humanist enemies have swept in like a flood. It's more than talk the Church needs, it's *God in action*, the restoration of nations. There is contradiction between creed and conduct. People are professing much and performing little.

An apocryphal story describes a Christian arriving at the gates of heaven. He was warmly greeted by the archangel Gabriel, who offered a personally guided tour around the vastness of heaven. The first building they visited was an enormous aircraft hangar lined with narrow shelves. Each shelf was filled with neatly wrapped presents all addressed to the new arrival.

'What's this, then?' enquired the Christian.

'Oh, those,' replied Gabriel, 'they're all the gifts which God had for you to use on earth and which you never bothered to claim!'

Teaching – prophecy – service – giving – exhortation – hospitality – leadership – acts of kindness or mercy – word of knowledge – word of wisdom – faith – healing – miracles – discerning of spirits – tongues – interpretation of tongues – apostle – help – administration – exorcism – evangelism – pastorship – celibacy – voluntary martyrdom – mission – intercession and encouragement.

All those gifts are clearly recorded in Scripture. Some will come by natural means, others are supernaturally endowed. The more our lives are filled by the Spirit of God, the less we will demand to rule ourselves by human logic. When we bring to God our natural inclinations and abilities, asking Him to bless what *we* have planned for *Him*, it is an invitation to spiritual disaster. Instead, our surrender to the direction of the Holy Spirit opens us to receive from him every gift which he wants to bestow on us.

When Paul wrote, 'Be filled with the Spirit' (Ephesians 5:18), the tense used in the original Greek is the 'aorist' tense and does not refer to a once-and-for-all event but an ongoing experience. A more accurate translation (although very bad English) would be, 'Continue to be being filled with the Holy Spirit.'

Dwight L. Moody was once addressing a nineteenth-century British congregation on this theme and many were offended. Afterwards several leaders and clergy took Moody to one side and demanded, 'Why do you say that we need to go on being filled with the Holy Spirit – we've been filled, 20 or 30 years ago. Why do we need to be filled again?'

Moody's reply remains, to this day, an absolute classic of spiritual commonness. 'I need to be filled with the Spirit every moment of every day – because I leak.' Today we remain a very leaky people; we desperately need to know God today, not just hark back to our memories of His activity.

A sense of holy dissatisfaction with the poverty of our knowledge of God and our love for him would quickly change the situation.

As A. W. Tozer has ably summarized:

In this hour of all-but-universal darkness one cheering gleam appears: within the fold of conservative Christianity there are to be increasing numbers of persons whose religious lives are marked by a growing hunger after God Himself. They are eager for spiritual realities and will not be put off with words, nor will they be content with correct 'interpretations' of truth. They are athirst for God, and they will not be satisfied till they have drunk deep at the Fountain of Living

Water. This is the only real harbinger of revival which I have been able to detect anywhere on the religious horizon.

As I travel around Britain the major sin which I encounter among Christians is not jealousy, immorality or greed. It is that so many of us have a wrong view of ourselves. We examine ourselves from such a jaundiced view that we easily draw the conclusion, 'I'm useless.' We long to have the gifts of others. We struggle on with little recognition or encouragement. Increasingly we become sucked into feelings of self-pity and insecurity. We attack people God is using, we criticize and grumble. We deny the Lord the control of our lives. All because we have a wrong view of ourselves.

We must be careful to recognize those gifts which God has given to us – and those which he has not. As J. B. Phillips has paraphrased Romans 12:3: 'Try to have a sane estimate of your capabilities.' And do not be surprised when God gives you the opportunity to use gifts of which you are not even aware! They are given so that we can use them to bless and encourage others. 'Each one, as a good manager of God's different gifts, must use for the good of others the special gift he has received from God' (1 Peter 4:10).

As C. Peter Wagner has stated:

Every spiritual gift we have is a resource which we must use and for which we will be held account-able at the Judgement. Some will have one, some two, and some five. The quantity to begin with does not matter. Stewards are responsible only for what the Master has chosen to give them. But the resource that we do have *must* be used to accomplish the Master's purpose.

This is not time for ordinary lives but for extraordinary living – *God is calling us*! Rally the remnant who know their God and can illuminate the world ... no longer must believers creep around in the dark, but flood the world with light.

Many Christians sing, 'I'm standing on the promises', but they are sitting on the premises. One pastor said to me, 'Keep in with the key men in your denomination, Melvin.' I replied, 'I only keep in with the keeper of the keys.'

- Many believers appreciate the Word – but never appropriate the Word!
- We have plenty of correct heads and few consumed hearts!
- Many ministers recently have resigned but need to be re-assigned!
- We are urged in Hebrews to remember, 'His messengers are [like] winds, the servants are tongues of fire...'

Peter the apostle put it:

Your life is a journey, you must travel with a deep consciousness of God, it cost God plenty to get you out of the dead-end life ... He paid with Christ's sacred Blood ... He did it by an unblemished, sacrificial Lamb ... it's because of this sacrificial Messiah ... raised from the dead and glorified ... that you have a future.

1 Peter 3:7–19 The Message

Many of the successful minor prophets in the Old Testament, or apostles in the New Testament, would hardly win any popularity contests with many people, but they won their generation often to a new-found faith in God – such people as Jonah in Nineveh, and Micah, Hosea and Isaiah making Hezekiah's righteousness prosper.

Paul was thrown out of some cities, as Orin Gifford used to say, 'He saw either a riot or a revival'! They moved in mighty power with a timeless message. Often the world challenges us too: only God in action is our salvation. We will prevail. God is acting for us.

8

ACTION WITHIN US

On the front of one of our brochures that goes into some 2 million homes of the British general public each year, to invite the vast non-churchgoing communities to one of our gospel crusades, is the phrase (it upsets over-holy people) 'SEEING IS BELIEVING!'

The philosophy of the society in which we live is quite simple: if it works then it must be right! Seeing that all doctrine, precepts, commandments and statutes are not always immediately visible, and neither are our prayers always perfectly interpreted into immediate actions, this is not always the soundest of systems to work by. However, too much emphasis in the Church has been made on what God does not do, rather than on what He can, does and is willing to do, and is in fact now working for us.

And in our advertising we are interpreting to and communicating with a gospel of power. A gospel of Christ crucified, glorified: He lived and does live again. This gospel is a gospel of *action*: it works.

'How can God bring this about in me? Let Him do it and perhaps you will know,' George MacDonald said.

THE COST

It is a struggle to the breaking of day. 'All I have seems to teach me to trust the Creator for all I have not seen,' Emerson said. Seeing – trust what you see.

God reveals it step by step, as T. S. Eliot said, 'Man cannot take too much truth about himself' at one time. God allows a little by little. Christians, ministers, churches that have allowed themselves to get into a place of scepticism, caution, doubt over miracles, and settled down with the status quo system, cannot see any of the supernatural miracles of Christ. Amy Carmichael said we ought to have 'a contentment with the unexplained'.

Through trial, struggle, darkness, costs, we get more of the miraculous of God. Thoreau wrote, 'The things for which we visit a man were done alone in the dark and the cold.' W. Jenkyn said, 'As the wicked are hurt by the best things, so the godly are bettered by the worst things.'

The pressures, darkness, the storms against us, can show what is really in us. De Gaulle said, 'In difficulties a man finds himself.' The poem goes:

What lies behind us,
and what lies before us,
are tiny matters compared
to what lies within us.

Dante told how 'midway on my journey through life I found myself in a dark wood, the path was lost!' It's easy to lose our bearings, get off the road a little.

I was travelling with my wife in an area quite familiar from some years before, when I had preached around that district in mid-Derbyshire. I was sure I had to go straight on to find the turning off on the right, on to the town I wanted. My wife insisted I had taken the 'wrong road', I had gone too far, I must turn back, detour, double-back on myself and find the old road, the direct road. I firmly replied that I knew the area well, this was it, the turning would come up soon! But after another five minutes, unfamiliar markings, churches, pubs I did not recognize appeared on the landscape. I was in strange territory, on the wrong road. She sat quietly till I drew up, and slowly turned around. There was no 'I told you so' – that's not her style. On I pressed, back over the way I had foolishly come to find the correct turning, and true enough it was still there! As my wife had described, soon I was at the venue, having learnt a lesson from my drive in the dark.

When God is withdrawing some light, he is trying to teach us something better than light – faith! We need to learn how to believe, how to trust in the dark.

An old drunk, bottle in one hand, cigar in the other, said, 'Hey, Rev. Banks ... I've seen your miracles ... wonderful...' he hiccuped, tried to catch his breath and staggered, then went on. 'My wife has read all your books ... I believe in your miracles!'

I replied, blushing and with tongue in cheek, 'Are you a Christian?'

He chuckled and staggered. 'No, I'm not a Christian...' He reeled forward. 'I can't believe what it says in the Bible, that God wiped out little children, a God of love can't do that.'

I looked him straight in the eye and commented, 'No, He cannot.'

He seemed to sober up suddenly. 'You agree!'

I replied, 'I agree.'

'But you are a preacher, you are supposed to believe in the Bible.'

I said, 'Well, I do believe in it – all of it – yes, all of it.'

'I'm confused,' he blurted out.

I went on, 'You see, I understand most of the Bible, but there are a few passages I don't doubt but I don't understand and those I accept by faith!'

The Church is still frightened of what it cannot explain. It wants to know everything, caution reigns and is destroying the river of revival for so many. D. J. Hall put it, 'The Church has allowed and permitted its message to be filtered through the sieve of worldly power and glory.'

'The natural man receives not...' he cannot understand the spiritual revival, he rejects what he cannot explain. Jacob could say, 'I've seen God face to face.' Jeremiah, moving through suffering to understanding, could say, 'God has plans for welfare not calamity, to give you a future and purpose' (Jeremiah 29:10–11 NASV).

Faith is:

1. The wisdom to see the treasure in the trash.
2. The courage to face things as they are, not as we wish them to be.
3. The boldness to embrace things and say, 'I will not let you go till you bless me.'
4. The making of our great weakness our greatest strength!

I like Heather Blackwell's lovely lines:

O Lord,
You know my heart.
Keep me from despair.
Keep me from losing hope;
From assuming there will be
No change.
No new thing.
No clean wind of your Spirit.
No stirring and shaking
In the tops of the trees.
Keep me from prayer without asking
For fear of not receiving...
Keep me from prayer without pleading
For fear of pain that pierces...
O Lord, you know my heart.
Help me to fearlessly see what *is*
And to joyfully perceive what will be.

IS YOUR FAITH RUNNING OUT?

You can run out of energy into exhaustion
You can run out of love into barrenness
You can run out of commitment into the mundane
cycle
You can run out of resolve into a rat race programme
But you cannot run out of God

In a valley in South Wales where I was preaching, a
pastor gave me a verse, which reads:

What opposes you
is nothing,

what you are to face tomorrow
is an abysmal affair compared
with what God is doing within you...
FAITH IS IN US!
VICTORY OR DEFEAT IS IN US!

The teenager looked in the mirror and said sadly, 'I'm looking older.' What's happening to him? The heating system broke down in a block of offices one bitter cold winter's day, and the engineers found it was a tiny dead ant in the thermometer that caused it all! A man lost his hearing in one ear – it was all off balance, it echoed and rang, the surgeons found out that this pain and annoyance was one tiny hair, almost unseen by the human eye, that had caught on to his eardrum! Whether we are old or young, stress catches up on us, little things wear us down, cause a blockage, a disconnection, and misery, disorientation, loss, coldness, blight and even torment.

There are many pressures – family pressures, employment pressures, professional pressures, career pressures, education pressures, money pressures. The more you gain and accumulate, the more can break down! Pressures produce stress. You find you cannot handle it any more. It's the straw that breaks the camel's back.

I stayed recently with a Baron in a large 1,000-year-old castle in Holland. Here was a man who had a vast, old, stone building to maintain: although he lived in such a grand-sounding place, he was not rich, all his inheritance was in that old, historic building. It was magnificent (although very cold at night), its six-metre thick walls, its moat, its cobbled court, its tall towers. This man ran it with his wife and one part-time helper. It took all he had to maintain such a place: he said he had to pay 50 per cent taxes before he could begin to make enough to keep the great edifice viable. But this man – I still see him laying stones on the 150-foot tower top – was as free as a bird, stressless, at peace, full of joy. He had found Christ a short time before and was radiant and victorious, and calm as he moved among his sheep, his cockerels, his peacocks, his vast castle estate, poor yet rich in spirit! Stress free. God was in action in this man's life.

It's time to sit, to think, to listen, to learn to receive from our Maker. A recent survey showed more people fall asleep in church than in any other public place. What a compliment! Think of all those people with their eyes shut meditating, in another world, dreaming their dreams, 'O Thou that sleepest, awake!' God wants, however, to speak to us. Jesus said, 'When you pray, go inside, *shut the door*, and whatever you ask of your Father in *secret*, He will give it to you.'

SHUT THE DOOR

Go somewhere without your husband, without your wife, without your business problems, without your children, without your friends, without your pleasures. You have become overloaded; it is time to cast things aside and listen to the living God. He is out there!

Have a clear, open line, no disconnection, an open heart to the Master's voice. Philip Brooks, a writer, had many stresses, disappointments, a breakdown. He went to the Holy Land, and found himself sitting on Christmas Eve in the shepherds' fields just outside Bethlehem, where Christ was born. I've sat there myself, on the green grass and brown hillsides with the Arab shepherds. He had been so distraught, but was overcome with peace that dark night. He wrote some verses – it was the beginning of his restoration – and he went on to become a great preacher in the USA. You can see his statue outside his old church in the centre of the old town in Boston, Massachusetts. The words he wrote expressed his peace and victory over pressure and stress. We still sing them today.

> O little town of Bethlehem,
> How still we see thee lie,
> ... as the silent stars go by ...
> Yet in the dark streets shineth
> An everlasting Light,
> the hopes and fears of all the years
> are met in thee tonight.

Let the signal come through. There is someone out there. An answer to pressure is at hand.

9

MODESTY: A BACKBONE TO FAITH

'He who speaks on his own does so to give honour for himself, but he who works for the honour of the One who sent him [Christ] is a man of truth, there is nothing false about him' (John 7:18 NIV). Here is factual modesty, no pushing of one's own name, no 'feathering his own nest'. Christ is 'par excellence', 'a man of truth': we must be like Him. 'Whoever claims to live in Him must walk as Jesus did' (1 John 2:6). If we seek our own ends and glory, we are on our own. If we modestly, humbly seek God's glory, there will be a ring of truth about us. Someone said about D. L. Moody: 'He never seemed to have heard about himself.' There is power, there is faith, there is an indelible anointing, when we die to our selfishness and ego, walk humbly in faith. Then great honour comes to our Heavenly Father. Did our Lord not say, 'He who honours me I will honour'? 'You did not choose me, I chose you' (John 15:6).

Count Zinzendorf tried to burn a piece of parchment. Again and again, he attempted to do it, but it would not burn. Finally he read the two lines on it:

> O let us in the nailprints see
> our calling and election free.

It resulted in his life-changing salvation experience, and eventually 40 years of dedicated service to Christ, during which thousands of people were saved.

FAITH'S BASIS

God through His word put faith in our hearts. Justified by faith, we have peace with God, through our Lord Jesus Christ. Martin Luther had written on the margin of his Bible next to Romans 1:17, '*Sola fide* – faith alone'.

Faith needs both prayer and the word to savour it. Charles Simeon said, 'It is easier for a minister to study and preach for five hours than pray for his people for half an hour.' Samuel Chadwick, the Methodist giant, said, 'I would rather preach than eat or sleep or do anything else on earth.' Jesus said, 'If you believe in your heart and ask anything it will be done.' Paul wrote, 'Faith begins by taking in the divine words of the Lord...' 'Seek faith more than anything,' he said to the Hebrews (Chapter 13), 'imitate their faith.' Again, 'Impart spiritual gifts ... be encouraged by each other's faith' (Romans 7:12 NIV).

The original Methodist preachers were called the 'Now' preachers, for they always proclaimed faith is now, full salvation is now! The wonder of the access now by faith should always arrest us – a privilege, confidently, constantly exercised. 'Let us then approach the throne of grace with confidence ... helping us in our times of need' (Hebrews 4:16). Keep a soft heart towards God. Richard Baxter wrote, 'It is the dearth of our faithlife to have hard thoughts towards God.' 'By him, in believing we say – "My Father"' (Romans 8:15).

His name – JESUS, JESUS, JESUS – is everything. His character is everything, His works, His love, His glory is everything. Plan to pray, plan to make His word predominant. Fail to plan and you plan to fail! Plan to succeed and you will!

Begin each day with Him. 'Morning by morning ... Lord I hear your voice, I wait in expectation...' (Psalm 5:3). The Greek proverb says, 'The beginning is half of the whole.' 'Seldom does a day's end finish more blessed than its beginning,' says Derek Prince. Give God the best. A well-known company has marketed the slogan: '...when you care enough to send the very best'. God is worthy of the best, from the start to the end of the day. John Wesley said, 'It seems that God is limited by our prayer life, and that He cannot (or will not) do anything for humanity unless someone asks Him!'

God has always done His work through humble instruments. Most Bible students know that Moses lived for 120 years, and that his life was divided into three periods of 40 years. The first 40 were spent in Egypt where Moses learnt to be somebody. The second period was spent in the backside of the desert of Midian where the man who had been somebody learnt to become a nobody. And for the last 40 years of his life God showed the world what He could do with a somebody who had become a nobody. Paul tells us that God is pleased to use the 'are nots' (1 Corinthians 1:27,28).

I often talk of the old saints from Norfolk I knew 40 years ago. They often spoke of the early revival days. In 1921 a mighty awakening swept along the east coast from the north of Scotland down to Yarmouth. There were two outstanding human instruments – Jock Troup and Douglas Brown, a successful Baptist minister. Speaking at Keswick of his own personal experience, he said, 'It may take more than one meeting to get the truth right home. It took me more than four months. I had been a minister of Jesus Christ for 26 years. Then God laid hold of me. He laid hold of me in the midst of a Sunday night service and nearly broke my heart while I was preaching. I went back to my vestry, locked the door and threw myself down on the hearthrug in front of the fireplace, broken-hearted. Why? I don't know. My church was filled. I loved my people and I believe my people loved me. I do not say they ought to, but they did. I was as happy as a man could be there. I had never known a Sunday there for 15 years without conversions.

'That night I went home and straight to my study. My wife came to tell me that supper was ready. "You must not wait for me," I said. "What's the matter?" she asked. "I have a broken heart," I replied. I had no supper that night. The Lord Jesus laid His hand on a proud minister and told him that he had not gone far enough, that there were reservations in his surrender. I knew what He meant. He wanted me to do a piece of work that I had been trying to evade. I knew God was right and I was wrong. I knew what it would mean for me and I was not willing to pay the price.

'I went to my bedroom, but not to sleep. I spent the night in prayer. As I left the bedroom next morning, I stumbled over my dog. Mike licked my face. He thought I was ill. When Mike was doing that, I felt I did not deserve that anybody should love me, not even my dog. I felt such an outcast. Then something happened. I felt myself in the loving embrace of Christ, and all the loving embrace of Christ, and all the power and blessedness rolled in like a deluge. God had waited four months for a man like me. I have not had time to prepare addresses for this Convention. This is my 1,700th service this last 18 months.'

In the revival which followed, thousands were brought to Christ.

Faith lifts us up above the realm of our own ability, and makes God's possibilities available to us. Faith relates us to two unseen realities – God and His Word. It is God's saying, God's quotation, God's divine verbal leftovers, His divine words that brings faith within us. Faith is in the heart. 'For with the heart man believeth unto righteousness' (Romans 10:10). True biblical faith originates in the heart. A long time ago I renounced confidence in my apparent senses, and in the ambitions of the eyes. I trusted what God has said, witnessed to me of, told me in His Word, and lived by that alone for over 45 years. It makes us as strong as a rock. 'Those who trust in the Lord are as Mount Zion which cannot be moved, but abides forever.'

Faith asserts the supremacy of the invisible realm of God and His Word, requiring me to humble myself and acknowledge my dependency upon God. Faith and trust must be cultivated. Hence the study, the scouring, the searching of the Bible, which is the Word of God. 'The righteous man shall live by faith' (Romans 1:7). There is no alternative to faith. 'I believed therefore I spoke' (1 Corinthians 4:13). Again, 'He is my rock and my salvation, my stronghold. I shall not be greatly shaken' (Psalm 62:2).

When I was a boy and my mother took me to the doctor, he would say, 'Open your mouth, show me your tongue!' Sometimes he would put a thermometer in my mouth. 'Keep it on your tongue, keep your mouth closed,' he would advise. He could soon find out if I had a fever, by this examination in my mouth – amazing! He always said in the end, 'There's nothing wrong with this boy!' Matthew 12:34 says, 'For the mouth speaks out of that which fills the heart.' An old English version runs, 'for the mouth speaks what the heart is full of'. Faith is in the heart, but the mouth and our actions *reveal* what is in the heart. Faith is a walk, an outcome of an ongoing relationship with our Maker. 'With the heart man believeth unto righteousness and with the mouth [tongue] confession is made unto salvation' (Romans 10:10).

True faith rejects both dimensions of the senses and the boastful, self-exalting pride of the soul. More pride, less faith; the more humility, the greater the possibilities of faith expanding us. This enables a righteousness based on trust, and not on ourselves or our senses, to grow in us.

Man's destiny is determined by his response to faith's requirements. Faith, in order to grow dynamic, fruitful, must reject pride, the humanistic, natural reliance, as it says in Habakkuk 2:4: 'Behold the proud, his soul is not upright in him; but the just shall live by faith.' The Jewish version from the Hebrew Scriptures reads, 'Behold his soul is puffed up, it is not upright.' A paraphrase says, 'The soul that exalts itself becomes perverted.' It warns us of the folly of trusting in our own senses, the man who takes faith as his basis for living, humbles himself before God, accepting God's Word as the standard and rejecting all confidence in the flesh and his senses, is on the Shining, radiant path to victorious Christ-like living.

True faith is incompatible with pride. Faith reverses the process of the fall. Faith is the antidote to the effects of the fall.

It re-affirms our confidence in the invisible powers of God, His kingdom and His redeeming mercy and grace, and in the efficacy of the Blood of our Redeemer and Lord – confidence in His divine teachings, His irrefutable Word, the Holy Bible.

This is no time to run out on the Scriptures – the world is collapsing, we need the good news more than ever before. We live in perilous times. Shake off apathy, shake off fornication, shake off idols, shake off caution, timidness, tradition: make a 100 per cent surrender.

God cares, His Word is changing the hearts of hundreds of people in my missions across the land, miracles of healing are happening, Jesus is front-page news. 'Get back to the old paths,' the prophet warned, 'return to the Word of God,' Jesus told us. 'While ye have the light believe in the light.' Again, 'Trust in the Lord with all thine heart, lean not to thine own understanding.'

A mother had a problem with her little girl, getting her to bed. She never wanted to go, bedtimes were a real struggle. One day she was taking her for tea with an old auntie, a real saint of God. The little girl piped up, 'She'll talk about nothing but God and the Bible, and she's so good, it's the only time I want to go to bed early!' A woman not living in the flesh, but in the Word of God, a soul strong in faith, even bringing conviction to a six-year-old! Here is the reality of the Bible today:

it is challenging, it is changing us, it is charging us up!

Don't let ignorance, unawareness, apathy, idleness keep you from re-discovering its wonders, loveliness, beauty, power.

God is in action through the Word of God, but impeded, impounded, limited by our flippant, un-knowing lightness towards it, our forgetfulness of it, our lack of diligence with it.

10

DOUBT: THE THIEF OF
GOD'S VICTORIES

I have quoted this psalm and the corresponding passage in Mark so many times in nearly 45 years of preaching ministry, that some believe in the UK that I wrote it! But I can assure you I did not! God wrote it long before I ever came on the scene. It is Psalm 1: 'God blesses those people who refuse evil advice (of doubters) and won't follow sinners. Instead they think about the Word of the Lord day and night. They are like trees growing beside a stream, trees that produce fruit in season and always have leaves. Those people succeed in everything they do. That isn't true of those that are evil (doubters), because they are like straw that is blown by the wind.'

Then Jesus said in Mark 2:23,24 'Have faith in God! If you have faith in God and don't doubt, you can tell this mountain to get up and jump into the sea, and it will. Everything you ask in prayer will be yours if you only have faith.'

I was at the close of an enormous revival movement of God in mid-Staffordshire. A man who had been blind for six years, and never saw anything but darkness those long years, was there, with his wife and lovely, light brown guide dog by him.

Suddenly, after my prayer – I had in fact moved on to a young 10-year-old lad, who suffered three years with a crushed foot, every bone in his ankle, foot and leg had been broken – a shout behind me came from the pastor of the church. 'This gentleman can see my tie and its colours!' he announced, then he added, 'My hand, then my handkerchief!' The man's wife was by now crying beyond measure her husband was blind but now he can see! Meanwhile, the lad, who wanted to be a professional footballer, was walking, his crippled foot straight, his pain gone. Three years of suffering was over, he could walk in a straight line, perfect, free, happy. The blind man was by now looking all over and the audience was clapping and cheering!

Soon a wheelchair was being pushed all the way down the gangway, through the open doors. What a miracle, what a revival! A hundred new people were born again, and the whole town talked about Christ and His miracles. From the cotton factories, the printing works, the farms, from everywhere people streamed in, bringing in their sick, even from hospitals, eventide homes, they came hours before the service. A normal, quiet country town was moved by revival. This was God's visitation. Then one man said to my assistant, Richard Hill, 'But how long will it last?' The doubters had begun. Determine not to let doubt steal from you the precious might, victories and works of God which He wants to pour out to you. *Starve your doubts; feed your faith*.

I remember once praying for the sick, and this man had a bad spine, much pain, and unrelieving disease and suffering for a long time. The man said, 'I have tuberculosis of the spine. My spine is as solid as a crowbar, and I can't bend over. The doctors say there is nothing they can do for me.'

I laid one hand on the man's back and one hand on his chest, just as the Lord had directed me to do. Immediately I felt the fire in my hands jump from hand to hand, and I knew an evil spirit had brought about that condition and was enforcing it in this man's body. So I said, 'Come out of him, you foul spirit, in the Name of the Lord Jesus Christ!'

But then I missed it. I said to the man, 'See *if* you can stoop over and touch your toes.' That was doubt! The man tried to bend over, but his back was as stiff as a board.

I said, 'We'll try it again.' Again, I was in unbelief, and I didn't even realize it. You see, faith doesn't *try* something; faith *does* it!

I laid my hands on his back and his chest again, and the fire began to jump from hand to hand like heat waves. I said, 'You foul spirit that oppresses this man's body, come out of him in Jesus' Name!' And without really realizing that I was missing it, I repeated, 'See *if* you can stoop over and touch your toes.' Of course he couldn't. His back was as stiff as a board.

We tried it a third time and nothing happened, so I sent him on. As he walked away, I was thinking about what had happened, wondering why it didn't work. Then as fast as you can snap your fingers, there stood Jesus right in front of me. No one else saw Him, but I saw Him just as plainly as any man I've ever seen in my life.

Jesus pointed His finger at me, almost touching my nose. He said, 'I told you, "If you feel that fire jumping from hand to hand like heat waves, there is a demon or evil spirit in the body. Call him out in My Name, and he will leave."'

I said, 'Jesus, I know You said that. But I told the demon to leave, and he didn't'.

He repeated, 'I said, "Call him out in My Name, and the demon *will* leave in My Name."'

'I know You said that, Lord,' I answered. 'It seems as if it were just last night that You appeared to me. But I told him to leave, and he didn't.'

> For verily I say unto you, That whosoever shall say unto this mountain, Be Thou removed, and be Thou cast into the sea; and shall NOT DOUBT in his heart, but shall believe that those things which he saith shall come to pass; he shall have whatsoever he saith.
>
> Therefore I say unto you, What things soever ye desire, when ye pray, believe that ye receive them, and ye shall have them.
>
> MARK 11:23,24

The one who doubts in his heart shall *not* receive whatsoever he saith. *Doubt* is the thief of God's greater blessings.

Let's look at a few scriptural illustrations that show how doubt robs us of the greater blessings that God intends us to receive.

> [25]And in the fourth watch of the night Jesus went unto them, walking on the sea. [26]And when the disciples saw Him walking on the sea, they were troubled, saying It is a spirit (the same Greek word translated *spirit* is also translated *ghost*);

and they cried out for fear. [27]But straightway Jesus spake unto them, saying, Be of good cheer; it is I; be not afraid. [28]And Peter answered him and said, Lord, if it be Thou, bid me come unto Thee on the water. [29]And He said, Come. And when Peter was come down out of the ship, he walked on the water, to go to Jesus. [30]But when he saw the wind boisterous, he was afraid; and beginning to sink, he cried, saying, Lord, save me. [31]And immediately Jesus stretched forth His hand, and caught him, and said unto him, O Thou of little faith, wherefore didst thou doubt?

MATTHEW 14:25–31

Note verse 30: 'when he saw the wind...' He was looking at the wind, at the sea, at the problem. Don't tell God how big your mountain is, tell your mountain how big your God is! Don't look too long at the waves, the mocking unbelievers, the seeming triumphs of darkness, look at the greatness of the living God!

Again in verse 30, 'But when he saw the wind boisterous, he was afraid; and beginning to sink...' Peter was blessed to some degree because he did walk on the water for a while. But when he quit walking by faith and got into doubt, doubt robbed him of the greater blessing of receiving *all* that God had intended – for him to walk all the way and not sink.

Now in connection with this thief called doubt, I want you to see something concerning the ministry of Jesus in His hometown, Nazareth: 'And He [Jesus] did not many mighty works there [in Nazareth] because of their unbelief' (Matthew 13:58).

Why do you suppose Jesus didn't do many mighty works in His own hometown? Wasn't He the Son of God – God manifested in the flesh? Wasn't He anointed with the Holy Ghost and power, and didn't He have the Spirit without measure as John 3:34 says?

The answer to each question is emphatically, 'Yes!' And yet Matthew 13:58 says Jesus '*did not* many mighty works there'. Why? The rest of that verse tells us: *because of their unbelief*.

Now let's take a look at Mark's account of this incident: 'And He [Jesus] could there [in Nazareth] do no mighty work, save that He laid His hands upon a few sick folk, and healed them' (Mark 6:5).

I think it's interesting to note that Mark's Gospel doesn't say Jesus *wouldn't* do mighty works in Nazareth. It says that He *couldn't* do them! Now that messes up some people's theology because they believe God can do anything He wants to do, any time He wants to do it. Well, if that were true, then we'd have to throw out Matthew 13:58 and Mark 6:5!

God is not willing that *any* should perish. Well, then, why doesn't He just make everyone get saved? Because He doesn't operate that way. God says, 'Whosoever *will*, let him come' (Mark 8:34; Revelation 22:17).

No, there are a lot of things God can't do – not always because He doesn't want to, but because people won't co-operate with Him. That's what we just saw in Mark 6:5 '...*He* [Jesus] could *there* do no mighty work, *save that He laid His hands upon a few sick folk, and healed them.*' In other words, just a few folks got healed.

Think about that! Just a few people were healed in Jesus' hometown of Nazareth under the ministry of the

Lord Jesus Christ Himself! Why? Because of the people's *unbelief*.

So, first we saw that Peter was robbed as an individual of the greater blessing that God had intended for him to have. Jesus never intended for Peter to sink. He intended for Peter to walk all the way to Him, but when Peter saw the boisterous wind, he became afraid and began to sink. So he was robbed of God's best because of doubt.

Then second, we saw that almost an entire city was robbed of God's best because of unbelief. When Jesus left the city of Nazareth, He left people sick who *could* have been, *should* have been, and *would* have been healed because it was the will of God to heal them all. But they never received that healing because of their unbelief.

Now I want you to notice that your doubt and unbelief will not only steal God's greater blessings from *others* to miss out on God's best.

¹⁴And when they were come to the multitude, there came to Him a certain man, kneeling down to Him, and saying, ¹⁵Lord, have mercy on my son: for he is lunatick, and sore vexed: for ofttimes he falleth into the fires, and oft into the water. ¹⁶And I brought him to thy disciples, and they could not cure him ... ¹⁹and they said, why could not we cast him out? ²⁰And Jesus said unto them, because of your unbelief: for verily I say unto you, If ye have faith as a grain of mustard seed, ye shall say unto this mountain, Remove hence to yonder place; and it shall remove; and nothing shall be impossible unto you.

MATTHEW 17:14–20

A ROOM FILLED WITH GREAT TREASURE

This is what is at hand for the believer grasping faith's promise, so said wise Solomon in Proverbs 24.

It's ours to grasp. Rare and expensive riches to meet our every call and requirement. If you go into the British Museum, you can see the gates of Nineveh, that the evangelist Jonah passed by as he waded into that sinful, godless, wicked place with the gospel. Yet God had promised all their wealth was his, indeed the 'wealth of the wicked is laid up for the righteous'. He required then and he looks for now a few men or women, or even one with the faith to go. Nineveh became the Lord God's dominion, and so is your world, if you have the fervency, the committing spirit, the earnestness, the faith longing, to action, to do.

W. S. Richards used to say to the Assembly of God pastors when he preached to them at conferences, 'You know these things, brethren, but you must go and *do* them!' Make the vision fit. Let there be collaboration in your disciplines. Solomon spoke in that chapter of 'a man who saved a city by his wise actions'. Have Bible – will travel! Become a ministry of the new covenant. We can all do something, we don't have to wear a dog collar, or be paid by the church. *God calls you*. Take in hand God's work.

Have a ministry of consolation, give heart to others, get the treasure out of them. For every demon that attacks us God has an angel ten times as strong to help us! Stand on the head of Satan, be a blessing to someone today, act in faith. I often say I live with an ingrained anger – I hate Satan! I love to give him a hard time when

I arrive in a city to preach the gospel. I give the old devil a bit of hell! Replace the kingdom of devils with the kingdom of God, the nature of God is the nature of God's kingdom – it is fiercely powerful, fresh, full of light, triumphant!

Embrace the greatness of what God is doing. Don't be spiritual grasshoppers. Don't look for Satan, but beat him on the head with your Bible if he comes to you today. A man said to me, 'The devil came into my room.'

I replied, 'I'm glad he did, that means he's not in mine!'

Walk in power, run in faith. The chief ministry of the Church is not to actually meet people's needs all the time, but to make the high priority of the glorious good news of the gospel to all men available by proclaiming daringly the Cross and Crucifixion of Christ. It always succeeds when we believingly do God's work, in God's way, through God's people!

Unbelief is a curse

Unbelief never got anyone into heaven, never brought any satisfaction or joy to anyone. Unbelief fills hell and empties heaven. Unbelief never got any incurable person healed, it never gave anyone any peace of mind, it never brought anyone into Christ's salvation or kingdom.

We don't have bad news for you, we have good news. I preach to reach! I'm no doom-and-gloom preacher: open the gates of your heart and the King of Glory will come in. Isaiah 40 tells us, 'God is not weary nor is he faint.' He is true to his Word, 'He has exceeding greatness of power.' Unbelief will keep you out, faith will bring you in. God is a doer, 'God is able to do above what you ask or think.' He makes not just bad people good, but dead people live! No more crying, no more dying, no more tears, no more sorrow, no more disease, in God's heaven. It's the 'No More' land! And Jesus said, 'As it is in heaven so be it on earth'. Heaven has bent low, God's Word is coming real to us. I believe what God says.

One man said to me, 'How can you believe that as the Bible says – a whale swallowed Jonah?'

I replied, 'I trust the Word of God so much, that if it said that Jonah swallowed the whale I'd believe it!' We have an active God, a true God. 'Let God be true and every man a liar.'

A rich man in the USA many years ago felt the call of God, and in faith left all to go and preach the gospel. Bill Borden, of the famous 'Borden Milk' family in America, turned his back on fame and fortune and went to China as a missionary. His friends in America thought he'd taken leave of his senses, to walk away from a life of comfort and riches to build churches, win souls and preach the gospel in China. When they found his body he was already three days dead. They found him in a tent, with a note under his thumb which read, 'No reserve! ... No retreat! ... No regrets!'

Romans 6:13 says, 'Give yourself completely to God, every part of you to be tools in the hands of God, to be used for His good purposes.'

Isaac Watts' great hymn says:

Were the whole realm of nature mine,
That were an offering far too small.
Love so amazing, so divine,
Demands my soul, my life, my all.

FAITH PURIFIES

Faith enables us to keep clean. John the apostle said, 'Young men who have overcome the world, you have kept yourselves clean by believing that Jesus Christ...' Isaiah said, 'If you do not stand firm in your faith, you will not stand at all.' The Word keeps us standing, upright, pure, wholesome, clean.

As legend has it, a man went to Sodom one day, hoping to save the city from God's judgement. He tried talking to first one individual, then to the next, but nobody would talk to him. Next, he tried carrying a picket sign that had 'Repent' written in large letters, but nobody paid any attention. Finally, he began going from street to street and from marketplace to marketplace, shouting, 'Men and women, repent! What you are doing is wrong. It will kill you! It will destroy you!'

The people laughed at him, but still he went about shouting. One day, somebody stopped him and said, 'Stranger, can't you see that your shouting is useless?'

The man replied, 'Yes, I see that.'

The person then asked, 'So why do you continue?'

The man said, 'When I arrived in this city, I was convinced that I could change them. *Now I continue shouting because I don't want them to change me.*'

Let faith in God's Word stop you being moulded by the filth of this world.

FAITH IS A WAITING GAME

A noted preacher said, 'Patience is faith.' It's certainly vital in procuring and growing in trust.

From *God's Little Devotional Book* comes this wonderful story. A man's car once stalled in heavy Friday evening traffic just as the light turned green. All his efforts to start the engine failed. A chorus of honking rose from the cars behind him. Frustrated, he finally got out of his car and walked back to the first driver and said, 'I'm sorry, but I can't seem to get my car started. If you go up there and give it a try, I'll stay here and blow your horn for you.'

'Do not be quickly provoked in your spirit, for anger resides in the lap of fools' (Ecclesiastes 7:9).

My grandmother used to say, 'Patience is a virtue.' In Walter Wangerin's novel of the Bible, *The Book of God*, he writes in Chapter 28 of Nehemiah, the yearnings after patience, prayer, character living, he is offered to return to the old city his home in Jerusalem and finish the work:

There has been an aweful democratic spirit in the church, which has almost ruined the church. God is looking for GOD RULE, men submitted to God's supreme anointing and control. A MANI-FEST REALITY. Make a once and for all break with sin.

SEEK A PURE HEART FROM THE LORD. 'GOD IS NOT DEAF THAT HE CANNOT HEAR'.

We have had today heads full of ideas but no power, and other hearts full of the spirit, but no divine revelation or scriptural theology. This is not a work done in a corner; God has big plans for you. Begin where you are, get heaven's vision, contact the headquarters of Glory. Small deeds done are better than big deeds only planned.

Don't be a wobbler, not a poverty spirit, not a spiritual vegetable, gripped by icy fear, but men and women of structure, truth and integrity. Be spiritually motivated, exuding spiritual authority, delivered from legalism, getting the grip of God, giving it all that you have got.

A fine man said to God, 'I'm with you, if you're with me.' God's works are so mighty and numerous, I don't know what He is going to do next! I am exhausted by the wondrous things God is doing. But I am constantly on the watch that doubt does not steal my thunder.

'Watch and pray.' Say today:

I am no longer my own, but yours;
Put me to what you will,
Rank me with whom you will;
Put me to doing,
Put me to suffering;
Let me be employed for you,
Or laid aside for you;
Exalted for you,
Or brought low for you;
Let me be full,
Let me be empty;
Let me have all things,

Let me have nothing;
I freely and wholeheartedly yield
all things to your pleasure
and disposal.

FROM THE 'COVENANT SERVICE PRAYER',
THE METHODIST CHURCH

11

When We Work

The only place where you find success coming before work is in the dictionary. Get it done!

A newly hired salesman stunned his superiors with his first report, for it revealed that he was nearly illiterate. He wrote, 'I met this outfit, who aint got a dimes worth of nuthin from us, and I sole them sum goods'! The Board decided he must be fired, but before they got to passing the information down, a second badly written letter arrived. It read, 'I came to Chicawgo an sole them haff a million.' The President of the Company decided he must keep the man, and promptly ordered that his letters, in large script, be pasted on all the firm's noticeboards with an addition – 'We ben spendin two much time trying to spel instead of sell ... Gooch is doin a grate job, and you should all go out and do like he done!'

Gooch became top salesman, the greatest the firm had ever seen, bringing in millions upon millions of dollars of orders. Sometimes the Church gets so preoccupied with appearance that we lose sight of our primary purpose.

We cross the 't's, and dot the 'i's, and get it all perfect, but that's not God's way in revival. He came into the house when it 'was noised abroad'; Jesus worked in the midst of noise and mayhem; on the day of Pentecost it seemed as if they were all drunk! Yet God moved and planted his Church there!

God uses the imperfect. 'We have the excellency of this power in earthen [old clay] jars,' Paul recorded. 'My speech and my preaching were not with persuasive words of human wisdom but in demonstration of the spirit and power' (1 Corinthians 2:4).

FAITH THAT WORKS

Faith never stands around with its hands in its pockets. Mary is a senior citizen with many health problems. She is also a widow with a home to keep up. No use expecting Mary to do much in the church or community any more, right? Wrong! In spite of her limitations, her faith continues to work.

Although Mary and her late husband had no children, they had a ministry to other people's children. Now alone, she co-ordinates a new ministry in her church for women who might be considering abortion.

Mary writes, 'If we are preaching against abortion, we should offer pregnant women our help. Within 2 days I've had 4 volunteers to help me. Now we must meet to set up a plan of action.'

A plan of action – how typical of a working faith! How different from people who see a desperate need and moan, 'Why doesn't somebody do something?' but are unwilling to be that somebody!

In James 2 we read that Abraham obediently offered his son Isaac on the altar. This act is cited as a work that proved the reality of his faith (vv. 21–23). Mary, like Abraham, has a faith that works.

Faith is the power that prompts us to
And give to the hungering, bread;
Faith means much more than a doctrine or two,
For faith without works is dead.

James Dobson, a well-known authority on the family,
tells a story about his father, who was greatly loved by
all who knew him. James Dobson Sr spent much time in
intercessory prayer, considering prayer for others his
most important business on earth. In fact, he specified
in his will that only two words were to be put on his
tombstone following his name: HE PRAYED.

Of the thousands of verbs in our language, by which
one are *you* likely to be remembered? He *served*. She
cared. He *supported*. She *praised*. Faith must act or die!

A minister in Chicago was having a difficult period
when he felt as if his soul was becoming a desert. His
people were making so many demands that he was
becoming spiritually drained. While in this state of
spiritual drought, he struck up a conversation with
a devout Christian woman. He told her he felt like a
pump, and his people so constantly pumped him that he
was running dry. Straight from her heart, she answered,
'Didn't you volunteer to be pumped when you prayed
to be used by the Lord? Don't ask your people to quit
pumping. Drive your pipe deeper. You need to get down
where there's water again.'

Perhaps you've had the same experience. Remember
that God may entrust you with duties that seem to
be drought-inducing burdens. Yet they are God-given
assignments designed for your spiritual growth.

Drive the pipe deeper! The more sapping, the more

exhausting, the more you act in God. Act and God acts! Draw from Him and go and do it! Man has no lack when God is his supply.

'Whatever you do in word or deed, do all in the name of the Lord Jesus' (Colossians 3:17). If you sense your spiritual well drying up, drive your pipe deeper. God gives an unlimited supply of grace. Gustafson wrote the lines:

> We shrink from this life's challenges – we plead
> For watered pastures never touched by pain;
> But God will often let us sense our need
> Before He sends His cool, refreshing rain.

Do something – God sustains and enables – God delays because we do not push ourselves and act!

When God looks down and sees someone who says, 'I will not give up', He says, 'There is someone I can use.' Paul said, 'Let us not be weary' (Galatians 6:9 NIV). Have backbone not chicken bone. In Luke 18 Jesus commended the persistent woman who got the miracle in the end. The only way we lose in life is when we quit. Some people talk and talk and talk, then go and pack in themselves. Preach what you practise, and practise what you preach. Some people make a lot of noise and then produce nothing. Mark Twain wrote, 'The hen brings the house down with her noise, yet produces only one egg, yet she cackled as if she was producing an asteroid!'

George Bernard Shaw said, 'Nine out of ten times what I wrote was a failure, but then I would go and do ten times more work and was a success!' Edison, who often did 1,000 experiments before finding what he wanted, said, 'Most opportunity is missed by most people, because it is dressed up in overalls and looks like work!' We must press through, busy at it. 'Work while it is day,' Jesus noted – don't yield to the world's pressures, don't stop now, your miracle is on the way. Don't waste time day-dreaming and doing nothing. Ten per cent of nothing is nothing. The father of success is work and the mother is ambition. Who are the people who failed? The people who stopped!

It's like riding a bike: if you don't go on you go off! 'Be steadfast ... unmoveable, always abounding...' (1 Corinthians 15:58). The usefulness of the postage stamp is that it sticks to something till it gets there!

You may be up against it, you may be marooned by the storm, but not shipwrecked. The world passes away, but the Word of the Lord abides forever. Cling to God's Word, trust it all the way, don't go out – go up! Don't give in – give out! Don't get down – get around! Finish your course, let nothing put you off. Phillips wrote (Colossians 3:23), 'Whatever your task, put your whole heart into it...' Jesus said, 'Lo, I am with you always till the end...'

Many things you had high hopes for have not worked out, you feel like giving up. The Russian saying goes, 'God closes a silver door, and opens a golden one.' Joan of Arc claimed to have heard God's voice, but the Church found her guilty of heresy, did not believe what she said, and later burnt her to death. The King of France said to her, 'I am the Dauphin of the whole land, and I have not heard God speak to me, yet you say He has spoken to you...' Little Joan replied, 'Then you must listen, sir, and you will hear Him speak to you!'

God is speaking to each of you through the divine oracles, the Holy Bible today. He is leading you on, He is saying, 'Don't give up!'

The old saying went, 'Men are born with two ears but only one tongue, which indicates we were meant to listen twice as much as talk.' Listen to God. Proverbs 8:34 says, 'Blessed is the man who listens to me.' Again, 'Listen to me ... the Lord has called' (Isaiah 49:1). He is saying 'Go on.'

God will change your desert to fertile ground. The Lord is your keeper, saying, 'I will not fear what man can do unto me.' He is turning your setbacks to stepping stones. Lack is not your portion, failure is not your portion.

His angels are around you guarding and guiding you. He fights for you. Cover yourself with the blood of Jesus.

Don't give up. Give it all your push. As Moses asked, 'Does God speak and then not act?' Don't lag, don't lack, don't lie down, God will keep His word to you. 'Be not fainthearted for the Lord God goes with you.' Live for Jesus today and tomorrow will be great!

Have faith in tomorrow. If you have no plan for tomorrow, then it is a passing dream, don't stay where you are, act on your revelation, act on your vision. A person without actions yet has faith, is like a bird with wings but no feet. 'Ask for the old paths, walk in it and find rest' (Jeremiah 6:16). Paul said, 'Go on living ... in simple faith' (Colossians 2:6).

'If you do what the Lord commands you and cleave to Him ... none shall stand before you' (Deuteronomy 11:25).

Elderly minister sees revival

My great personal friend Pastor William Van der Berg and his dear wife I have known for the past 10 years. I have had many crusades with them reaching out across South Holland, which is 90 per cent Roman Catholic. He has built a strong church there on the Belgian borderlands. Together we have taken restaurants, cafés, coffee bars, pubs, community halls, and seen them filled to capacity with up to 90 per cent non-Christians, or sometimes 100 per cent Catholic people. Wheelchairs have been walked home, crutches left on the bar-top counters, the blind have seen, people have flocked in hundreds and we have found great favour in an area difficult to evangelize.

A few years ago in my absence as I was campaigning in Ireland, I heard how he had gone off for six weeks on his own down to Indonesia to preach the gospel. More visits followed, soon miracles were flowing, hundreds of people touched, in one area where the church had never been before he saw a new church planted. Soon he was revisiting yet again, leaving his church to his able wife to run. He was reaching further and further out into the remote villages of Sumatra. In some jungle places they had not seen a white man for 40 years, soon whole villages were moved. Eighty per cent of sick people received a healing deliverance or miracle; hundreds were finding Jesus Christ.

At a point where he could well be retiring, God was raising him up to help move multitudes of people. God gave him great strength to cope. He kept returning to his native Holland always revived himself, re-invigorated, re-awakened, with burning vision to reach more of his own people. His church now full, he would call me to fly over to nearby Dusseldorf in Germany, the nearest airport, pick me up and take me through his little Belgian, Flemish and Dutch towns with the gospel. I would preach, miracles happened, I would be reaping this man's sacrifice. God was also rewarding him at home for his hard work abroad in Indonesia.

God wants more from your life in your later years. Don't give up. God is not finished with you yet. It is the older people who are seeing dreams come true.

12

SAY GOODBYE TO DEFEAT

I love the words of the ancient and rather obscure prophet Zephaniah, who likens the Lord God to 'a courageous, gallant Holy Warrior, unconquerable and invincible'. Medieval chivalry would have called Him a 'perfect Knight' – He is calm in battle, confident, braver than 'Braveheart' the Scot! It is a daring anthropomorphism – 'The Lord God is with you, He is mighty to save, He will take great delight in you, He will quiet you with His love...' (Zephaniah 3:17).

Someone said to me, 'I'm fighting the BIG "C" [cancer].'

I replied, 'You're not, you're fighting the little "c" with the BIG "C" – Courage!'

Why is God not working for much of His Church in western Christianity, in spite of boastful human claims, grand theology, better preaching, theorizing, seminars, conferences, teams, programmes and ongoing organizations? Yet only in a small number of places is there daring, breakthrough, action, revival! *It is because of our wrong thinking.*

HOW DO WE THINK RIGHT?

The two words are used together 365 times in the Bible – 'Fear not' – one for every day of the year! It does not advise us to 'grieve not' or to 'weep not', in fact it encourages us to 'weep with those that weep'! But it does say hundreds of times, 'Fear not'.

Webster's dictionary tells us that courage is 'to be bold enough to challenge'. Courage is the opposite to fear. Courage is to think right. Zephaniah says, 'Do not fear ... do not let your hands hang limp' (3:16). Courage is the passion of God working within you, a hunk of boldness, it's becoming something, turning the world into something beautiful. It's a divine call we all have – 'Be thou very courageous.'

In Mini Street, Los Angeles, the murder capital of the eastern seaboard of the USA, where drug-peddling gangsters, touts, whores and the lowest in society mix, fight, gamble, hustle, live and die, one of the most dangerous spots on the face of the earth, two men during the past two years have made a difference. They are two policemen, Tony Romero and Don Aneddero, two fine Christians. They decided to go and live right there in the midst of the criminals – and their presence, their golden hearts, their tough work and prayers have made a difference. They have had to dodge the bullets, and the knife in the dark, to become friends with their desperate neighbours. In the first year alone the crime rate dropped by 45 per cent. The Bible in men's hearts, and in practice *changes things*. The Christian truth – God in action – transforms situations.

This is thinking right, doing right, this is courage.

Dr Lawne Schlesinger, the famous American child psychologist, on prime-time radio in *America Weekly*, was asked how you deal with rebellious teenagers, who are smoking, uncouth, becoming anti-social? She replied that she dealt with her two 13-year-olds in this way: she took their cigarettes and other doubtful material and put it on the beds of their tiny brothers and sisters. When the teenagers came and could not find their 'weeds', they dashed into the rooms opposite to see the youngsters handling them with inquisitive looks. They were so ashamed that they took them away and destroyed the cigarettes and the mother had no more rebellion again over the matter! Ashamed by innocence!

Shame is an opposite to courage. Daring, faith, boldness in truth vindicates, lifts, inspires. We silence the voice of our enemies with courage.

Daniel, in spite of the law that praying to the Living God was an offence punishable by death, still took heart and prayed. I like Daniel 6:10, which says, 'Now Daniel heard that the decree had been made, went home ... got on his knees and prayed, just as he had done before.' Here is consistency and courage. C. H. Spurgeon put it like this: 'It was absolutely impossible for the lions to eat Daniel because most of him was backbone and the rest grit!'

With hungry lions snapping at his heels, he would need a double dose of faith and courage. But the root of his deliverance was formed earlier, when he was challenged with a smaller compromise. He 'refused the royal food and wine'. A great Russian writer said, 'God is in the detail.' He is in the small things. Daniel got the smaller trees down first then tackled the larger ones. Because he regularly climbed the steps to the upstairs room and communed with his Lord, he was able to gather the courage for the tiny and later the catastrophic demands that faced him. You may not need grace to fight lions today, but start with the small detail, the minor challenges that need a courageous decision today, and stay in the upper room as much as possible, so that you can fight the big lions tomorrow! *The Bible is the book of courage.*

Surrounded by a large, hostile Nazi navy, dive-bombed hourly all day long for months by Italian fighter planes and bombers, General Dobie, Governor General of Malta and his brave islanders and small British force, defied all that came, near starvation, cut off from friendly aid. The General said, 'We will never surrender, we will fight to the last man and woman!' He won through, and the island was given the George Cross, every islander alive at that time has the right to add GC – holder of the George Cross – after their name.

General Dobie told in his autobiography that, 'The Bible was the sole source of my courage.' After the war, whenever a general, leading politician, cabinet minister, BBC personality, film star, or Field Marshal came to visit him (or even the household cook, waitress, private soldier or maid), they would not be allowed to leave for their home without the great general opening up the Bible and reading a few verses to them. This was a man not afraid to own his God, a man of great determination and courage.

I urge people in my meetings everywhere, don't join a religion, don't just sign up in another club, make a personal commitment with Jesus Christ: that is the source of all daring, courage, right thinking, integrity.

As we often sing in my services,

Great is thy faithfulness,
Springtime and harvest, summer and winter
Great is your mercy and love ...

Morning by morning new mercies I see,
Lord unto me ...
Pardon for sin and peace that endures,
Thine own dear Presence to cheer and to guide
Your strength for today, your grace for tomorrow
and 10,000 beside ...
Great is thy faithfulness Lord unto me...

Ask the Lord to give you courage today. Take heart
from the promises of Isaiah, Chapters 42 and 43.

THE LORD'S SERVANT

Here is my servant! I have made him strong.
    He is my chosen one; I am pleased with him.
I have given him my Spirit,
    and he will bring justice to the nations.
He won't shout or yell or call out in the streets.
He won't break off a bent reed or put out a dying
flame,
    but he will make sure that justice is done.
He won't quit or give up until he brings justice
    everywhere on earth,
    and people in foreign nations long for his
teaching.

I am the LORD God...
I chose you to bring justice, and I am here at your
side.
I selected and sent you to bring light
    and my promise of hope to the nations.
You will give sight to the blind;

you will set prisoners free from dark dungeons.
My name is the LORD...

Tell the whole world to sing a new song to the LORD!
Tell those who sail the ocean and those who live far
away
    to join in the praise.
Tell the tribes of the desert and everyone in the
mountains to celebrate and sing.
Let them announce his praises everywhere...

I will lead the blind on roads they have never known;
    I will guide them on paths they have never trav-
elled.
Their road is dark and rough, but I will give light
    to keep them from stumbling.
This is my solemn promise...

THE LORD HAS RESCUED HIS PEOPLE

Descendants of Jacob, I, the LORD, created you
    and formed your nation.
Don't be afraid. I have rescued you.
    I have called you by name; now you belong to me.
When you cross deep rivers, I will be with you,
    and you won't drown.
When you walk through fire, you won't be burned
    or scorched by the flames.

I am the LORD, your God, the Holy One of Israel,
    the God who saves you.

God called and prepared and filled men and women with holy courage! Look at the courage of Peter, yet he had been a short time before an awful failure. Despite that he's used marvellously with a gratifying, glorious vision, in one of the most dramatic and supernatural moments in the Church's early history. A crucial hour that demanded a courageous choice – he did not miss it – Peter broke the mode.

Acts 10:23–48 describes to us how Peter tells Cornelius about faith in Jesus and Gentiles receive the Holy Spirit.

The next morning, Peter and some of the Lord's followers in Joppa left with the men who had come from Cornelius. The next day they arrived in Caesarea where Cornelius was waiting for them. He had also invited his relatives and close friends.

When Peter arrived, Cornelius greeted him. Then he knelt at Peter's feet and started worshipping him. But Peter took hold of him and said, 'Stand up! I am nothing more than a human.'

As Peter entered the house, he was still talking with Cornelius. Many people were there, and Peter said to them, 'You know that we Jews are not allowed to have anything to do with other people. But God has shown me that he doesn't think anyone is unclean or unfit. I agreed to come here, but I want to know why you sent for me.'

Cornelius answered: 'Four days ago at about three o'clock in the afternoon I was praying at home. Suddenly a man in bright clothes stood in front of me. He said, "Cornelius, God has heard your prayers, and he knows about your gifts to the poor. Now send to Joppa for Simon Peter. He is visiting in the home of Simon the leather maker, who lives near the sea." I sent for you right away, and you have been good enough to come. All of us are here in the presence of the Lord God, so that we can hear what He has to say.'

Peter then said, 'Now I am certain that God treats all people alike. God is pleased with everyone who worships him and does right, no matter what nation they come from. This is the same message that God gave to the people of Israel, when He sent Jesus Christ, the Lord of all, to offer peace to them.

You surely know what happened everywhere in Judea. It all began in Galilee after John had told everyone to be baptized. God gave the Holy Spirit and power to Jesus from Nazareth. He was with Jesus, as he went around doing good and healing everyone who was under the power of the devil. We all saw what Jesus did both in Israel and in the city of Jerusalem.

Jesus was put to death on a cross. But three days later, God raised Him to life and let Him be seen. Not everyone saw Him. He was seen only by us, who ate and drank with Him after He was raised from death. We were the ones God chose to tell others about Him.

God told us to announce clearly to the people that Jesus is the one He has chosen to judge the living and the dead.

Every one of the prophets has said that all who have faith in Jesus will have their sins forgiven in His name.'

While Peter was still speaking, the Holy Spirit took control of everyone who was listening. Some Jewish followers of the Lord had come with Peter, and they were surprised that the Holy Spirit had been given to Gentiles. Now they were hearing Gentiles speaking unknown languages and praising God.

Peter said, 'These Gentiles have been given the Holy Spirit just as we have! I am certain that no one would dare stop us from baptizing them.' Peter ordered them to be baptized in the name of Jesus Christ, and they asked him to stay on for a few days.

Courage is attractive – Plymouth's revival

This southern city, noted for its great English characters, enthroned in history, such as Sir Francis Drake, Sir Francis Chichester, the pilots and air crews of the RAF and men of the naval destroyers and the rest of the fleet, who fought with such determination in 1940–1945 from here. Plymouth was the most bombed city of any in the Second World War (next to London). Winston Churchill said, 'They were the heroes of heroes when the enemy stood at the gate.' The great man came personally to thank the city in 1945, welcomed by a tumultuous multitude.

It is the city of the Puritan fathers, who went and colonized America from there, also the world-wide

Christian group the Plymouth Brethren, who spawned such great historic figures such as Dr George Muller, who fed and cared for and brought up 10,000 orphans, in the greatest philanthropic work seen last century.

It was my privilege to hold a crusade that many have said had the greatest evangelistic impact since Stephen Jeffries' famed visit in 1930, when thousands were saved and healed.

COURAGE GRIPS

Ian Fleming, the creator of the James Bond stories, is buried in a small country churchyard in Wiltshire near to where I live. It is an unmarked grave, amidst a very rural and pretty background. Fifty per cent of the world's total population at some time have apparently either read a story, article, or seen a film or TV broadcast of a Bond adventure. His pull and attraction to the populace of the late twentieth century has been immense.

What is this interest? Is it not his courageous and daring spirit? It is said that at least somewhere in the world, a James Bond movie, video, or TV broadcast is being viewed every minute of every day. It's all about courage, grit, adventure, right against evil, and this has a very powerful draw on mankind. We need these strengths in our constant spiritual battle as well, as God's people call for spiritual determination, audacity, persistence, faith and a courageous will.

As James said to his boss, 'M', in the secret service headquarters one day, 'Governments change but the evil stays the same!' How true. The directive we have is to bring a God of action into human affairs, and that takes immense cost and courage.

LOOK AT YOURSELF

Are you building up spiritual resources for the day of demand and testing? In Tolstoy's *Dr Zhivago* one character comments, 'The searchlight cannot look at itself.' Who is going to watch the watchers?

It's true, but we can guard ourselves. Jude said, 'Keep yourself pure.' Communion with God does not weaken us, but toughens us, gives us zest for the ultimate challenges, so we then discover courage.

The old pioneer in the American West 160 years ago told how strong his wagons were. 'I go to the top of the hill, that's where the wood in the trees is hardened by the storms.'

The courageous find that the impossible is the untried. Try – do – search, commune in fellowship more and more with Jesus Christ and you will find that in that height of blessing you are tough, strong wood that endures on the long journey. There the steel of courage is forged and sharpened in you. 'As He is so are we in this world.' Jesus was the most courageous man who ever lived.

FIND VICTORY EVEN AMONG THE RUINS OF DEFEAT

Count Ciano said, 'Victory has 1,000 fathers, but defeat is an orphan!' At Wimbledon the All-England Club decided three or four years ago that, after the finals on Centre Court of the world-famed tennis tournament, the defeated finalists should receive their medals first – then the victor steps forward.

Professor of Philosophy Adam Morton of Bristol University called defeat 'potentially explosive', for it can destroy all our future thinking and efforts or can blow us out of lethargy into eventual successful living. You can brood on defeat and that will corrupt and diminish you, or you can learn from it, then put the past behind you and look to the future. Failure can be character building, but it depends on how you react to it. Few who achieve anything worthwhile in this world have an unbroken record of success.

Years in the wilderness strengthened Churchill and de Gaulle and prepared them for their greatest work. Ulysses S. Grant, who led the Union armies to victory in the American Civil War, had experienced much failure and humiliation before his triumph. Failure forged the steel in his character. Defeat and failure provide a testing ground for the spirit.

People have flocked in enormous numbers to the Cezanne exhibition to admire the work of the man who is now regarded as perhaps the greatest of French painters and the father of Modern Art. But Cezanne spent most of his life being mocked and disparaged. He enjoyed almost no success with critics or the public. In effect, he suffered defeat after defeat. But he went on working in his own way, following his own vision. He would have been a lesser man and a lesser painter if he had buckled.

The story of many great artists is similar. Innovators such as James Joyce suffered years of neglect and contempt. For others, like Scott Fitzgerald, defeat and the wilderness followed years of glittering success; it steeled him to face what he called 'a long, slow, uphill climb'.

Disraeli was howled down when he first spoke in the House of Commons. Colleagues exploded with laughter at his manner. He vowed that the day would come when they listened to him, and it did.

Defeat is a matter of how you take it. Hemingway said, 'Man can be defeated, but not destroyed.' He was not quite right, for man can indeed be destroyed if he succumbs to defeat; if he lets it dismay him or make him resentful. Yet defiance in defeat is not, by itself, enough. The most defiant speech in English literature is found in *Paradise Lost*. But it is given to Satan, and while we may admire his 'unconquerable will and courage never to submit or yield', all that he can otherwise offer is 'the study of revenge, immortal hate' – nothing constructive, merely that which Hitler offered the Germans.

Defeat can be enriching, but only if you learn its lesson, accept responsibility, put bitterness and self-pity aside and look to a brighter future.

You can fail 1,000 times, just make sure the last time you try and don't fail!

A missionary who had spent years in an overseas country in service to the poor returned after 30 years and, after arriving at the airport, saw the blue 'TAKE COURAGE' signs everywhere outside breweries, pubs and on hoardings. She declared, 'It's wonderful to have that in lights to be encouraged to be brave in faith and courageous!' She thought Britain had become a very religious people. God, however, *does* want us to be of great courage!

13

THE WITCH WHO SWITCHED

I love a battle, soft Christianity is not for me. Some Pentecostal leaders and evangelical Bishops get the keys to the city when they come to town in the United Kingdom and other nations, but I get locked up in prison, occasionally, when I arrive to preach the gospel! In Malaysia I was detained after a great revival there a few years ago, but a Pentecostal Bible School Principal visiting from Britain was fêted and given a padded pew!

I love a fight, I love to give the Devil misery, I love to give the Devil a hard time. I was in the middle of a strongly Republican IRA estate in Northern Ireland, where a gospel tent put up there shortly before had been burnt down on the second night. Visiting Pentecostal young folk had been roughly treated and chased out of town. Yet here I was with crammed meetings, holding two or three meetings daily, so many sinners attending, 99 per cent of them unsaved. God has called me to many trouble spots of the world – I am the apostle of lost causes, I think!

But so many miracles had happened that these people welcomed me with open arms. Then the police armoured cars came, many troops surrounded the building, helicopters flew overhead with large searchlights, long queues forming up the streets had drawn a security net around us. There was a scare by the defence forces, I was told of possible ensuing trouble, so I ran out. When I was seen and my English Oxford accent picked up outside, I got a shocked British Intelligence Officer's sharp rebuke: 'What are you doing here?' The people of this world are shaken by our audacity of faith.

GOD'S LOOKING FOR MEN OF FIRE

That's why He sent me to the East End of London, to Bethnal Green, where no one would go – the Bronx of London, the home of the gangsters – the Kray brothers and the Great Train Robbers. That's why He sent me to the fishermen, whalers and sheep farmers of the Falkland Isles and gave me revival; to the biker gangs, completely unreached, wild Hell's Angels; to the untouched Muslims, never going to a Christian church, yet packing my meetings in hundreds often, especially the Turkish immigrants, Pakistanis and the Bangladeshi people.

I go into town and say, 'The Devil is not going to operate here any more! We are going to enforce the bounds of the Kingdom of God!' Many churches are frightened of signs and wonders. I don't like things too smooth. Satan controls too much ground, multitudes are in the bondage of hell. Many believers are settled down to their lovely little prayer meeting, their worship and praise time. They have changed the Great Commission in the UK to, 'Go into all the world and prophesy and hold worship services.' I believe in *going into all the world and preaching the gospel of power*.

'The spirit of the Lord is upon me to preach the gospel to the poor ... to heal the broken hearted, to set the captive free, to open the eyes of the blind...' The world's leaders don't mind the posh Evangelical preachers, the nice Full Gospel Charismatic ministers, but they hate the men of fire, who heal the sick, chase the Devil and raise the dead.

I started in a town in the North of England. The local vicar attacked me like a madman – soon the front page headlines in papers read by 100,000 people shouted: 'VICAR WARNS OF HEALER'. He blabbered on about people being prayed for and they could be disappointed. It was like saying don't preach about Christ, don't tell anyone He saves the soul in case they don't believe it and nothing happens. It was idiotic, crazy beyond words.

Soon interest bucked up. I started with six people, and now there was hardly any room, or seats left in the tent! A woman arrived; her husband would not even come into the tent, but sat outside in the car. Soon she came running out of the tent without crutches: she ran, she danced, she laughed, she shouted, she jumped – Jesus had set her free. The husband ran out of his car and hugged her. The next night he came back and was saved within a few days. The papers carried in huge headlines: 'THE VICAR WAS WITHOUT ARGUMENT – IT WORKED, JESUS HEALED, THE GOSPEL WAS WITH POWER'. He was lost for all argument, and the Word of the Lord was vindicated – 'Hath He not spoken it, shall it not come to pass...?' The vicar was made a real fool in the eyes of the world and the Church.

'NO VOICE RAISED AGAINST YOU SHALL BE SUCCESSFUL' (ISAIAH 54:17)

Many great miracles were seen in that tent. When the Devil starts messing, the Lord starts blessing. When you come through the fire I will bless you, He said. 'After the fire, the still small voice.' Opposition, hindrances, all hell let loose, controversy, I love it all! Go and fight in His Name, He always gives us the victory. Do not fear what men or devils will do against you. The more fire I pass through, the greater the opposition, the mightier the miracles and the more valuable I am to God.

Many were the miracles in the tent after the Devil had sent that vicious, slanderous and lying broadside, but God always upholds the truth. We must cut the Devil down to size by the Word of God, that is our source of strength. The old evil one knew how many captives would be released from his foul snares.

THE WITCH WHO FELL UNDER THE SPELL OF JESUS

A woman who was a witch had gone along to the local library. She asked for a book on spiritual power, and the librarian sent her to the 'religious' section. While there she picked up my book, *The Healing Revolution*. She went to her house and was so moved by the acts of the apostles in the UK today, as told in that book, the great miracles of Jesus, that she was shaken to her core. God laid His hand on her. She could not sleep, she could not rest day or night.

Then amazingly she had read all the controversy about my coming, and ventured into the gospel tent on Knutsford Common. God gripped her and stunned her, cutting, convicting and melting her hard occult heart.

She was wonderfully saved. It took some months of counselling, care, love, constant shepherding, prayer and deliverance, but she came through. I was there with the new church six months later, when she gave her testimony and was shining for Jesus. Her story has touched many in that area. The fear of God has touched the whole district. How lovely are His leadings, when we are in His presence. He leads us to the right towns, the right people and the right situations to give victory to His Body.

Who would have thought God had spoken in a library to a witch, then the preacher whose book she reads, of all the ten thousands of towns in the UK, comes to her town a few weeks later and hits the main headlines. And she gets into a meeting and is delivered, by the matchless name of Jesus. This is all part of His planning and presence. This is what it means to live in His personal fragrance, in His ways, in His immediate favour. Lord, you never fail.

Up against opposition

When I came back from the border counties last time, where I had been holding crusades never held in such places, the police virtually detained me for questioning for some time because of my preaching, visiting and staying for such a long period in IRA territory. (When the nice, posh teachers and preachers came back from their Bible conventions in Ulster, among all the Christians no one took any notice of them. It was different with me.) For some months lately, neighbours of mine, who watch our house for us, have told of people calling and questioning them about my lifestyle, whereabouts and ministry.

Perhaps MI5 is after me? But I don't mind, I tell them, I'm a red-hot Jesus preacher: I will preach the gospel where God sends me. It doesn't matter what trouble it brings.

Obey God and you are in trouble – walk in His presence and it will set the cat among the evangelical pigeons. You will be far from a man-pleaser. But God will send mighty conversions – drunkards are made sober, witches made saints, adulterers made pure, broken homes made new, religious bigots humbled, all by the mighty, all-prevailing Spirit of God.

There is trouble, shake-up, adversities, but 'after the fire, the still small voice', after the trouble, the revelation, the presence of God Himself.

I realize I am a marked man, I have embarked on an all-out war, I've got no time, like most Christians in this country, to play tiddly-winks in the pew. It's time for the Church to snap back into reality. This is the battle of the ages, God's people have let the Devil gain ground and take cities and towns. Wherever I go I serve notice on the Devil, that he no longer reigns in that place. When I enter a city the kingdom of God has come. The Holy Ghost is in control now. You see, the kingdom of God is in us, so wherever I go the kingdom is there in power through me. It's time to wake up the Devil, war has broken out, no nice Church Missions with the

Mayor giving you the right hand of welcome, where once they threw our preachers into prison! Jesus took our battle scars, Jesus has all things under His feet. 'The Kingdom suffereth violence,' Jesus said, 'the violent take it by storm.' Stand up for Jesus, ye soldiers of the cross.

'I've had to fight for everything I've got, I'm used to opposition,' Roger Forster said. 'The warfaring Church is not a respectable Church.' We must keep the Devil where he belongs. Be bold, the Holy Ghost is in control. Only the children of God, the elect, the anointed ones, can penetrate the kingdom of darkness. 'Greater is he that is in you than he that is in the world' (1 John 4:4). Again, in the Epistle to the Romans, 'I give you power to bruise Satan under you...'

When I enter a town I announce that it no longer belongs to the evil one but to the King of Kings. A millionaire one day hailed a taxi at New York airport, to drive into the city. The cabby asked, 'Where do you want to go?' The big man said, 'Anywhere, I own it all!'

'Whatever you bind in heaven you bind on earth.' Satan is under our feet, bound, beaten, on the run. When I hold a crusade I state, 'I've come to take back what the Devil has stolen.' God has given us the kingdom of love, power, healing, a sound mind, peace, joy and victory. In the worst IRA town, when police said to me, 'You're crazy to take your crusade into that place, you're not likely to come out alive in this dangerous ghetto, you're not likely to live!' I replied, 'I'm dead already!'

Others said, 'You're wasting your time in East Birmingham, which is 70 per cent Muslim.' They had stoned people at an open air meeting, conducted in their street by some Christian young people, a few months previously. But as soon as miracles happened these hitherto completely untouched Asians flocked in, in scores and hundreds. In Luton, a Mullah came to the meeting with his people.

I went right down to the Falklands, where no evangelist had ever been in 150 years of history for a major crusade. God shook the islands. It cost £2,000, but nearly 200 were saved; half the population of the territory's families came to the meetings.

When I enter a town that God Almighty has sent me to, I come to heal the sick, cast out devils, raise the dead, set captives free, heal the broken-hearted – and lead the people into the mighty Holy Ghost baptism and fire!

I've got to go in and let the Devil know that God's Church, His people, that God Almighty is in charge once more. I died a long time ago, I just obey what the King tells me. I go to bind Satan and loose the Church, to fight sin, sickness, poverty, despair and heal disturbed minds, to tell people we have the answer – for, 'If Jesus is lifted up, all men will be drawn unto him.'

– 14 –

THE WORD OF GOD PROSPERS

The Scripture tells us, 'O Lord of Hosts, blessed is the man who trusts in you' (Psalm 84:12). God wants us to give every ounce of faith to reach His goals. 'The Lord takes pleasure in His people, He adorns the humble with victory' (Psalm 149:4). You can be a winner in faith.

God's living Word is the only hope for a dying world. The Word of God in us produces faith. Dean Inge said, 'He who marries the spirit of the age will find himself a widower.' The spirit of Anti-Christ is in the world. True faith obeys without delay or doubt. 'Your word have I hidden in my heart that I might not sin against you.' Faith is not of this world.

As you approach a barrier at the car park, it will not move till the car bonnet touches the invisible sensor. You can stand still and get nowhere, but as you move forward and touch the unseen ray, up goes the barrier and you are free. Faith is to go forward.

Walk on in faith, see beyond the human eye. Faith brings invisible powers from the Almighty into being. Sometimes faith is like a ton weight which has fallen on me – I feel by His power so much anointing on me, the sick are healed, countless sinners released from generations of guilt, joy comes to broken homes now reconciled, there is peace, heaven comes down, the Blood of Christ is applied to thousands. Ezra prayed the great faith call, 'Give us a measure of reviving, of new life, in our bondage ... this is your work, this is your day O God' (Ezra 9:8).

One little girl heard the story of John's vision of the lampstands from Revelation as the preacher gave his sermon. She turned to her mother. 'Wouldn't it be lovely if all the lamps were shining on Jesus?' Great faith in God's people causes all the light in us to show up Jesus.

Showerman wrote the verse:

> God give me the faith of a little child,
> Who trusts, so implicitly,
> Who simply and gladly believes Thy Word,
> And never would question Thee.

If doubts arise in your head, if the flesh cries out the opposite to faith, if your mind plays tricks with you, if you are about to quit – don't, don't, don't! For 'greater is he that is in you [Christ], than he that is in the world [alone with no faith or power]'. Let Jesus carry your burden today.

- By faith He is in you to change the situation.
- Faith in God takes the limitation off yourself.
- Faith in yourself takes the limitations off God!

End your doubt, end your mutiny. Jesus said, 'Why do you call me Lord, and don't do what I say?' (Luke 6:46 NIV).

OBEY THE KEY TO FAITH

The acid test is obedience to Christ. John 4:12 says, 'Anyone who has faith in me will do greater things than these.' God is a faith God, He works through believing people, through His Word in us. 'No Word of God is void of power'. Keep your trust strong.

I like the story of the mother on her way to meet her son Donald – who had only just started school. Suddenly she realized she was 10 minutes late. She hurried to the school gates. Not a soul about. She went indoors anxiously. There in the hall was Donald happily 'helping' the janitor.

'Sorry, dear,' murmured a contrite mum. 'I met somebody. You weren't worried, were you?' Donald beamed.

'No,' he said. 'I knew you'd come – you said you would!' That's what I call faith!

TURN TO FACE GOD

Once when the Church of Christ was under severe Roman persecution by Nero, the apostle Peter wrote to Christians scattered all over the Roman provinces, to encourage them.

He had seen Christ in the flesh, walked with Him, eaten with Him, watched Him do great miracles, and had even witnessed His transfiguration. How did he encourage those believers? Did he tell them things were much better in the old days? Did he harp back to the days of Christ's walking on water, and inspire them with such words as: 'You should have seen it'?

No. Peter lifted his pen and wrote those fabulous words: 'Whom having not seen, you love ... Though now you see Him not, yet believing, you rejoice with joy unspeakable and full of glory: receiving the end of your faith, even the salvation of your souls ... which things the angels desire to look into (1 Peter 1:8 AV).

Faith in an *unseen* Christ has a vigour, an independence of all circumstances, a power to defy attempts to extinguish it, a buoyancy, a heavenward ardour, a love, a depth, a height, which faith in a *seen* Christ could never have had. 'Blessed,' said the Saviour, 'are those who have not seen, yet believe.'

The night I came to Christ in a meeting at the cinema in Bristol, I did what Charles Wesley did 250 years ago: I 'laid my reasonings at Jesus' feet'. The moment within my heart when I learned to yield to Him I felt what the great English poet felt – 'The wild winds hushed, the angry deep [within] sank like a little child to sleep...'

O to learn to rest in Him. This victory of faith is claimed on the strength of what God has said and done in His word. *Faith is a philosophy of life, not just when we want something badly. It is a system of living.* It is diametrically opposed to the secular thinking of our age.

Faith sees the invisible, believes the incredible, and receives the impossible, as the old saying goes. It means believing what God says solely *because He said it* to us. Abraham and Isaac all started on God's naked Word, risked all on God's Word, submitted to the fact that what He said He would do. What we read we must believe, it is not only true but practicably reliable for our generation. Believing is to stake everything, your very life, on the fact that He is true to His words. Dr

Martin Lloyd Jones said believing is 'to take the bare word and act upon it'. The urgent, glorious, eternal, transforming gospel is applicable, every bit of it, for today.

We must believe by acting, practising it. A Chinese student got saved in London and wrote home in broken English and got mixed up: 'I am reading the Word of God and *behaving it*...' Well, not far out; we must live it, be an example, act on it. A saying the Wiltshire preachers had when I was a boy was, 'Faith never stands around with its hands in its pockets...'

I love the book of Habakkuk, a prophet of trust, faith, revival (see 3:17–19). 'Yes,' Habakkuk prays, 'I know that judgement is coming on us. But, Lord, I trust You in the midst of the whole thing. I trust You to act. I trust You to work out Your purposes. I will trust You through thick and thin.' Then he comes out with the most joyful affirmation of divine sovereignty one can possibly read anywhere: 'Though the fig tree does not bud and there are no grapes on the vines, though the olive crop fails and the fields produce no food, though there are no sheep in the pen and no cattle in the stalls, yet I will rejoice in the Lord, I will be joyful in God my Saviour. The Sovereign Lord is my strength.'

We can best summarize the attitude of Habakkuk by asking some questions. Do we doubt? Are we troubled by the silence of God? Do we doubt because of disappointments? Do problems confuse us? Somebody has said that, given the world we live in, if God is God He is not good – and if God is good He isn't God. That shows a very shallow understanding of who God is. But that is where many people are. They have doubts. One more question: If you have doubts, will you wait? Will you wait on God and trust in Him? You should, because if you consider the alternatives they are too unspeakably horrible!

As you are waiting on God, are you being faithful? Are you full of faith? Are you trusting Him where you can't see? Will you trust in Him where you don't have all the answers? Will you still have that firm rock under your feet even though there are all kinds of doubts? Faith is the very basis of life. Try living without faith and you will discover you can't.

A friend of ours spent a few lovely days in the Cairngorms. He climbed a hill or two, and there, while he rested and enjoyed the view, up came a young couple. The girl was in a bad temper, complaining they ought never to have tried to climb that steep slope on such a hot day, and it was all the young man's fault, and she was going down. And down she went, slithering a bit.

Within minutes an elderly man and his wife, both taking their time about the adventure, came slowly uphill, pausing often to admire the view and get their breath, chatting pleasantly and obviously enjoying every minute.

My friend comments: same steep climb; same weather; same difficulties. One party mad; the other glad. One failed; the other reached the top. Isn't this faith? Determination? The spirit of endeavour? Of risk? Of faith and perseverance?

PERSIST – KEEP ON GOING FORWARD

Through tests, trials, setbacks, keep letting God lead you, guide you, use you. Many fail, for they give up for different reasons, while on God's road. Let tough times strengthen and fortify you. I like the verse,

> When you feel like giving in,
> And you're sure life's got you beat,
> Take a second breath – then try
> With more energy and heat,
> You will find, if you go to it,
> You have learnt the way to do it!

ONE HEART – ONE MIND

John Bunney lives opposite a bowling green. One day as a visiting party waited for their bus, John strolled over to chat with them. He noticed that an old couple, well over eighty, looked tired. So he asked them if they'd like to step over to his house for a rest and a cup of tea. Soon they were all chatting as if they'd known one another all their lives. It turned out the old man was a keen gardener, and was especially proud of his tomatoes. He'd grown them for years, and always had a grand crop.

John asked his secret. 'Well,' said the old man, 'next time you plant your tomatoes make sure you press the soil down hard on top of them. You see,' he added, 'the harder it is for the plants to come up the stronger and better they'll be.'

Soon, the bowlers' bus arrived, and John bade goodbye to his new friends. But he couldn't help thinking that the old man's advice is very like life. So often those who, like the old bowler's tomatoes, have known difficulty and setbacks, not only stand firm in life's storms but bear better fruit.

> For every hill I've had to climb,
> For every stone that bruised my feet,
> For all the tears and sweat and grime,
> For blinding storms and burning heat,
> My heart still sings a grateful song;
> These were the things that made me strong!

Perseverance may conquer mountains. That was true of the greatest of the Greek orators, Demosthenes, who, realizing his voice was weak, practised hard against the sound of the waves beating on the shore. Or Disraeli who, on his first speech in Parliament, was mocked and sneered at as a Jew. 'You will hear me yet!' he shouted and, persevering, became Prime Minister.

Or take the simple courage of Robert Louis Stevenson who, when finding he had lost the power of writing with his right hand, taught himself to write with his left. Mountains are made not to be looked at but to be climbed, if we have the will and the determination.

> You can't keep on? You've tried so hard?
> You've battled on so long
> This is the end. You're finished now –
> For everything's gone wrong.
> In spite of dark despair and pain
> Look up! Hold on! Begin again!

Joseph Lister, a Glasgow doctor, found the secret that doctors had searched for almost since time began. In 1864, 45 out of every 100 patients who underwent operations did not live. Then, on an August day in 1865, a Glasgow lad called Jimmy Greenlees was brought to Lister with a badly broken leg. The doctor smiled encouragingly at the lad as he examined him, though he knew he would almost certainly die from blood poisoning. It was the killer for which there was no known cure.

But Professor Lister had worked for years against great difficulties to find the answer. Now, despite the sneers of others, he decided to put it to the test on Jimmy. It was simple carbolic – the first antiseptic ever to be used. I cannot imagine what Lister's feelings were as he waited by the bedside of that Glasgow boy, hoping against hope. Praise be, Jimmy lived! The miracle of the antiseptic was proved beyond a shadow of doubt and the whole course of medicine was changed. *He persisted*.

Lister was showered with the highest honours. But he could never know that millions all over the world would owe their lives to him in the years to come and, as is inscribed on his grave, that 'all generations would call him blessed'.

He kept on – in faith. Those who are faithful to the end *reap the harvest*.

'If at first you don't succeed...' How many of us have given up in despair after a few attempts to do something, and have marked this quotation down as nonsense? And yet, so many great people have proved it true. G. B. Shaw, for instance, spent nine years in extreme poverty before he found a publisher for his books. During that time he earned only six pounds. But he never gave up – he always tried again. Perhaps there is a message here for you. Try again and this time, God willing, you will succeed.

GOD BREAKS THROUGH WHEN WE DON'T GIVE UP

It's when things seem worst that you mustn't quit! It's over 225 years since Horatio Nelson was born. He was, of course, the hero of Trafalgar. But whenever I think of this famous admiral I think of the Battle of Copenhagen, in which, at one time, the engagement was so fierce that Sir Hyde Parker felt it expedient to signal Nelson to withdraw.

Nelson, however, did not wish to obey. When his attention was drawn to his superior's signal of recall, the 'bad boy' of the Navy put his telescope to his blind eye and, as he could not see the signal, he went on fighting ... and won!

When you begin to lose heart because the going's hard, are you looking here and there for excuses to stop trying? Are you prepared to beat a retreat? Or have you something of the Nelson touch? I trust you have – and that, however long or hard the struggle, you'll keep on and on, with a grin as well as courage and determination, until you, too, win a splendid victory.

I dare say you feel that you cannot keep on,
And I dare say the call is so tough,
The job is so hard or the waiting so long,
There's nobody fit for such stuff.

But I'm telling you – and I know this is true –
That whatever the road you began,
With courage and faith you will do it, for sure ...
If you THINK GOD can do it, YOU CAN!

Robert Schuller's words can be used about faith:

Treat faith tenderly – it can get killed pretty quickly.
Treat faith gently – it can be bruised in infancy.
Treat faith respectfully – it can be your most valuable
   possession.
Treat faith protectively – don't lose it.
Treat faith nutritionally – feed it well.
Treat your faith antiseptically – don't let it get
   infected with germs of negative thoughts and
   doubts.
Treat your faith responsibly – respond, act, do
   something with it!

ADAPTED

God takes pride in our faith. He says in the last book –
almost the last words – of the Bible, 'Come, I will show
you the bride [the Church – the people of real faith] –
the wife of the Lamb' (Revelation 21:9). It's a joy
forever to Him that we have overcome through His
blood and by faith in Him.

Sir Christopher Wren, the architect of St Paul's Cathedral in the city of London, chose on his retirement to live in Camberwell, on the other side of the River Thames, where it was possible to view the cathedral, the construction of which had been his crowning glory. Erected between 1675 and 1710, the cathedral is recognized as being one of the most spectacularly splendid buildings in Britain. Sir Christopher Wren lived to be 90 years of age, and could sometimes be seen sitting with spyglass in hand, looking out across the Thames and surveying with pleasure and pride the cathedral he had designed. What an interesting sight it must have been for those who witnessed it – the master contemplating his masterpiece.

So God looks down today on the masterpiece of the Christian with rising, growing faith. He is looking for you, at you, to you; is your faith strong? Getting stronger? In need of pepping up? Weak, shallow, at a loss? Or being revived? Let God be proud of you His masterpiece, because of your faith, love, fruits, maturity, soul-winning, joy, peace, tender, blossoming believing. I pray so much it shall be like this for you.

When the disciples asked Jesus why they had no power to cast the demon out of the afflicted child in Matthew 17:8–20, He replied, 'Because you're not taking God seriously ... the simple truth is, that if you had a mere kernel of faith, a poppy seed, say, you would tell this mountain – "Move!" and it would move. There is nothing you wouldn't be able to tackle!' (*The Message*).

IMPEDED BY UNAWARENESS

Shortly before his death, the Duke of Burgundy was presiding over the Cabinet Council of France. A proposal was made that would violate an existing treaty but would secure important advantages for the country. Many 'good' reasons were offered to justify this action. The Duke listened in silence. When all had spoken, he closed the conference without giving approval. Placing his hand on a copy of the original agreement, he said with firmness in his voice, 'Gentlemen, we have a *treaty*!'

This was a man who wanted to stay true to his word. It's a strong temptation today to abandon some of God's Word in favour of being popular, for personal advantage or even financial gain. I heard some say in a very good gospel church, about some scriptural songs: 'We don't sing those any more, they are old hat!' We must remain true, if not to the 1950s gospel hymns, at least to Scripture itself. We must stay true to God's own Divine Word all the way. 'I have sought your precepts' (Psalm 119:94).

Three top American authors recently made the following comments about the Bible:

'Lay chosen faith aside and read this beautifully written book,' wrote Loren D. Estleman.

'It is the foundation stone of the English language,' added Madeleine L'Engle Franklin.

John Jakes urged people to read the Bible 'for the magic, and the possibilities, of English'.

The books that men make are nothing compared to the book that makes men. I like Dean's verse:

> God's Word is deeper than the sea
> and broad as all eternity;
> And there may we time's meaning know,
> But only as we dare to go
> Into the depths with God.

There is a great unawareness of God's teaching at this time. George Verwer put it: 'The Word of God ignites the reader!' The people spoke of Christ: 'His Word was with power', again, 'Never spake a man like this man.' One soldier requested, 'Speak the word only and my servant will be healed.' Among the prophets previously it had the same stinging effect and 'He sent His Word and it healed them.' 'Listen to these sayings; they are health to all their flesh.'

Later, in the first days of the Christian Church the Bible records: 'When they heard this [the Word of God] they were cut to the heart.' Orin Gifford, the well-known Baptist preacher in the USA, put it: 'Paul's preaching of the Divine Word brought either a riot or a revival.'

The problem today is that there is so much ignorance of the Holy Bible. Sinners have no background, it is not taught in the schools properly, not read much in homes (a recent survey showed less than 10 per cent of British people had read from the Bible once in the previous month! Ninety per cent had not read from it at all; some 50 per cent hard core hardly ever in their lives!)

Yet some 96 per cent of British homes have a Bible somewhere in the house. Recently we helped to send some 600,000 Bibles to Ethiopia. One church there has grown from 1,000 to 20,000 very rapidly. They expect that to make 2 million new Christians in the next five years!

But what about the UK, the sceptics say? In most of my meetings, we are crowded with often 80 per cent non-church people. When it comes to the Bible reading some are looking through the song sheet to try and find where the Scripture is! In Europe it is an amazing fact how few people actually read the Scriptures. Moving along the Belgium–Dutch border towns, and the German–Dutch towns like Kerkrade, Stein, Sittard and Maastricht, many villages have never seen an evangelist in history! Or as one English insurance agent said to a friend of mine, 'Who is Billy Graham?'

The darkness is appalling. In the Flemish–German towns hundreds crowd my meetings, in bars, cafés, clubs, town halls, community centres, 70 saved in a night, in another place 50 converts in an afternoon. Every miracle recorded in the book is witnessed to, as cripples walk free, disabled chairs are left redundant! This is the Bible coming alive to a new generation.

But in the 'dark ages' copies of the Scriptures were chained to the pulpit in the secret language of the clergy and the public were kept ignorant of the life-changing nature of its truths. Men like Tyndale were burnt alive for trying to get the Scriptures into the hands of the common people. In those days biblical ignorance was forced. Now, in our day, it is voluntary. In fact, the more versions of Scripture we have, the less the Bible is read.

A teacher quizzed a group of college-bound high school pupils on the Bible. Here are some of the answers he received.

- Jesus was baptized by Moses.
- Sodom and Gomorrah were lovers.
- Jezebel was Ahab's donkey.
- The New Testament Gospels were written by Matthew, Mark, Luther and John.
- Eve was created from an apple.
- The most hilarious, if sad, answer to the question, 'What was Golgotha?' was, 'Golgotha was the name of the giant who slew the Apostle David.'

Despite the fact that millions neglect the Scriptures, it does not take away the reality that there is no other place where better guidance can be found for everyday living. To move away from the pages of Scripture is to enter the wastelands of subjectivity. The Bible is a divinely provided map containing directions and markings to guide people to the true order for family or nation. To ignore its teachings leads to moral and spiritual shipwreck.

There is, of course, nothing magical in reading the Scriptures. They need to be obeyed and you need to know the author, which is possible through Jesus Christ. We know very well that professional religious types have been merely reading the Scriptures and disobeying them for centuries. It is obviously important that the Scriptures are obeyed.

IGNORANCE AMONG BELIEVERS

Most appalling of all is the lack of knowledge among Christians of God's Word. Many falter, are weak, led astray, live carnal lives, are mainly unfruitful in winning the pagans; others grumble, grouse, criticize, many have got hardened hearts, dry doom and gloom living, defeated, unrealistic, and they often fall into sadness, depression, fears and guilt and sin, because they do not know of the glorious power, the victories that are on offer, through neglect, ignorance of God's offers, God's revelations, God's blessings, that are properly theirs.

'Many are sick among you and many die, because you do not rightly discern...' So Scripture tells us: they do not understand, they do not know God's Word! *You must read it and know it and live it.*

When Christians come to my meetings and see so many lost sinners converted they are set aflame, 45 the other night in one service in the small country town in Bedfordshire where I was preaching. Last week 100 were born again, first time seeking Christ, in one service in Aylesbury in Buckinghamshire. The meeting went on till nearly midnight!

Believers want to start reading their Bibles again when they see God so working. God's actions inspire Bible searching and studying.

I try to read 150 chapters a week of Scripture, but often don't manage that – sometimes – I read more! After one revival in Devon when so many got saved, everyone wanted to read the Bible, and there was such a rush at our bookstall for copies, I was nearly pushed over, and 100 Bibles were sold in a night. We then put up a sign:

WHEN BIBLES ARE SOLD AS CHEAP AS THESE IT
MAKES THE DEVIL TREMBLE IN HIS KNEES.

GET INTO DIVINE TRUTH

As Sherlock Holmes used to say to Dr Watson, 'These
are deep waters, Watson!' Let's look at the benefits just
in one portion of the Word of God. Psalm 119 spells it
out graphically for us – with 20 facts.

1. *God's Word makes us pure* – vv. 9 and 11. 'How can
   one cleanse His way? By taking heed to His Word ...
   your Word I hide in my heart that I may not sin...'
2. *God's Word grants me counsel* – v. 24. 'Your
   testimonies are my delight and give me counsel.'
3. *God's Word shows all that is false in us* – v. 29.
   'Remove from me the way of lying.'
4. *God's Word leads me into true reverence for God* –
   v. 38. 'Your Word causes your servant to be devoted
   in fearing you.'
5. *God's Word gives me courage* – v. 46. 'I will speak of
   you before Kings and not be ashamed.'
6. *God's Word comforts me* – v. 50. 'Your Word gives
   me life and comforts me in afflictions.'
7. *God's Word brings me through panic* – vv. 61 and
   62. 'The cords ... bound me, but I have not forgotten
   your Word ... I will rise and give thanks...'
8. *God's Word teaches me knowledge* – vv. 65 and 66.
   'You have dealt with me according to your words,
   teach me good judgements and knowledge, for I
   believe...'

9. *God's Word teaches me patience* – v. 87. 'They almost made my end ... but I did not forsake you.'

10. *God's Word spiritually peps me up* – v. 93. 'I will not forget your precepts, for they give me life.'

11. *God's Word gives me much happiness* – v. 111. 'They are my heritage for ever, the rejoicing of my heart.'

12. *God's Word aids me to reject wrong and do right* – v. 128. 'Your precepts ... I consider to be right, I hate every false way.'

13. *God's Word causes me to walk in truth* – v. 133. 'Direct my steps, that no sin dominates me.'

14. *God's Word gives me victory over stress and trouble* – v. 143. 'Trouble and anguish have overtaken me, yet your commandments are my delight.'

15. *God's Word inspires strong praying in me* – v. 147. 'I rise before the dawn and cry for help, I hope in your Word.'

16. *God's Word rescues me out of trials* – vv. 152–154. 'You have founded them forever ... from my afflictions, deliver me ... plead my cause, revive me according to Your Word.'

17. *God's Word fills me with praise and adds peace to my soul* – vv. 164–165. 'Seven times a day I praise you ... great peace have I ... nothing makes me to stumble.'

18. *God's Word saves me when I drift away* – v. 176. 'I have gone astray like a lost sheep. Seek your servant, for I do not forget Your commandments.'

19. *God's Word sustains me when I am helpless* – v. 116. 'Uphold me ... that I may not be ashamed of my hope.'

20. *God's Word guides me in the true way* – v. 5. 'My ways are directed to keep Your statutes.'

GOD CAN'T BE STOPPED

'Biblical religion,' says Eugene Peterson, 'is aggressively internationalistic.' Our churches ought not to be cosy places to which we retreat but centres from which we draw inspiration to make both individual and corporate evangelistic forays into the world. Jesus' last words were not 'come', but 'go' (Matthew 28:19).

Has the Word of the Lord come to you? Has God spoken into your life and given you clear direction concerning the path along which He wants you to go? Then go for it – and never give up. Doing the work of God faithfully is the excellence He looks for. The Word of the Lord is your strength. Give Him praise and honour and glory.

I think of Sir Winston Churchill's picturesque remarks concerning one of the generals who led the Russian armies against Germany in the Second World War. 'He reminded me of a frozen peg hammered into the ground, firm, solid, immovable.' That is the picture I hold in my mind of Jeremiah. We can all choose how we will live – cautiously or courageously. Which one will it be for you?

A BOOK OF HOPE

Pascal, the great French Christian and philosopher, said, 'It ought to be the soul's habit whenever discouraged or in need of guidance to first call out to the Lord before calling out to anyone else.' It is not wrong to seek help from others, but our first port of call ought to be the Lord and His Word.

'Then the Lord ... said to me, "Now, I have put my words in your mouth"' (Jeremiah 1:9). 'God does not send us into the dangerous and exacting life of faith because we are qualified,' said Eugene Peterson. 'He chooses us in order to qualify us for what He wants us to be and do.'

One person put it like this: 'Standing in a church singing a hymn doesn't make us holy any more than standing in a barn and neighing makes us a horse.' It's not so much *what we say* but *who we are* that's important.

Doubt is best dealt with in prayer before God, not peddled in public. A minister whose sermons were often filled with doubts was told by one of his congregations, 'I have enough doubts of my own. When I come to church I come to hear convictions.'

– 16 –

GREATEST WHEN WE ARE LOWEST

In order to serve God we need drive and positiveness, but we also need humility. In fact, all of the most successful Christian leaders I have rubbed shoulders with have been modest people. Also, quite a number of the famous figures of the past have been unassuming folk, seemingly unaffected by their fame.

George Washington was once out riding with some friends in the country. One of their horses happened to kick a few stones from the top of a wall it had leaped over.

'We'd better put those stones back,' said Washington.

'Oh, we can leave that to the farmer,' said one of his companions.

But when the ride was over Washington went back to the wall and began to carefully replace the stones.

'But General,' protested one of his friends, 'you are too big a man to do that!'

'On the contrary,' replied Washington, 'I am just the right size.'

Samuel Chadwick once humbly volunteered to clean someone's boots. As he was on his knees doing this menial task he felt Jesus' presence. There and then he vowed that in future, whatever he did he would do for the Lord. He went on to become one of the greatest Christian teachers of his age!

Once one of the Dukes of Norfolk happened to be at the railway station near his home, Arundel Castle, when a little Irish girl stepped off the train with a very heavy bag. She had come to join the Duke's household staff as a maidservant. Timidly she asked a porter if he would carry her bag to the castle, which was about a mile away. She offered him a shilling, which was all the money she had, but the porter contemptuously refused. Then the Duke stepped forward, in somewhat shabby dress as usual. He picked up her bag and walked the mile with her, chatting to her as they went. At the castle gate he took the shilling she offered him and waved goodbye to her. It was only the next day, when she met her employer, that the girl knew that it had been the Duke of Norfolk himself who had carried her bag from the station for a shilling! The truly great man does not think of his place or prestige. It is only little people who are concerned with their status.

King Edward VII had been having lunch with his friend, David Sassoon, at his home in Hove in Sussex. As he left Sassoon's house, a schoolboy who had been waiting outside asked him the time. The King consulted his watch. 'Half past three,' he said. 'Half past three?' exclaimed the boy. 'Crumbs, it's later than I thought. They say the blooming old King's inside this house – I've been hanging around since one o'clock to see him! But I ain't waiting no longer – he ain't worth it!'

King Edward had turned 60 but had never quite grown up. Instead of being annoyed he was tickled pink by the loyal but weary laddie. 'You're right,' he declared warmly, 'absolutely right, sonny. He just ain't worth it. I'm the blooming old King, and here's something to remember me by.'

A few silver coins changed hands, and the astonished boy went off with his head in a happy whirl.

Isobel Baillie's beautiful voice made her a household name in her time. But although she was famous she was also remarkably modest. In her autobiography the actress Beryl Reid recalls that when she was a child she used to visit Isobel's home to play with her daughter. Beryl grew up and didn't see Isobel for years, but there came a time when they happened to be on the same programme at the Albert Hall. Beryl was delighted to see Isobel again. The great singer told her that she had always followed her career with great interest and had gone to see everything she had done on stage.

'But why didn't you contact my manager and personally come and see me?' asked Beryl.

'Oh,' replied Isobel, 'I didn't think you would remember me.'

I like this story which Sinclair Lewis, the famous American novelist, once told against himself. One day during a crossing of the Atlantic on a liner he and a friend were pacing the deck. They passed a woman who was sitting in a deckchair reading. Lewis was delighted to see that she was reading a book which he had written. Pulling his friend aside, he whispered to him, 'Look, she's reading one of my books! That's fame! There is an obviously intellectual woman absorbed in what I have written!' But the next moment the woman shut the book with a snap and contemptuously tossed it overboard. Lewis felt very humbled!

One of the things I love best about children is that they can be so natural and so lacking in the pride which adults display. Princess Margrethe, who is today the popular and lovely queen of Denmark, was as a school-girl once asked by a new girl in her class, 'What's your father?'

She replied, 'He's a King. What's yours?' We adults need to emulate the unselfconscious humility and modesty of children.

A certain well-known preacher was recently conducting some crusades in Queensland in Australia. He was invited to meet with and speak to a gathering of 14 young ministers and evangelists in a remote part of the Outback. He agreed, and flew 600 miles and drove 250 miles on some very rough roads to meet these Christian workers. He was used to speaking to crowds of hundreds and thousands, but didn't mind that there were only going to be 14 people listening to him. He felt that God wanted him to go and speak to them, so off he went. He knew that even one person is of inestimable value to Jesus. I suggest that the minister who is too big to speak to just a handful of folk is *too* big!

An amusing story is told of a church service at which the preacher was to be a visiting dean. The vicar rose and proceeded to give the dean a long and elaborate introduction, listing his many splendid achievements. At last the vicar stopped, and the dean, who had been rather embarrassed by all this praise, was greatly relieved. On his way to the pulpit the dean turned to the vicar and said, 'Thank you. After an introduction like that I can hardly wait to hear what I've got to say!'

I heard a lovely story recently. When the House of Commons was being constructed, a painter requested permission to paint one of the large frescoes. He added that if that request could not be granted, he would like permission to paint one of the small frescoes. Then he said that if that request could not be granted either he would like permission to mix the paint for the man who did the painting. He was so eager to be involved in the work that he was willing to do even the most humble part of it. That should be our attitude. If someone else is asked to the 'big' jobs which get all the attention, so be it. We should be content to be able to serve God in some way, no matter how small. Let us pray, 'Lord, keep us humble and modest!'

Hudson Taylor once said that humility was 'being small enough for God to use'. The great evangelist D. L. Moody used to say, 'You can be too big for God to use, but never too small.' To 'eat humble pie' is the only way to move upward and forward in Christ. Augustine said, 'It was pride that turned angels into devils, and it is humility that turns men into angels.'

John Bunyan wrote glowingly of this blessed virtue of humility:

> He that is down, needs no fall,
> He that is low, no pride;
> He that is humble, ever shall
> Have God to be his guide.

Here is a paraphrase of a story told in a Quaker song from about 200 years ago:

Having spent a time alone in the desert, Saint Anthony came to the conclusion that there could be no holier saint than he. Later, in the back streets of a great city, he met an old cobbler named Conrad. Anthony asked him, a little haughtily, what he had ever done to please the Lord. 'Me?' Conrad replied. 'Me?' I have done nothing but mend sandals. 'But,' he said, raising his head, 'I have mended each pair as though they belonged to my Lord and Saviour.' That simple cobbler taught Anthony a lesson he never forgot.

If we think we are humble, then we are not! Three monks of different orders were talking together one day. One of them, a Dominican, said, 'Our order is the best, because we are the intellectuals of the Church.' A second, who was a Jesuit, said, 'Oh no, ours is the greatest order, because it is the most disciplined.' The third, who was a Franciscan, piped up, 'We are the most noble of orders because we are the humblest!'

> It's a gift to be humble,
> It's a gift to come down to where we ought to be.
> When we see ourselves in a way that is right
> We will live in a valley of love and delight ...
> When true humility is gained ...
> To live and to love we will not be ashamed.

If people parade their 'humility' they show that they in fact have none! A man once wrote a book entitled *Humility and How I Achieved It.*

A schoolboy who had been cheeky to a teacher was given a severe dressing-down by the headmaster and was warned that if he erred again he would be in for some tough punishment. 'You ought to be more modest and humble, boy,' the head told him. The boy promised to obey. The following week the boy was again brought before the head for bad behaviour.

'You promised me you would be more modest and humble!' he said.

The boy sheepishly replied, 'I tried for a week, sir, but no one noticed!'

Here is a true old saying: 'Modesty does nothing to be noticed, but cannot in the end be missed.'

History contains many examples of humility but, of course, Jesus Himself is the supreme example. He gave up the glory of heaven to come to earth for our sakes. Paul wrote, 'Christ Jesus ... being in very nature God, did not consider equality with God something to be grasped, but made Himself nothing, taking the very nature of a servant, being made in human likeness. And being found in appearance as a man, he humbled himself and became obedient to death – even death on a cross! Therefore God exalted him to the highest place' (Philippians 2:5–9).

Humility is mentioned many times in Scripture. It exhorts us to 'put on ... humbleness of mind' (Colossians 3:12), to 'walk humbly' (Micah 6:8), to be 'clothed with humility' (1 Peter 5:5). God has said, 'This is the one I esteem: he who is humble and contrite in spirit, and trembles at my word' (Isaiah 66:2). Jesus said, 'Come to me ... learn from me, for I am gentle and humble in heart' (Matthew 11:28–29).

The Bible places great emphasis on humility as a vital condition for gaining success in life: 'Clothe yourselves with humility towards one another, because "God opposes the proud but gives grace to the humble." Humble yourselves, therefore, under God's mighty hand,

that he may lift you up in due time' (1 Peter 5:5–6). God
has promised special success, exaltation, blessing, victory
and prosperity to the humble. As Jesus said, 'He who
humbles himself will be exalted' (Luke 14:11).

FAITH AND HUMILITY BRING STABILITY

Will you wait and let God speak to you? You are not
going to understand Him quickly and you are not going
to come up with solutions overnight.

As you are waiting on God, are you being faithful?
Are you full of faith? Are you trusting Him where you
can't see? Will you trust in Him where you don't have
all the answers? Will you still have that firm rock under
your feet, even though there are all kinds of doubts?
Faith is the very basis of life. Try living without faith
and you will discover you can't.

One day I got in a little plane to make the flight
home. The guy who was to fly the aircraft said it would
take us two hours and ten minutes to get there. I
believed him, and got into the plane. On the way home
we were in the cloud cover all the way. We couldn't see
a thing – we just trusted the instruments. Then a voice
spoke to us on the radio, telling us to descend from
7,000 to 2,700 feet. The voice promised us we would
come out of the cloud, and we did. The minute we came
into the clear at 2,700 feet a runway appeared right in
front of us. We trusted the voice, we trusted the instruments, I trusted the pilot, I trusted the plane.

That is how life operates. Do you ever trust God?
The nice thing I liked about that pilot was that he said,
'Let's pray.' He was a man of faith too.

God is stable. We're the ones who are unstable. He is the One who can be relied upon. We're the unreliable ones. However, when we begin to take Him seriously, we begin to get our lives in line with His. My wife has a lovely expression. She used to think that prayer was sitting in a little dinghy pulling on the rope trying to get the big ship to come alongside. What she discovered was this. As she pulled the rope, her little dinghy was drawn alongside the big ship. Often our attitude is to try to get God (the big ship) alongside us. In actual fact what the Lord tells us to do is to pull on the rope and get ourselves alongside Him. When we understand who He is, and what He is doing, then we have a chance to get our act together. But as long as we refuse to do that we will be in trouble.

Your faith can draw you near to God and then He will draw near to you. I like the words of Scripture regarding the faith of King Hezekiah, as recorded in 2 Kings 18:15–18 (NIV), 'He trusted in the Lord ... there was no one like Him [among Kings] either before Him or after Him; he held fast to the Lord, and did not cease to follow Him, he kept the commandments ... The Lord was with him ... he was successful in whatever he undertook.'

AN ANSWER TO FEAR

God works for faith in the heart. A ray of hope appears and that little ray of hope is the way God always operates. 'I will surely gather all of you, O Jacob; I will surely bring together the remnant of Israel. I will bring them together like sheep in a pen, like a flock in its pasture; the place will throng with people. One who breaks open the way will go up before them; they will break through the gate and go out. Their king will pass through before them, the Lord at their head' (Micah 2:12,13).

God promised that day to Micah the prophet to save the faithful, to be their head, to act for them, if fear was turned round to believing. The key to conquering the fears in us is to humble ourselves, to give way to the mighty hand of God.

Jack Hayford, writer of 'Majesty', spoke of it as 'the inevitable triumph of the humble'.

Colossians 3:14–16 in the NRSV translation reads, 'Above all, clothe yourselves with love, which binds everything together in perfect harmony. And let the peace of Christ rule in your hearts, to which indeed you were called in the one body. And be thankful. Let the word of Christ swell in you richly...'

A vicar told how, 'Our church could not be used for several weeks when redecorating and cleaning were being done. It left the pews covered in dust. One day I was walking through the church and I saw a man sitting there cleaning the dust off the pews. I asked him if he was enjoying himself. "Oh yes," he replied and his face absolutely lit up, "What could be more wonderful than working in God's house?" He was doing a task that many people would find mundane and boring but he was genuinely finding it satisfying. I walked away realizing that that was the most profound sermon I had heard for some time. He was doing it to the glory of God.'

HUMILITY

I know men and women who are prepared to set out seats in halls prior to a revival service, clean toilets, make cups of tea, give a night's rest to an evangelist, make a meal for a homeless person, some even wash my car and polish my boots for me – for *me* – week after week. Their reward will be great in Glory. They are truly humble people.

Humility is seen so often as inaction, a quiet, go-slow policy, a deeply devotional person's unmoved attitude, inward-looking, sublime, while the goons in evangelism are all action, the hasty, ever-running, talking, gabbling, evangelistic types, bear all the visible fruit, but the extroverts are not the humble! Not at all. In fact, some of the most dynamic, hearty, soul-loving people, who have built large, strong churches, leading the people of God forward into great blessing, revival, growth, victory, have been among the humblest, just as those who have never preached a sermon but done all the so-called menial tasks are also often humble.

I like Paul's words in Philippians 2:3–4 in the Good News Bible: 'Don't do anything ... from a cheap desire to boast, but be humble towards one another, always considering others better than yourselves.'

Sociologists call 'self-improvement' or 'self-esteem' 'upward mobility'! We can be modest, humble yet confident and go places, there is a happy medium and balance. The basics of humility have nothing to do with self-righteousness, snivelling, cringing Uriah Heeps, like in *David Copperfield*, the famous novel of Dickens. Remember his words, 'I am well aware I am the humblest person going!' True humility is rather a life by which we are willing to listen, help the hurts of others, share and get down to the needs of pitying mankind.

Humility is often there *until* we know it's ours – then we are no longer humble! D. L. Moody used to say, 'Faith gets the most, love works the most, but humility keeps the most.' Jesus said, 'Blessed are the meek.' And, 'The humble shall be exalted.'

'You know that men who are rulers ... have power over them ... this is not the way among you, if one of you wants to be great, he must be a servant of the rest ... want to be humble ... then be slave of all' (Mark 10:42–44 GNB). The Greeks were not humble, they cried to the disciples, 'Sirs, we would see Jesus.'

The Greeks were not at all humble. I've heard preachers say dozens of times, these people who came in John 12:21 and asked Philip, 'Sirs, we would see Jesus', were deeply humble people. Far from it. They came to Jesus second-hand, indeed third-hand, for Philip goes to Andrew, then they come to our Lord. Jesus never did meet them, He knew they were not truly humble, in fact He replies to their request – in verses 24–26 – 'Unless a grain of wheat is buried in the ground, dead to the world, it is never any more ... it sprouts and reproduces itself many times over ... hold on to life and you destroy it ... let it go, be reckless in your love and you'll have it forever ... if anyone wants to serve me – follow me ... the Father will honour and reward anyone who serves me.' This is the plan for humility which Jesus gives.

There is a marvellous friend I have in Swindon, Wiltshire. He has never preached a sermon, he is an outstanding artist, I have some of his fine bird sketches on the wall in my front room. He lives by painting. He had a great healing and conversion in one of my services a few years ago. He will get up at 3.30 in the morning to drive 25 miles, to pick me up in the country, and drive me down the M4 to Heathrow Airport, to get the first flight at 7.30, to some international city to preach the gospel of Christ. This is humility for such a noted artist to do this small job, and never take payment from me, but send the servant of God on his way to bless thousands of lost and sickly and desperate people. Ken and Beryl Beint say, 'I feel a part of this revival when I do this job.' God will and is rewarding them.

Someone tried to teach the mighty forerunner of my ministry, the anointed healer Smith Wigglesworth, a lesson in humility. They noted that later in life (in his seventies and eighties) he always journeyed by first class. The brother challenged the mighty man of God, saying, 'Why do you waste the Lord's money by travelling on the train by first class?'

He replied, 'Because I want to preserve the Lord's servant!' He walked humbly, but took good care of himself (second and third class carriages were crowded and full of smoke in those days). He lived to be 88 years of age and preached to the end full of fire!

God has sent His Son to die, to rise again, and to ascend to the Father's right hand. This Son has promised to return again in glory. In light of all these facts, what does the Lord require of us now? This is the crux of the matter and the answer is very simple and straightforward. As far as my relationship to God is concerned, I am to walk humbly. Is that all he says? No, there's more. God requires me to walk through life humble *with Him* – day in, day out. I am to walk into the office humbly with my God. I am to move through my day-to-day affairs humbly with my God. This means I operate under His control in humble obedience to Him. I am humbly repentant for that which grieves Him. I am humbly dependent upon Him at all times and for all things.

How will the world know that I am walking humbly with my God? They will know by the way I treat people. Those who walk humbly with their God have a passionate desire to please Him.

WHAT DOES GOD THINK OF YOU?

Some years ago, my friend Fred Train, an old missionary from Paraguay, was teaching at a Bible school in England. At the school there was a particularly obnoxious student who was so arrogant it oozed out of every pore. People avoided him; they just couldn't cope with him. They literally couldn't stand him. This student didn't care much for the ministry of missions. He didn't like to be told about people going out to reach the unreached.

One day he approached Fred Train and said, 'I've just been on the phone to my father with regard to what you've been teaching. And my father says that he wants you to know that he thinks it would be the most dreadful waste of my life for me to go to the mission field. And he also wants you to know what he thinks about your message.'

Old Fred Train, who was never one for backing up, looked at the student and said, 'I'm very interested to know what your father thinks about you and me and my message and the Lord Jesus. But what interests me far more is – I wonder what the Lord Jesus thinks of your father.'

What does God think of your words, your talk, your attitude, your humility, or lack of it? Is fear of what others think, fear of the world, fear of yourself, very real in your life?

'Seek the Lord, all you humble of the land, you who do what He commands. Seek righteousness, seek humility; perhaps you will be sheltered on the day of the Lord's anger' (Zephaniah 2:1–3). What a tender invitation! God is saying, come with others of like mind before the presence of the Lord and seek His face. Make *Him* your ambition. Make knowing Him your prime concern. Do what is right in His eyes. Be made right with Him. Be humble instead of proud. Get rid of your self-sufficiency and arrogance.

The famous golfer, Jack Nicklaus, tells how as a lad his father was showing him the ropes regarding golf. The old pro was patiently teaching him, when one day, frustrated, Jack threw down the clubs and stormed across the green. His father spoke gently and firmly over to him, 'Do that once more and you will never get another lesson ... ever again from me!'

Why didn't Jack Nicklaus ever throw another club? I think I know why – he knew his dad meant what he said. If he'd had the slightest inkling that his dad would say, 'Oh, I didn't really mean it,' Jack would still be petulantly throwing his clubs today. Instead, he's a self-controlled, capable, professional athlete with an admirable reputation. That's what God wants for each of His children. He invites us to step into true greatness – commitment to Christ and a life lived obediently under His direction.

Jack learnt humility that day and conquered his lack of confidence and his fears!

GOD'S PLAN FOR HIS PEOPLE

Look at God's plan for His people: 'Then will I purify the lips of the peoples, that all of them may call on the name of the Lord and serve him shoulder to shoulder. From beyond the rivers of Cush my worshippers, my scattered people, will bring me offerings. On that day you will not be put to shame for all the wrongs you have done to me, because I will remove from this city those who rejoice in their pride. Never again will you be haughty ... But I will leave within you the meek and humble, who trust in the name of the Lord. The remnant of Israel will do no wrong' (Zephaniah 3:9–13).

What is He promising here? There will always be those who will stand out from the crowd of unbelievers. They will humble themselves, and seek the Lord. Asking for His forgiveness and His grace, they will respond to His tender loving call.

Humility is tender but tough on our fears. A young fellow, busy stealing cars in California, was eventually caught and hauled before the judge. Wisely, the judge didn't just send him to jail. He knew that there the boy would be introduced to all the advantages of a jailhouse education. There was a high probability that this amateur car thief would become a professional. Yet, on the other hand, the judge knew that he couldn't just let the boy off. So he tried to blend some toughness with tenderness. He sent the young fellow to a ski camp and told him to stay there until he mastered the sport of downhill skiing. The boy had to fit into a gruelling training programme – but those who are interested in downhill skiing are glad that the judge dealt firmly with Bill Johnson. He became the gold medal winner in Alpine skiing at the Olympics. The judge wasn't so tough that he broke him – but he wasn't so tender that he let him get away with his crime lightly.

WITH GRACE AND GLORY

We can so easily put our foot in it. Like the little girl when the vicar called who said to him, when her mother was out of the room getting some tea and cakes ready, 'You aren't very handsome, are you?' (she was only about five years old). He was taken aback and when her mother came in with the goodies, he told her seriously what the little one had said. The mother thought for a moment then added, 'It's amazing how children come out with the truth sometimes, isn't it?'

But thank God, with the Saviour we can have the right words, be always on the ball, not miss the mark or opportunity, be a part of God's all-time action, share even His glory and grace.

OUR LORD IS ALWAYS VICTORIOUS

An old icon in the Orthodox Church shows some engravings, picturing Christ descending to Hades, meeting with Adam and Eve fallen in sin, lifting them by the wrists, and coming up in glory and triumph, reclaiming our first parents, and presenting them before the Father's throne in glory. Not quite scriptural, but certainly symbolical of His mighty power and victory over all the effects, destructions, pollutions of sin and fallen man.

This is the glory offered to us, through the Cross of

our Lord Jesus Christ. As we give Jesus away we have more of His activity in us!

The story is told of two men who had worked together in a factory for 10 years. One arrived for work looking somewhat sheepish that morning. With a real effort he plucked up his courage and stammered out, 'I think I ought to tell you that I've become a Christian.'

'Praise the Lord!' replied his colleague.

'What on earth do you mean?'

'Why, I've been a Christian for years.'

The newly converted factory worker was flabbergasted. His was no sudden decision. He had been struggling towards faith for years but had always looked at his friend and thought, 'Well, Fred looks all right. He seems to manage without Christianity!' All those years and Fred had only to open his mouth, but never did!

One friend became a committed Christian through the witness of a 15-year-old girl and the patient sharing of a number of older Christians. He went back to school full of fire and enthusiasm. The Christian Union was revolutionized by this one young convert. In the weeks which followed dozens at the school committed their lives to Jesus Christ. One, at least, is a full-time evangelist today because of the work and witness of a schoolboy who met Jesus and couldn't bear to keep his faith hidden in a corner.

I share Jesus with countless others, such as with the wild biker gangs, or the terrorists in Ireland, with the gypsy encampments across England, in the Flemish–Belgian villages which are hitherto totally Roman Catholic, or in hamlets of the Austrian Alps. Right out in the outback of Australia, I arrived on my third plane of the day, this one a tiny five-seater, landing on a dry, hot, dusty airstrip, in the deepest Aussie interior. I was met with the sight through the sandstorm of a hut with 'XXXX – FOSTERS' on the side. I thought it was the name of the township! Then a big Australian outback Assemblies of God pastor heartily welcomed me. 'We're just going up the road to the church a little way, about 400 miles!'

It's a big country. But as I led many alcoholic farmers to Christ, I felt as I do everywhere in all these places: 'another man' is present with me, I bask in the company of Jesus. He is the truth of God, the very life of God. He brings His glory down on my preaching, witnessing, healing and teaching. I may be speaking to members of the criminal fraternity, or preaching in one of Her Majesty's prisons, it may be in a tent on the Welsh borders, in the Church of England at the high altar, in a cathedral, in some small mission hall, or in Selhurst Park football ground to many thousands, but wherever I am, God in glory and grace has been there with us.

So thousands can testify as in Tennyson's words, 'back from the mouth of hell they came'. Or in the hymn writer's lines:

> I wandered in the shades of night
> till Jesus came to me,
> and with the sunlight of his love,
> bid all my darkness flee.

There are no hopeless situations, only people who have lost hope. But by our going forth with positive glory and faith and love, they can see God in action for them, they can feel Him with us, whatever the despair, we can rise again. No matter what the failures, you can rise again. No matter what the heartbreak, you can rise again. Nothing is too hard for the Lord.

GOD RISES AMONG THE GANGS
OF MOTORBIKE RIDERS

As John said, He 'holds the key ... What He opens, no-one can shut' (Revelation 3:7).

Another fringe social group which has been touched by the present revival is the bikers. There are about 30,000 of them in the UK. They are an unmistakable and rather intimidating sight, with their leather jackets, ragged denims, beards and helmets. Some of them are in their early teens, others are in their twenties or thirties. Living with their girlfriends, drugs, alcohol and violence are often all elements of their wild, amoral lifestyle. They are frequently in conflict with the police. Some of them are mixed up with the occult and the New Age Movement. Never before have these people been seriously touched by the gospel, but today there is an amazing moral and spiritual revival going on amongst them.

A while ago I was taking part in a divine healing service at a Pentecostal church. I was just about to stand up to preach, when we heard a huge roaring noise coming from outside the church building. I thought it was just some noisy youths passing through, since the church was on a busy main road. But in fact it was about 50 bikers turning up to attend the service.

Unaware of what was about to happen, I got up on to the platform, and the pastor introduced me to the congregation. Then the doors at the end of the church crashed open loudly, and a small army of leather-clad young men marched in. The stewards didn't know what to do, and the bikers just swept past them and made for the empty seats. One after another they trooped in, the door swinging back and forth. There seemed no end to them! Some of them were very big, muscular men. Most had beards, and many were carrying their helmets. On their jackets were swastikas and the name 'Hell's Angels'. Some of them had bands tied around their foreheads. They filled every available seat, and some of them had to stand.

The pastor wiped his brow nervously and said, 'We've got trouble here, I think. What do you think we should do?'

'Get them converted,' I replied.

I preached a sharp gospel message about sin, repentance and forgiveness; I told them they had to change their whole way of life, by God's mercy and grace. The bikers listened intently all the way through. When I appealed for those who wanted to become Christians to come forward, the bikers were on their feet before anyone else. They rose like one man and rushed down the aisles. The pastor, closing his eyes with fright, whispered, 'This is it!' They stopped at the pulpit, their hands reaching out penitently! These big, tough men – their swastikas shining under the overhead lighting – were weeping, tears dropping from their beards. Some of them cried loudly as I led them in a simple, sincere, heart-rending prayer. 'Lord, Lord, forgive me!' They prayed, some of them almost shouting. The place was flooded with the supernatural power of God. What a night!

The local Christians were surprised by all this, to say the least. Some of them thought this mass conversion would be just a seven-day wonder. But in fact there was a lasting change in these bikers' lives. And gradually some of their women were won over as well. The work amongst the bikers has grown since then, and there are now between 300 and 500 fully discipled bikers in the UK. They are truly saved and sanctified; they have been baptized and they are now following the Lord. Bridgewater in the West Country and Wokingham in Berkshire have seen the bikers touched in a powerful way, but encouraging things are happening in other parts of the country too. Some bikers are now working among their fellows as full-time evangelists.

There has been a striking moral revival amongst the bikers who have been converted to Christ. When they become Christians they either part with their women or marry them. They are also learning to obey the law – breaking it used to be one of their pastimes! They are learning to have consideration for others, and they no longer rev their machines near people's homes late at night. On their backs and bikes the name 'Hell's Angels' has been crossed out and replaced by 'God's Angels'. Now they roar up the motorways at the top (legal) speed with texts like 'Prepare to meet thy God' and 'Where will you spend eternity?' written on their bikes. But they still have long hair – even the evangelists!

They hold Bikers' Rallies, where they hear the Word preached and worship God with great enthusiasm, singing loud choruses, dancing before the Lord, clapping and shouting the name of Jesus until they are hoarse. The police come to keep an eye on things, but there is nothing for them to do. There is no fighting, drug-taking or immorality – only Christian joy. They used to swear at the police and fight them, but now they give them cups of tea and gospel tracts and tell them about Jesus, to the amazement of the bobbies!

However, it is proving to be difficult for them to become integrated into the life of the mainstream churches. Some converted bikers once went to an Anglican parish church. They advanced down the aisles, smiling at the vicar. There were about 40 of them. They were wearing black leathers and had chains on their arms and heavy boots on their feet.

The vicar walked nervously down to them. 'What d-do you w-want?' he asked.

The leader of the bikers replied, 'We've come to do our stuff!' – meaning they had come to worship God. But the vicar clearly thought he meant they were going to smash the place up!

Even some evangelical churches have not welcomed them for long. It seems that their loud, exuberant worship is too much for some rather sedate Christians. They have asked me for advice many times about the increasing problem of their relationship with the established churches. The Church just isn't ready for this biker revival – it wasn't ready for many of the great awakenings of the past. I have advised the Christian bikers to start their own churches and fellowships, where they can worship freely within their own culture. I thank God that such churches are now in existence and 'that God did not give us a spirit of timidity, but of power, of love, of self-discipline … never lacking in zeal, keeping your spiritual fervour and serving the Lord' (2 Timothy 1:7; Romans 12:11).

– 18 –

Look Out – God at Work!

Wheelchair invalid's miracle on BBC

Mrs Brumby was almost in despair with herself – long hours waiting in hospital wards for doctors to give further diagnosis, continuous long journeys to and from hospitals, hours of pain, drugs and medicines, frustration, pain, declining health, no answer, weakness and immobility and finally crushing discouragement and depressions as a result. Enough to knock the stoutest heart out!

Then she read in the newspaper of some 'healer' coming to town, there in the heart of the Stafford countryside. Nothing like this type of event had been held in the town before. 'Can it be true? Can someone have the powers to cure people's ailments and sicknesses?' This was the media's story in newspapers, articles and on radio. 'I'll certainly give it a try,' Mrs Brumby told her husband. 'Get two seats reserved, I see there's an afternoon meeting!'

So they arrived early at the church where the services were scheduled. There was quite a queue already at the door when she drove up in the taxi. The cabby was very helpful, getting the disabled chair out of the boot, helping her husband to fix it up, lifting her up the steps into the building. Soon the place was suffocatingly packed, and roisterous singing started. She had never heard such a good sing-song for years.

She had not been to church for ages, had gone in her young married life, and as a child, but had drifted away. Soon the short stumpy-looking middle-aged preacher stood up (that was me), and she heard the message from the Bible about how to be saved and know it, how to be sure of your salvation, to really know God and His deep assurance of peace. She asked Christ to come to her, as so many did in that place that afternoon. She said she forgot everyone around her as hands were placed on her head as she sat in pain in that wheelchair. A warmth shot through her, pain seemed to have gone as she moved her back, even her legs were free. She quickly stood up, encouraged by my assistant Rev. Richard Hill.

'I was walking like a two-year-old everywhere, up and down the aisle of the church,' she recalled. 'Fred pushed the chair out. You should have seen the look on the taxi man's face, he could not believe it as I jumped into the taxi. The next 10 days were crucial. The ministers told me to walk, use my faculties, believe, thank God, keep walking. I did just that and grew stronger each day.

'Two weeks later the BBC rang me, sent a car for me, and I turned up in their city studio to be questioned. I just told them how I felt. I was incurable but now could walk. It worked, it was real ... my whole life has changed since that afternoon in September two years ago. I have never been the same since – God is a living person to me.'

From experiences of pain and failure and nothingness, we can experience the blessings of victorious praying. Only as we are humbled and broken at the

Cross can we see God work in this way, and our prayer times become truly efficacious. Alan Redpath, noted Keswick preacher of the 1950s–60s (later pastor of the great Moody Bible Church, Chicago), in a private chat I had with him just before he died, said, 'Prayer is not primarily a means of getting something, it is concern for the glory of God.'

The working presence of God is a missing factor in British–European church life. Dr Martin Lloyd Jones says, 'I can forgive the preacher almost anything – if he gives me a sense of God!'

Through persistent prayer the power of God is released in our lives, in the lives of others and in the life of our nation. The celebrated preacher Smith Wigglesworth often prayed well into the small hours of the morning. The Puritans held four prayer meetings every day of the year, and for a time they took control of England! The daughter of a minister once told a friend, 'When my father's trousers got threadbare at the knees, it was always a sure sign that revival was on its way.' Former Archbishop of Canterbury Donald Coggan once said, 'When a man or woman is praying the appropriate notice is not so much "Quiet! Man at prayer!" as "Look out! God at work!"'

Prayer never fails to astonish me. It is health-producing and power-generating; it restores and recreates us; it increases and exercises our love for others. It makes us Godlike – it makes our hearts throb with His love and power.

When we pray we are meeting with the Living God. There would be no point in praying to Shakespeare or Napoleon – they are just dead men, and they cannot hear us or help us. But Jesus Christ is the One who died and rose again, and He is alive today and forever. We cry to Him, 'Dear Jesus, melt me, change me, cleanse me! I praise and glorify You! Hear my cry – answer me, Lord!' He hears us and He never fails to answer our prayers.

As I have driven home late at night from meetings and campaigns in different parts of the country I have often seen young people streaming home from discos and night-clubs, sometimes as late as three in the morning. The sinners have been worshipping their false gods, who will in the end destroy them. *Where are the believers who pray into the small hours, beseeching God to revive the land?* I often pray, 'O God, get this unbelieving generation of Christians on their knees!'

People are dying without the bread of life. We must look to the spiritual welfare of the unsaved people around us, we must throw God's light on the dark places in our land. We must offer people new hope instead of their utter *hopelessness*. What has the world to offer them? Nothing. We must point the hungry masses to God and to the heavenly city of which He is the builder and maker. We must call the people out of their lostness, coldness, barrenness, darkness and bleakness into the light, warmth and laughter of the kingdom of God.

The spiritual climate goes through different seasons, but we must be constant. We must never give up. We must pray, pray, pray. We must seek revival and build, build, build. We must live in the fear of the Almighty and put His will and His Great Commission first in our lives.

But when we pray we first need to make sure that our hearts are right with God. The Psalmist said, 'The Lord God is a sun and shield; the Lord bestows favour and honour; no good thing does he withhold from those whose walk is blameless' (Psalm 84:11). We must be right with God if we are to receive what we ask for in prayer.

In one of his last sermons the famous American evangelist D. L. Moody preached from this psalm. After the service a woman asked him to pray that her husband might be converted. She said she had been concerned about him for many years.

'I will pray with you for him on one condition,' Moody told her, 'and that is that you have fulfilled the requirement of verse 11 of Psalm 84. Tell me, are you walking uprightly?'

After some thought she confessed, 'I'm afraid I'm not.'

Moody told her, 'Ask God to forgive the past and save you from your besetting sins, and then promise that you will do His will.'

The woman got down on her knees immediately and admitted her own shortcomings and got right with God. Moody then prayed earnestly for her husband's salvation. The very next day the man turned to God. Moody had previously seen many similar, almost miraculous answers to prayer result when those seeking God's blessing had fully met the conditions of Psalm 84.

When we pray we do not come to God as beggars and vagabonds but as His children, as the heirs to His infinite wealth and boundless resources. Scripture promises us that in response to our sincere, earnest, heart-of-heart prayers God will supply all of our needs 'according to His glorious riches in Christ Jesus' (Philippians 4:19). God supplies our needs richly because He has endless riches from which to supply them. He answers our prayers plenteously, gloriously and liberally!

A man once visited a stately home that was open to the public. He was greatly impressed by the beautiful and fascinating paintings, furniture, valuables and suits of armour. However, in one room he noticed that on a chess table there were two items that were not listed in the official catalogue. He asked the curator about this. The curator looked at the table and realized that the visitor was right. There was one ornament of solid gold and one of solid silver. Both were very valuable. He was baffled.

'Well, that's strange,' he said, scratching his head. 'They weren't there last night!'

'How do you think they got there?' asked the visitor.

'I think the master of the house must have come in last night and left them here for us,' decided the curator.

Out of his great riches the wealthy master had put out a few extra items for the pleasure, education and inspiration of the visitors.

Our Heavenly Master is like that. He has an infinite storehouse of riches, and so He always has something more to share with us and give to us. He always answers prayer and we can never ask too much of Him. God said to Abram, 'I am your shield, your very great reward' (Genesis 15:1). He is our very great reward too. We have only to ask, and He will reward our asking. *Ask, ask, ask and keep on asking!*

MOORLAND TOWN IN REVIVAL

It has been since well before the war, many years since Christian meetings drew so many non-church people in the town of Leek, near Cheshire.

Sounds of miracles, walking sticks being left for the dustbin collectors, a blind man coming into the evangelist's meeting with his guide dog, then going out seeing, that has caused such a rumpus right through the county there. Seventy to eighty per cent of congregations have never shown such an interest in organized religion for generations. Wheelchairs left empty, deaf people hearing the sound of the TV when they got home, people with tinnitus, loud noises day and night for years, beyond themselves and medical help, are telling their neighbours they are well again, can sleep without tablets, hear okay, not missing a thing; even hitherto unbelieving husbands are convinced when they tell their better half everything they've been whispering behind their backs. Hundreds are blessed – 140 new converts turn up for the converts' supper and first teaching meeting for new believers. It's a revival! Nothing has shaken the moorlands countryside and town like this for donkeys' years!

What encouragement to faith in a district! It is a bastion against failing faith. Sometimes Christians find their faith faltering. Then they turn away from faith and start to rely on human endeavour and ability. If you take your eyes off God and abandon faith, you soon become a tragic shadow of what you were. For your spiritual exploits and victories and miracles become things of the past. That is what has happened to the modern Church.

King David tasted this bitter experience in his life-time. When his life was threatened by King Saul his faith slipped. 'There is only a step between me and death,' he told his friend Jonathan, Saul's son (1 Samuel 20:3). That was the way it seemed to him at the time, but in fact it was very far from the truth. Indeed, God had promised him that he was to be the King of Israel. And yet now he took his eyes off that promise, and his faith faltered as a result.

His life still under threat from Saul, David went to a quiet highland village called Nob. There was a sanctuary there where 86 priests lived. When he arrived a priest named Ahimelech asked him, 'Why are you alone?' (1 Samuel 21:2). It is sad to have to write that David, in a state of panic, lied. He said he was on secret business for King Saul and was meeting up with his men later. Oh, what tangled webs we weave when first we practise to deceive!

David asked Ahimelech if he had a sword anywhere. Did he have a sword? That's like asking your local preacher if he has any guns in his house! The priest replied, 'The sword of Goliath the Philistine, whom you killed in the valley of Elah, is here; it is wrapped in a cloth behind the ephod. If you want, take it; there is no sword here but that one' (v. 9). When people panic their faith is often eclipsed. David had not needed a sword to defeat the giant Goliath, but he felt he needed one to defend himself against King Saul. So the sword which had been in the sanctuary for years as a trophy of his faith now went in his hand as a symbol of the collapse of that faith. He said to the priest, 'There is none like it; give it to me.' Those have got to be some of the saddest words in the Old Testament.

Down, down, down went David – down to Gath, down to live among the Philistines, down to act the madman. There, in the presence of King Achish of Gath he feigned madness in order to protect himself, 'making marks on the doors of the gate and letting saliva run down his beard'. Achish exclaimed, 'Look at the man! He is insane! Why bring him to me? Am I so short of madmen that you have to bring this fellow here to carry on like this in front of me?' (vv. 13–15). David then escaped to the cave of Adullam. What a sad story!

David was in a sorry state. He was the man who had been especially chosen by God to be the King of Israel; he had been a man after God's own heart – pure, sincere, kindly, good-hearted, full of faith – and yet now he had deserted faith.

May we all learn the lessons which this sorry episode in David's life teaches us. Let us keep our eyes on God and on His promises. Let us not doubt Him when things become difficult in our lives. We should not, like David, look at God through the mists of circumstances, and so lose sight of Him. Instead we should look at circumstances through the promises of God.

GOD KEEPS HIS PROMISES

I had just returned home after being away for some weeks on a mission. My son Philip came to me and reminded me that I had promised to take him to see a Donald Duck film at the cinema that evening. I told him I was too tired to go out. 'But you promised me, Dad!' he protested, tears on his cheeks. As I looked at his sad face my conscience rebuked me. So I gave in and took him to see the film after all. Children expect their parents to keep their promises, and rightly so.

Some people's promises aren't worth much, because we know that they probably won't keep them. However, God always keeps His promises. In the Bible there are 7,487 promises made by God personally! The missionary Adoniram Judson used to say, 'The future is as bright as the promises of God.' He eagerly claimed God's promises, and as a result there is a rapidly growing church in Burma today. Man may be unreliable, but God is absolutely reliable. Scripture says, 'The Lord our God ... remembers His covenant for ever, the word He commanded, for a thousand generations' (Psalm 105:7–8). It also says, 'For the Lord your God is a merciful God; He will not abandon or destroy you or forget the covenant with your forefathers, which He confirmed to them by oath' (Deuteronomy 4:31).

God has promised to 'meet all your needs according to His glorious riches in Christ Jesus' (Philippians 4:19). Another translation of this verse reads, 'Out of the greatness of His wealth He will give to us.' What a wonderful promise! I can testify that He has never failed to meet all my needs. On four occasions in my life God has kept this promise in a truly miraculous way. Three of those miracles occurred some time ago when I was working in Malaysia. The fourth happened about four years ago when I was doing church-planting work in a rural area of France. There were no evangelical churches in the district and the local people had shown little interest in the gospel message. However, there had been an encouraging trickle of converts. There came a time when I badly needed some money to live on.

I carefully counted what I had left – just 50 francs. I put the money in my case and locked it for safety. No one could possibly open the case without knowing the code. Later, wondering how I was going to manage with so little money, I opened the case again and was amazed and delighted to discover that there were now 250 francs in it! It was an outright miracle.

How can one fail to trust a God who does things like that? Of course, He doesn't always keep His promises in such an obviously miraculous way, but He does always keep them. However, in return He requires us to obey Him. Queen Elizabeth I asked a great admiral, who had served her loyally and bravely and had now retired to an estate in the country, to undertake one more special and dangerous voyage for her. He tried to excuse himself from this, saying, 'I have my land, workers and business to attend to.' The Queen replied, 'You see to my business, and I will take care of yours!' Jesus our Lord has promised that if we do our part and obey Him, He will do His part and take care of us.

During a very exciting healing crusade in west Wales, a little girl was brought to me. She had a sweet face but she was scruffily dressed and was in need of a good wash. I was very busy and asked an assistant to deal with the matter. He replied that it was serious, since someone had seen the girl take a pound coin out of the collection. I was shown the coin, and I asked her if she had stolen it.

'No!' she replied.

A teenager standing beside her stated that she had seen her deliberately put her hand in the collection basket and take the coin out. My assistant supported this allegation and added that he had found the coin in her hand. I questioned the girl again: 'You say you didn't steal it. But it was in your hand – so where did you get it from?'

'Out of the collection basket!' she replied perkily.

I was confused. 'So you did steal it, then?'

'Oh no, I didn't!' she retorted. 'When you were here in this church a couple of years ago you told the people to give generously. And you said that if we were poor and didn't have anything to give and needed money ourselves, then we should take a pound out of the basket. So that's what I did tonight!'

I laughed with relief, and marvelled that a child should have remembered that offer I had made a few years ago.

'So what should we do?' asked my assistant.

'Let her go,' I said. 'She's done nothing wrong. She just took me at my word!'

We Christians should treat God that way – we should take Him at His Word, because He is a loving Father who always keeps His promises! God's promise is for folk like you today.

ARSONIST BURNS WITH THE HOLY SPIRIT

He was in prison for some years. He had burnt down property worth millions of pounds. He was browsing through the prison library – 'I felt so lonely, voices in my head said *take your life you are no good, you will never make anything.*' He felt no one loved him, a cast-off, a no-good, a life wasted. Then he saw a section at the end of the library labelled 'Religious Books'.

He became curious. He was about to turn back to the 'thriller' sections, when something drew him, his hand seemed to be pulled up to the top shelf of this section, and he soon found in his hand a book called *The Wind of Fire*. He began to read from the first chapter, just standing there in the library. He got into it, wild, long-haired criminals being converted, people who had never been religious finding peace with God. He soon carried it back to his cell. In a week he had read it through three times. He wrote to the author (myself) saying he felt a miracle had happened inside him as he read it.

We suggested a chat with the chaplain, sent him gospel literature, prayed hard for Michael in the office prayer meetings. Soon we heard that in a few months he was truly changed, found Christ, attended all the chaplain's Bible hour classes. He is now out, a new man, no more fires, only the fire of the Holy Spirit in his heart and mind.

The country has been saved millions in taxes, insurance companies millions in claims, and here is this former arsonist saved for posterity, working for his living, building up not destroying, all through the power of the action of God, the channel of mighty praying. The promises of Christ were real for a dark, sad, purposeless soul, now a disciple, a son of the living God by faith, a brand new creation.

WATCH OUT! LOOK OUT! GOD AT WORK!

19

MOBSTER'S WIFE GETS A MIRACLE

I was holding some meetings recently in a Dutch city near the Belgian border. I had been in the same church, a Dutch Reformed building which had been closed down, but recently re-opened by a young pastor full of the zeal of the Lord. He had a hard time getting people into his church – atheism, affluency, self-contentment, apathy, made the whole city cold towards the things of God. I had made a visit for one night four months previously and God broke through, some 40 members of one large family, grandfather, dad, mum, cousins, uncles, aunts, nephew, nieces had all got saved. The strength of the church grew overnight through a miracle in this family when a man left his crutches behind through healing in the Name of Christ, and had become strong and well again. Now when I returned for three services the church was trebled and much stronger in faith. The large building was quite full on this occasion and many were new people, many unchurched who had never been into a gospel mission before.

Then as I waited in a side room, my Bible before me, the pastor's wife entered the room very excited, she could hardly contain herself. 'Do you know who has come tonight? It's quite astounding!' she gabbled in broken Flemish and English. 'On the front row sitting with his wife is the chief crime boss (or that's his reputation) for the city. It's tremendous, he is not a bit religious, he is greatly feared by many, even police don't touch him.'

To me it was another night of the miracles I was expecting. God had called me long ago; I was here to preach the precious story of the theme of Scripture, the song of the Bible substitution, the Son of God who called all men unto Himself.

I remembered at the lady's words, the night in a dark town on the border with the Irish Republic meeting a known IRA terrorist – how we chatted with his henchmen guarding outside at a distance. And how he asked, 'Am I not beyond redemption?' I quoted to him the words of our Lord Jesus Christ, 'He who comes unto me I will not cast out [no one will be turned away].' If we repent and sin no more, God will take us in.

Soon the throbbing, rousing worship and song was sounding out through the old historic church. The well-dressed gentleman on the soft chairs at the front was hardly joining in, unused, no doubt, to such lusty music in church. His wife, however, was opening her mouth and really trying to join in.

The meeting soon came to the time for me to expound God's Word. He shifted to and fro looking down at the carpeted floor much of the time, smiling occasionally at my jokes. Soon, as people made their way into the side hall to be spoken to about their problems and have a happy little prayer with our local church workers, his wife got up and made her way through, but he sat motionless and went away after coffee thoughtfully. He had never enjoyed church so much before, he commented. His wife found a freedom from guilt and a deep darkness left her mind. She came to that fellowship with God's people regularly, and he said to people everywhere, 'I have a brand new woman!' Why, they asked him, have you changed your lady again or got another wife? 'No,' he told them, 'it's the same girl but she is different now, something has happened to her ... she is a miracle. It's changing me!' The mobster was affected by the awakening caused by God's Holy Spirit.

THE POWER OF CHRISTIANITY

This power is not simply in the intellectual power of its doctrines. This power is not merely in the moral strengths of its ethics. Neither is it in the philosophical powers of its ideas. Or simply its psychological advantages of its supremacy. It is in the ultimate limitless power – the power of the very presence of the living God Himself.

He created the Earth in seven days, divided the Red Sea with a stroke, stopped the sun for a day for Joshua, preserved the three Hebrew children in the furnace of fire in Daniel, made a donkey to talk and prophesy a great message with Balaam, caused a piece of iron to do a breast-stroke swim better than an Olympic star in 2 Kings, brought the mighty, high, rock-firm walls of Jericho down with one shout for the Israelite children. These are a few of a million other miracles which are His.

No one else is like God. 'I am the Lord, that is my name, I will not give my glory to another.' Only God is like God. Man must have what God alone can give. Yet this mighty, marvellous God wants to make us like Himself! He wants to give us the God-likeness of Himself. Nothing else will do. Man is so muddled, messed-up, defiled, shattered, vandalized – only God can restore him. God said when Moses asked Him His name: 'I AM WHAT I AM.'

When the Queen was a child, the story is told that she was playing at Balmoral with her sister. Inevitably they got lost and found themselves near a small house. The lady of the house had no idea who the two little girls were but offered them tea.

She said to young Princess Elizabeth, 'Who are you, dear?'

Back came the reply, 'Oh, I'm nobody, but my daddy's the King.'

We may be nobodies, the Church in Britain may be an insignificant speck on the horizon of society. But we worship and serve the King. In addition, we are His children – born and designed as containers for His Spirit.

We can face the future with hope, our society with courage, and ourselves with the knowledge that God can, and will, use even us. Because He *is* the King and we are His children. Because His Spirit has come.

A. W. Tozer rightly comments, 'The Church began in power, moved in power, and moved just as long as she had power. When she no longer had power she dug in for safety and sought to conserve her gains.' Christian history has always been divided into two phases, the *dynamic* and the *static*. In the former, men and women took risks in God, fearlessly communicating His love and truth to a largely hostile world. Exchanging the safety of inaction for the hazards of God inspired progress as they discovered that the power and miracles of God went with them.

Hari Krishna, attacking the Christian faith, declared, 'Christians claim Jesus Christ is the Saviour of sinners, but they show no more signs of being saved than anyone else.' That's good coming from someone who has got so many millions of young people into such an awful mess! But it is a challenge! The world wants to see more believers showing our God in action, in His power!

Two thousand years ago John the Baptist sent two of his disciples to discover if Jesus was the Son of God. In reply Jesus used more than words. He healed the sick and blind and delivered the possessed. Then He replied, 'Go and tell John what you have seen and heard; the blind receive their sight, the lame walk, lepers are cleansed, and the deaf hear, the dead are raised up, the poor have good news preached to them' (Luke 7:22 RSV). Only the Holy Spirit can bear witness to Jesus and only He can make the dead live, the sick recover and the poor hear the gospel. But the amazing truth is that He, the living God, chooses to work through ordinary sinful men and women like you and me. He works to demonstrate the power and glory of Jesus, not just all those years ago in Palestine – but as it is today!

We are the hands and feet of Jesus; we must be available for him to use us. Not because *we* are in any way special but because He is the King of Kings and He longs to demonstrate that fact among us today. By His grace He deigns to stoop to our human frailty and work within us by His Spirit. How dare we make complaint when he chooses to work in a way other than our own? We must ask that the Holy Spirit might do in our lives exactly what he wants to do; that by both miracles and acts of love Jesus may reveal Himself. God alone knows what the result would be for our nation if an army of ordinary people was subject to the Spirit of God.

The story is told of a preacher who was walking along a street in Soho and passed by a strip club. He sensed a clear word from God to himself: 'Stop. Go into the strip club.' Immediately he dismissed the thought as the product of a sinful imagination.

'Stop. Go into the strip club. Go up to the go-go dancer and tell her that I love her.'

He was a mature Christian who knew the voice of God and that resistance was useless. So, taking a quick look round to make sure no one was watching, he paid his entrance fee and went in! He didn't know where to look. So he walked straight up to the front and told the go-go dancer that Jesus loved her.

'Hey! You sit down there, I wanna talk to you.' Her reply amazed him. So he waited while she dressed and came to talk. In simple terms he told her about Jesus. In halting phrases she explained how, over the last few days, a hunger had grown to discover the love and affection of the living God.

Now that preacher's obedience made him break all protocol – but win a truly lost soul. He was moving in the power and guidance of the Lord.

Paul reminded us, 'It wasn't long ago that we ourselves were stupid, stubborn, dupes of sin, ordered every way by our glands [genes], going round with a chip on our shoulder ... but when God our kind loving Saviour stepped in, He saved us from all that. It was His doing, we had nothing to do with it. He gave us a good bath, we came out of it new people. Washed within and out by the Holy Spirit.'

'Our Saviour Jesus Christ poured new life so generously ... restored ... and gave us back our lives, and there's more life to come' (Titus 3:1–7 *The Message*).

Some young men were talking in a pub over a drink. They were young scientists, they were discussing the universe, its co-ordination, and if there was anybody 'out there'. Was their meaning up there *and* down here? One young man told how his mother had always taught him there was a supreme being, 'And your name is known to him personally!'

GOD AT WORK FOR ORDINARY PEOPLE

Phil Mitchell in the BBC's top soap opera *Eastenders*, went round for a long time full of a guilty conscience, he could not shake it off. He said, 'I can't get rid of it!'

God wants to work inside our lives, sort us out, forgive, cleanse us. Two sons went on an extended hike a couple of years ago, a bit fed up of 'Dad and Mum', they tried to get away from it all. The parents were quite wealthy, and put a huge, full-page advert in the national newspapers – 'COME HOME YOU'RE MISSED!' God says that too. 'I miss you, I died for you, I can change you inside, I can give you tranquil, glorious peace, I want you, I have a plan for your life!'

Inspector Morse, on the famous detective series on TV, always states to his buoyant young assistant, 'No one is ever guilty till there are eyewitnesses.'

Many are the eyewitnesses of our sin, guilt and failures and our doubts, fears and despairs, but God has dealt with them all, you are known personally by the Almighty.

Christ twisted in mortal agony on the Cross, took all your sins, not in part, but in their entirety and nailed them to the Roman punishment scaffold. The river of life was released, God's active, living, throbbing, divine blood was dropped down on all mankind. The divine visitor is amongst us. Christ crucified and risen and glorified is at work. Does He grip you, is He inside you?

If you ever enter Coventry Cathedral from the west side, you cannot see the many side windows, only the plain walling in between. Basil Spence, the noted architect, planned it this way, so that when you reach the Cross at the altar, then gaze down the full length of the nave towards the front doors, you then see every brightly coloured window. With the light shining in, it is a magnificent blaze of colour, dazzling murals and figures, light and beauty radiating before your eyes.

The view gives a reflection of the glory, the wonder, the marvel of the awesomeness of God. So from the Cross comes the power, from the altar of God you see the blazing riches, texture, facade of a hundred different colours. It's as if the worship, beauty, all-powerfulness of God is released, or pictured there. But you must come to the Cross, that's where the action begins!

As the Psalmist wrote in Psalm 139, 'I look behind me and you are there, then up ahead and you're there ... this is too much, too wonderful ... if I climb to the sky, you're there, if I go underground you're there ... you see me in the dark ... you are in the day and in the night ... your thoughts – how rare, how beautiful! ... I could never count them. O let me rise in the morning and always be with you' (vv. 3–6, 8, 10, 17, 18 *The Message*).

The Jewish goal for life is enshrined in one of their chief mottoes: 'Live in the world and yet hold faith close to your daily thoughts.'

IT'S FIRST THINGS FIRST

A fresh midshipman in the Second World War on a destroyer in the Far East, getting ready to go into a big battle with the Japanese aggressor, was given a lambasting by his First Mate for 'incorrect use of words'. He later told a friend, 'How will it help to beat the Japanese if I call a staircase a ladder?'

It's like that in much of the organized Church: correct minds, perfect wording, sound doctrine, cross the 't's and dot the 'i's, but many of these things have nothing to do with the practice, the power, the real task of winning the war against Satan, setting depressed minds free, lifting, healing, changing, saving decrepit, wavering, storm-tossed, bleeding, miserable, hell-tormented humanity!

We are called to go forth into society with faith's dynamic, God's all-action heroes. I like what Gerald, my good friend, says: 'We are sent out to enjoy life before mankind, to go partying, eating, drinking, dancing into the other world, with laughter, joy, humour, generosity!' Controversial, but there is some fact about it. I often say that Sunday is 'Funday'. With Jesus life is entirely different, your days are beautiful with Jesus. He is still the centre of my life, my sole attraction; my only fascination. God is in action in our lives, bringing peace and joy every moment of the day. I enjoy Jesus, enjoy life. It's an incredible life with Jesus.

> My eyes look up and see light.
> My heart looks up and sees hope.
> My faith looks up and finds strength.
> Life is fantastic with Christ.
> It's non-stop action.
> Does Jesus still fascinate you?
> Is Jesus still your greatest attraction in life?

The most rapidly growing church in the world is in mainland China. In 1949 Mao Tse-tung closed this vast nation to the outside world, and to all church influence, and missionaries were sent home. I knew a number of these fine Christian leaders and pioneers when I met them in the late 1950s – many were Salvation Army officers, outstanding, quality people. They always expressed to me their longing to go back to China; they lived, talked, slept and ate China. They all died before seeing the gradual opening of that land again. They never ever did return, but the seed sown, the years of hard labour, their converts and work has gone on. Miracle after miracle has been witnessed. The Chinese authorities today are beyond themselves to be able to control the massive church of 100 million plus members that has exploded in their nation.

That church was built by men and women of outstanding faith. In 1972, a message was intercepted by the authorities coming out of China. It baffled the secret police. It simply said, 'THE "THIS I KNOW"

PEOPLE ARE WELL'. They never did discover what it meant. But to the dying pioneers in Britain it meant hope; it meant everything. It meant the church in China was very much alive and thriving again, and the believers were in good heart. It came, of course, from Scripture, from 1 John 5:13: 'You may know...' and from Paul's words, ' I know in whom I have believed,' and, of course, from the Chinese Christians' favourite hymn:

> Jesus loves me, this I know,
> For the Bible tells me so,
> Little ones to him belong...

God is in action in that nation, much faith is being rewarded. The marvellous, thrilling life of Jesus is coming into millions of lives.

Jesus said, 'I, if I am lifted up from the earth, will draw all men unto me.' The Cross is the attraction, the sacred blood of Christ is God's action to redeem man, save our world. He is the people's power, He is at work.

WHAT SORT OF PEOPLE DOES GOD USE? WHO GETS THIS POWER?

Look at the varied characters in the Bible.

- The poetic Jeremiah – burning with God's love.
- The cool Luke – a medic, the analytical historian of the first Church.
- The heartbroken Hosea – his wife a scarlet woman – but what joyous passion he had for the lost.

- The rugged, rough Amos – stern, fearless, a herdsman of cattle, but a mighty prophet.
- The literary giant Isaiah – a gentleman – a colossal visionary who has touched the world.
- The mystical, mysterious Ezekiel, an aristocrat – a writer of enormous stature.
- The quiet fisherman John – contemplative, sweet, spiritual – who moved the heart of Christ.
- The severely practical James – with his 'epistle of straw', fascinating and down to earth.

We are all different. God uses some funny people, unique, strange, eccentric, even foolish! Wisdom knows best. Don't compare: the God of all peoples and all times has His way.

I've known many of the most fruitful evangelists of the last 50–60 years. There was, for example, Howell Harris, a crude Welshman. He emptied cinemas and night-clubs with his preaching, started over 20 Assembly of God churches, including one of the largest evangelical churches now in the north of England, and its daughter church is now centre of the so-called 'Sunderland refreshing'. He was once so long preaching, that his wife, tired after weeks of travelling, long hours and poor beds, called out from her position behind the pulpit, where she played the piano, so the packed house could hear: 'Get on with it, Howell, and let's get home for supper!' But the blind saw, cripples ran, miracles flowed from his fingertips.

Then there was the shy introvert, Tommy Hicks, an affable, quiet, painfully modest American. After over

30 years' preaching in small crusades, he lay dying, and he thought his life had been unfruitful. God spoke to him and told him, 'The latter house of my glory will be greater than the former.' God miraculously healed him, sent him to the then missionary country of Argentina, with few gospel churches, and only a few hundred believers. God used Tommy to heal the President of the country, Mr Peron. In his gratitude he gave the evangelist the largest stadium seating 100,000 people to use, plus radio and free newspaper coverage. The stadium was packed and overflowing for six weeks, 500,000 people were converted to Christ, and today that nation has 5 million full gospel-believing Christians.

Yet Tommy was so unassuming and shy. When he preached he was so very quiet, but when he made the appeal at the close of his 'revivals', to seek the Lord, nearly everyone in the building could not resist. He was an evangelist of evangelists!

Then there was A. C. Valdez Junior, a very corpulent, southern States evangelist. He was eccentric. He complained in Australia because he only had black-and-white TV in his hotel room and not coloured! He was a flamboyant, blunt character, he took huge offerings, but there was nevertheless a sincerity about him. His preaching was strange – he would always talk about this angel that was with him, and his southern USA drawl made it difficult to make him out, but when he suddenly declared that the fire was burning in his right hand, the whole service came alive, hundreds were truly converted again. In central Nottingham he stayed three weeks. Miracles hit the headlines, people queued up to get into his meetings. He restarted a run-down church – today it is Talbot Street Fellowship with 1,500 members, the largest in that region of the country.

I could tell you of many more: they were all so varied, in type, character, background, emphasis, presentation. But all were honest, good, genuine, called of God and anointed by the Holy Spirit. They all bore amazing fruit, and great was their reward. If God can use these, if God can use me – He can use you! He can use anyone!

GOD WANTS TO USE EVERY FACULTY YOU HAVE

I often say in a revival service calling people to dedication to Christ:

- God wants to come into your thinking through your head.
- God wants to come into your loving through your heart.
- God wants to come into your feeling through your emotions.
- God wants to come into your daily actions through your feet and tongue.
- God wants to swell in you constantly through each day.
- The light of Christ can shine through your personality.
- The fingerprints of Jesus can be stamped on your soul. God is always with you.

The Cross of Christ must be written on our hearts. Give Him your heart and He will give you His. I've seen that Cross in a thousand different towns, hamlets, villages, cities, estates, among the poor and the rich across the face of the earth, as I have preached the gospel for nearly 47 years.

I've seen it above the tiny churches in the outback of Australia among the dingos, kangaroos and alcoholic farmers, in Australia's remote interior. It's the only hope for these hardy people. I've seen it above the poor shanty towns in South Africa, among the noble Zulu people as thousands turned to the Living God. I've seen it above the cathedral I preached in at Port Stanley, in the Falkland Isles, among the fishermen, sheep herders, whalers and oil men. I've seen it over my crowded meetings in terrorist, bandit country in South Armagh, Strabane, and where Lord Mountbatten was blown up. Instead of the IRA sign, we put up a plain Cross of Christ and hundreds came and found deliverance.

In 45 nations of the world, in many of the crisis spots, to the neediest of people, I have gone and lifted up that Cross. It's God's sign of action – 'I am not ashamed of the gospel of Christ, it is the power of God unto salvation.'

I've learned to let God lead me, to let God work His action through me. Give yourself a thousand times. He cannot fail.

The old benediction of the reformed Church is so true:

God will be in your lying down and your rising up
He will be in your coming and your going

He will be in your laughter and in your tears
He will be in your labour and in your leisure.

When holding a notable revival in Bunyan's town of Bedford I sat in the vestry as hundreds filled the large hall. Later I spoke on the text of the famous minister – the Reverend Douglas Quy – who had pastored that historic church for over 30 years, and his favourite words hung on the wall: 'Can God? God can!' *That is our power!*

20

HINDERED BY OUR FEARS

IF WE FEAR GOD THERE IS
NOTHING ELSE TO FEAR

An old hymn, 'All through the changing scenes of life', has this line: 'Fear Him, ye saints, and ye shall have nothing else to fear.' Fear is a debilitating experience. In his classic sermon on fear, Clarence E. Macartney told the story of a peasant driving into a European city. The man was hailed by an aged woman who climbed up into his cart. As they drove along, the man became alarmed as he learned that his passenger was the plague, cholera. But the old woman assured him that only 10 people in the city would die of cholera. She even offered him a dagger, saying he could kill her if more than 10 died. But after they reached the city, more than 100 perished. As the angry peasant drew the dagger to deal a death blow, the old woman lifted her hand and protested, 'Wait, I killed only 10. Fear killed the rest!'

Fear kills faith, expectation, joy, anticipation, patience, nearly everything. When fear invades and is not repelled, then a mighty God in action seems to be missing. It nullifies God's ability. When God's people were filled with fear, the Psalmist wrote and reminded them: 'Don't forget His mighty works He did in the wilderness...' They had let fear limit the Holy One of Israel, and thus they saw no miracles, no works, no signs or God's glorious works. They had to be reminded of His abilities and goodness.

For many of us this truth is not enough. We stand on the wrong side of the Jordan, surveying the Promised Land, then turn sadly back to the sandy wastes of our old lifestyle. We regret the fears that prevent us going forward. But we are content with the Devil we know rather than the God who calls us on.

DON'T LOSE YOUR NERVE!

Fear prevents God acting. Many great advances for faith, many revivals and miracles were prevented, hindered or stopped by believers' fears. Fear causes many to give up. The spies who were acting for 3 million believers living in the wilderness, only an hour away from milk, honey, water, bread, lush green land, food and plenty, were hampered by fear. Huge numbers of people were doomed to die in the desert because just a few men were gripped by fear of their enemies.

Lack of security, faith wilting, lack of persistence to see God ready to act, all presents itself due to failure to deal with persistent fears! Fear is a killer, a destroyer. It brings much misery to millions of lives. The well-known author Philip Toynbee once wrote, 'Fear is always the enemy, the deepest of all roots of evil.'

Some years ago I led a crusade at the famous Mount Zion Church in Norfolk. A lady who had heard about the miracles of healing which had been happening came for prayer. She was convinced that she had cancer, even though her doctor and a cancer specialist had told her that she did not have it. But she was so sure that she had the disease that she was worrying herself into the grave. I warned her that this fear could bring the very sickness feared into her body. She would not listen to the Word of God or to medical advice. And later I heard that she had indeed died of cancer.

Fear itself is often worse than the thing which is feared. Many famous people have confirmed that most of the things they worried about never happened in the end. The comedy actor Bill Maynard, having faced many drastic ups and downs in his life, once remarked in a radio interview, 'Fear, which is at the back of worry, is almost always not so much fear of what is happening as fear about what is going to happen.'

I was conducting a crusade in a small Lincolnshire town. At the meeting I was to lead that night in a local church I was going to show a Billy Graham film. The minister was very nervous indeed, since this was the first evangelistic venture he had ever been involved in. As I was getting the projector ready he kept coming up to me and telling me, 'I'm sure something is going to go wrong!' I tried to calm him and assure him that all would go well.

People started arriving, and soon the church was packed out. Again, just as the service was about to start, he came up to me. 'What if the projector breaks down halfway through the film?' he whined. Finally he started the service. The first hymn was sung and there was a time of prayer. Then I introduced the film and started the projector. All went smoothly for the first five minutes. Then suddenly, just as Billy Graham was getting into full swing with his sermon, the film ground to a halt. The projector had broken down!

The minister turned the lights on and came up the aisle to me, red-faced and embarrassed. 'I knew this would happen!' he declared.

'It's your fault!' I told him.

'What do you mean?' he asked, amazed.

'Job says, "That which I feared has come upon me." You feared, and brought this upon us!'

There was to be no Billy Graham film that night. The people had to make do with me! But God was glorified and many were converted.

This story, although amusing, does illustrate that our fear can bring upon us many things which we would otherwise never have to suffer.

Most people have secret fears which they don't want anyone to know about. Often they are quite silly and irrational. Lord Roberts, the courageous Field Marshal, was so afraid of cats that he couldn't enter or stay in a room if he knew there was one in it. Some people can't bring themselves to step into a lift; others refuse to fly in aeroplanes. Some people are afraid of birds.

I remember seeing a fascinating television interview of a lion tamer. We saw him at work in a cage full of the most ferocious lions and lionesses. He looked like a tough and fearless man. 'Aren't you afraid of anything?' asked the interviewer.

'Yes, I am,' replied the lion tamer with an embarrassed laugh. 'It may sound silly, but I'm terrified of mice and spiders!'

To think that a man with the courage of a Daniel should be so afraid of such tiny, inoffensive creatures! Interestingly enough, Hitler was also afraid of spiders.

A beady-eyed newspaper reporter once asked me, 'Are you ever fearful, Mr Banks?'

Doubtless he thought I would boastfully answer that I was never afraid of anything. But he was startled by my answer. 'On the first night of a mission I'm petrified!' I said. This worldly-minded journalist and I then went on to have a lengthy discussion.

Yes, I often experience stage fright on first nights. It's the same whether I'm preaching on my own home ground in Chippenham Town Hall, or in one of the churches in Bristol or Exeter, or in the deep jungles of Malaysia and Thailand, or in the Australian outback in 'Crocodile Dundee' territory, or in the Zulu shanty towns in South Africa, or in New York City, or in Amsterdam or the Hague or Metz or Toulouse ... I am always nervous during those few minutes before facing so many sick, lost, helpless, broken people. I have preached in cathedrals, on ships, in buses, in house groups, in football and rugby stadiums, in dance halls and night-clubs, in some of the largest auditoriums and churches in Europe. I feel just as frightened when in front of 40 or 50 people in a tiny country church as when I'm about to speak to a crowd of 10,000 or 20,000.

I don't think it is a sin to experience such momentary fear, so long as we overcome it. A man of God, in whom I recently confided about this, said to me, 'When you lose that feeling of inadequacy you are finished as a preacher. That stage fright shows that you know you are just a man – it shows that you are relying on God alone for your gifts and power and not trying to serve Him in your own strength.'

Kathryn Kuhlman was always filled with 'trepidation' just before her great monthly rallies in Pittsburgh. Dr Paul Yonggi Cho, Derek Bingham, Ray McAulay, Reinhard Bonnke and Jackie Pullinger have all spoken about being afraid sometimes. And yet they have overcome their fears and have turned the world upside down to the glory of God.

I once went to see the grave of Edith Cavell in the close of Norwich Cathedral. She was a courageous nurse in the First World War who was shot by the Germans for helping Belgian prisoners to escape. While I was there a cathedral guide told me that about seven years ago a small boy from the cathedral school had accidentally knocked over and broken the cross on the grave while he was running about in the close. He could have said nothing about it and got away with it, since no one had seen him. He was afraid of the punishment he might receive. But he was a brave, honest boy, and so with a thumping heart he went and told the headmaster what he had done. A new cross was made for the grave. 'That boy will go far,' I said to myself. 'He will grow up to do what he believes to be right, whatever the cost to himself.' Both Edith Cavell and this little boy had fought fear – and won.

FEAR GRIPS ME BUT MIRACLES CONVINCE THE DOCTORS

I faced the sea of faces, of young medics, doctors of tomorrow, there in the University of Adelaide Medical School, South Australia. It had never been allowed before for a divine healing evangelist to visit and speak on campus. National TV was there, the three pastors escorting me were expecting a riot, a stormy reception. They could imagine press headlines the next day: 'EVANGELIST LYNCHED ON CAMPUS'!

God had given me a mighty revival in Adelaide Town Hall, so much so that not only were there hundreds of true conversions and noted healings, but it even touched the Government away in Canberra, when a Cabinet Minister's daughter had a marvellous miracle after a dreadful road accident left her with a fractured spine and wearing a steel-enforced back-length jacket. God had so cured her that x-rays revealed her spine was now normal, as against the former photos showing her spine split. She left off her jacket and was fit and pain-free. Her story stirred Australia.

So now I faced the wrath of the young future doctors of the nation. There was seething excitement, laughter, and a build-up of resentment and possible hype and unrest. The pastors were clearly unsettled and very nervous. The student leader thanked me for coming and introduced me. I had notes on this lady's healing, plus many other cases. I was aiming at the head, blinding them with science, convincing them from clear evidence that there were countless healings that medical advice and medicine could do nothing for, but God had clearly cured by prayer – and it was scientifically provable!

Then God spoke to me on the platform, facing hundreds of these young men (and a handful of young women): 'Preach the blood of Christ ... preach my blood, my Cross ... my death and resurrection to them.' It took them by surprise, as it had me, when I stood, threw aside my good and legitimate notes, and spoke from the Bible about Christ's sacrifice on Calvary. But instead of a riot, quiet fell on the place, God moved, and by a later count taken by the sceptical TV, two-thirds were convinced by or open to what I had to say. The press headed it the next day: 'GOD WINS, THE DEVIL LOSES', but it was no doubt the blood of Christ message that had brought peace, blessing and conviction to these many hungry hearts and minds. And my fear had been conquered!

Theologians have a term for this: *Eus Absconditus* – the God who is hidden. Richard Foster calls it the 'Sahara of the heart'. John of the Cross described it as the 'dark night of the soul'. However, it can spoil our lives:

> Fear saddens many a home,
> Shortens many a life;
> Worry keeps a husband glum,
> Makes an edgy wife.
> Worry never calmed a fear,
> Never rights a wrong;
> It is the worst thing quite
> That ever came along!

During the Second World War Charles Moran was Winston Churchill's doctor and travelled with him on some arduous and sometimes perilous journeys around the world. He kept a diary of that time, extracts from which were later published in his book, *Winston Churchill: The Struggle for Survival*. He records that on one occasion Churchill asked him, 'Is much known about worry, Charles?' Then, without waiting for an answer (which was typical of him!), he went on, 'It helps to write down half a dozen things which are worrying me. Two of them, say, disappear; about two, nothing can be done, so it's no use worrying; and two perhaps can be settled.' What good advice! Try it.

The story is told of a passenger on a train who wondered at the calm serenity of a little boy who was sitting alone in the carriage. 'Aren't you afraid to be travelling alone?' asked the passenger.

The boy looked surprised. 'Why should I be afraid,' he said, 'when my father is driving the train?'

We Christians have a heavenly Father who is 'driving the train' of our lives. Trust and faith in Him can deliver us from all fear. Trust in God is the only really effective answer to the problem of fear. Scripture says, 'The Lord is my light and my salvation – whom shall I fear? The Lord is the stronghold of my life – of whom shall I be afraid?' (Psalm 27:1).

We need real peace, and that is an inner quality that comes as a blessing from God and as a result of living according to His standards. Such living brings its inevitable reward. Scripture says, 'The fruit of right-eousness will be peace; the effect of righteousness will be quietness and confidence for ever' (Isaiah 32:17) – a fear-free life.

How does this God-given peace of which the Bible speaks work in the lives of those who possess it? It is a calm which was unknown before. The fears that used to fill the soul have died away, like the angry waves which subside after a storm at sea. Tranquillity pervades the heart, just like the sunbeams which break through the opening clouds after a tempest. Agitation and alarm are replaced by serenity and confidence that all is well because the soul is reconciled with God through Christ.

Pastor Martin Niemoller, the leader of the German Evangelical Church, was greatly feared and hated by Adolf Hitler. In order to silence him the dictator threw him into prison. Months later he was summoned to appear before a special court. Niemoller was suddenly very afraid – he had no idea what to expect. Was he going to have to face a firing squad? As he was taken along the seemingly endless corridors from his cell to the courtroom he heard one of the guards who accompanied him speaking in a low voice. He was quoting from the Latin version of the Bible used by the German Catholic Church. It was a verse from the Book of Proverbs: '*Nomen Domini turris fortissima...*' – 'The name of the Lord is a strong tower; the righteous run to it and are safe.' We don't know who this man was, but what he said dispelled Niemoller's fears and renewed his confidence in God's mercy. From that moment he was never afraid again.

This resolve will activate the believer to fight, oppose and conquer fear where before it conquered him. This grace will teach the believer to deny ungodliness and worldly desire, to live sensibly, righteously and in a godly way in this present age. This grace will assure the believer that God will finish the work He has begun. He will not tire of us, or our fears, or wear of our failures and weaknesses, but will persevere until in the end we are conformed to the image of His Son. As John Newton observes:

Through many dangers, snares and fears,
I have already come:
'Twas grace that brought me safe thus far,
And grace will lead me home.

Let us go forward in our lives, made courageous by our trust in God. Fear need not overcome us, because our Father is always with us. Let us make these words of the Apostle Paul our own: 'I am convinced that neither death nor life, neither angels nor demons, neither the present nor the future, nor any powers, neither height nor depth, nor anything else in all creation, will be able to separate us from the love of God that is in Christ Jesus our Lord' (Romans 8:38,39).

It irritates me when people say, 'Cheer up, things could be worse.' I did cheer up once, and things did get worse! And it's not masochism – 'Oh, I've got to suffer – whoopee!' We rejoice in the problem, we don't rejoice for the problem. So, how can we be happy in the problem? Because we know God has a purpose. He may be testing our faith, developing our endurance or maturing our character – even in the bad things that people do to us. They mean it for bad, but God allows it for good.

ENCOURAGE GOD'S PEOPLE

Our God has said:

Encourage my people! Give them comfort.
Speak kindly to them.
Your slavery is past; your punishment is over.

Someone is shouting:
'Clear a path in the desert! Make a straight road
   for the LORD our God.
Fill the valleys; flatten every hill and mountain.
   Level the rough and rugged ground.
Then the glory of the LORD will appear for all to see.
   The LORD has promised this!'

YOUR GOD IS HERE!

Flowers and grass fade away,
   But what our God has said will never change.
There is good news
   Shout it as loud as you can
Don't be afraid to shout to the towns
   'Your God is here!'
Look! The powerful LORD God is coming
   to rule with His mighty arm.
He brings with Him what he has taken in war,
   and He rewards His people.
The LORD cares for them
   just as shepherds care for their flocks.
He carries the lambs in His arms.

THE LORD GIVES STRENGTH

Don't you know? Haven't you heard?
   The LORD is the eternal God, Creator of the earth.
He never gets weary or tired;
   His wisdom cannot be measured.
The LORD gives strength to those who are weary.
   Even young people get tired, then stumble and fall.

But those who trust the LORD will find new strength.
They will be strong like eagles soaring upward on
wings;
they will walk and run without getting tired.

FEAR OVERCOME

Don't be afraid. I am with you.
Don't tremble with fear. I am your God.
I will make you strong, as I protect you with my arm
and give you victories.
Everyone who hates you will be terribly disgraced;
those who attack will vanish into thin air.

ISAIAH 40, 41

VICTORY IS OURS

Pritchard said, 'Fear is that little dark room where negatives are developed.' I sometimes put it, 'In trouble and fear, some men break – others break records!' What will you do? Scripture assures us that fear can be banned from our lives. As a friend told me, 'We can celebrate something every day.'

God said,

Fear not, for I have redeemed you ... you are mine, I will be with you ... when you walk through fire you will not be burned ... for I am the Lord ... do not be afraid, for I am with you ... do not fear the reproach of men or be terrified by their insults ... where is the wrath of the oppressor? I have put my words in your mouth ... do not be afraid; you will suffer no shame, do not fear disgrace; you will not be humiliated.

ISAIAH 43:4; 51:7; 12:13; 54:4; 15:17

As Campbell McAlpine used to say, 'God saw that His people had turned their backs on Him but not their faces!' God sees your face, but is your will – your back – against Him?

> Who among you fears the Lord
> and obeys the word of His servant?
> Let him who walks in the dark,
> who has no light,
> trust in the name of the Lord
> and rely on his God.

ISAIAH 50:10

The making of a man or woman of God will always be in those simple words, belonging to a child in its Father's arms, simply looking up in confidence and trust to respond, 'Father, I will.'

My tiny grandchild Helen Maria Banks (the first girl born in our family for generations) sits on my knee sometimes and says, 'Grandpa, I follow Jesus with you ... I go with Grandpa and tell people about Jesus...' She's just three years old!

Say today: 'I will – give all of me to you, precious Saviour.'

Say, 'I step from...'

- oppression – to freedom!
- fear – to faith!

- insecurity – to security!
- sinfulness – to goodness!
- depression – to hope!
- unhappiness – to joy!
- egotism – to healthy pride!
- shame – to glory!

OLD FEARS?

It's time to be rid of this crippling, dreading, killing, suffocating terror – and to have a healthy, soul-gripping, wonder-filled, awesome, godly fear of our magnificent, precious Saviour, Jesus Christ.

Old sorrows?
It's time to bury the dead.
Old sins?
It's time to accept Christ's forgiveness.
Old setbacks?
It's time to believe in beginning again.
Old insults?
It's time to let the past be the past.
Old hurts? Old angers?
It's time to accept the spirit of forgiveness.

Of course, we already know all this! But as Billy Richards used to say: '*Brethren, we know these things, but do we do them?*' Act with God to be free of these drudging fears.

One of my favourite jokes concerns a young man woken abruptly by his mother, very early on a Sunday morning.

'Get up!' she says. 'You've got to go to church!'

'I'm not going,' the son replies. 'I don't want to go.'

'You have to go,' the mother says, sternly.

'Why?'

'Two reasons. One because it's Sunday and we always go to church on Sunday. And two, because you're the vicar!'

GET UP, FACE AND WIPE OUT YOUR FEARS

Soon after his arrival in prison, an inmate had three teeth extracted. Then he lost a finger working in the kitchen. But when his appendix had to be removed the warden said, 'We'd better keep an eye on him. I think he's trying to escape bit by bit!'

You can defeat your fears 'bit by bit'. Faith comes when you are not really sure and you have to take that step in the dark. God gives you just enough light for the step. In Bible times they obviously didn't have any Duracell flashlights, so how did they get anywhere at night? They had little oil lamps that would give just enough light for each step. It wasn't a high beam so that you could see half a mile down the road: it was step-by-step illumination.

Likewise God's will is not laid down so we can know what's going to happen to us in the next 20 years. It would blow our mind if we knew and we probably couldn't handle it. God shows us the way one step at a time, telling us, 'My word, my truth, my Spirit will light your path.'

Firm faith in the promises of God is the best theology. 'Flaunt God,' as John Hopkins describes it.

Eugene Peterson, in *The Message* – his contemporary paraphrase of the Bible – makes the Psalmist say of his faith: 'I've got a good thing going and I'm not letting go' (Psalm 16:8). For once, the popular saying is right. 'If you've got it, flaunt it!'

Don't let go of God! You'll never build a reputation, business or relationship on what you *intend* to do. Your intentions may be honourable and sincere, but unless you *put them into action*, nothing is changed. Take hold – press in!

On our first visit to the United States, we stood in a long queue at the airport waiting for clearance through immigration. The officer carefully examined everyone's credentials. When our turn finally came I jokingly remarked that it seemed to be more difficult to get into the United States than to enter the kingdom of heaven.

Without hesitation the immigration official replied, 'Buddy, there's a lot more folks tryin'!'

Keep trying – throw your fears on the Almighty. Push fear out! I like the '20th Century Beatitudes', a parody on a part of Jesus' Sermon on the Mount. It was written by S. B. Philips –

> Blessed are the pushers,
> > for they get on in the world.
> Blessed are they who complain,
> > for they get their way in the end.
> Blessed are the blasé,
> > for they never worry over their own sins.
> Blessed are the slavedrivers,
> > for they get results.

> Blessed are the knowledgeable,
> for they know their way around.
> Blessed are the troublemakers,
> for they make people notice them.

Not Christian ideology – but it is certain that 'pushers' get results. We can afford to be 'pushy' when it comes to fighting fears and 'grabbing' the Blessing of God.

One of my favourite videos is the animated adventure *Aladdin*. As he enters the cave of wonders to find the Genie's lamp, Aladdin is instructed to take only the lamp – nothing else. However, the wealth of the cave is just too much for his monkey Aboo, who is mesmerized by a huge ruby and reaches out to take what isn't his. We can be 'takers' of the wonderful grace of God, which gives us victory over fear.

GIVE GOD ALL YOUR FEARS

During the American Civil War, Abraham Lincoln met with the generals of the Southern armies on a number of occasions as the war progressed, to seek a peaceful end to it. The Southerners wanted to keep on with these meetings because they were getting fairly profoundly bashed up. After one year of war they came to Lincoln and said, 'OK, we'll give in. Just let us have Texas, New Mexico, the southern bit of California and one or two other States. You can have everything else.' And Lincoln refused.

Another year went by and the Southerners became more desperate. 'How about letting us have just Texas and New Mexico? The North can keep everything else.'

Abraham Lincoln reached over the table, put his hand on the map of the whole of America and said, 'Gentlemen, this Government wants it all.' Then he left the negotiating table and refused to meet with his opponents again until they came back in unconditional surrender.

While we carry on trying to keep some sovereign states in our lives apart from God, He is unable to give us all that he longs to. He cannot fill us with Himself or direct us fully, because there is civil war going on inside us. God is putting His hand on the map of our lives and saying, 'My Government wants it all. Not just the bits you feel you can spare; not some bits and not others; I want all of your life.'

That is the key to break us of the hindrance of fear: all your life given to Him – then a God of action appears.

21

IDOLS PILED ON THE FIRE

As we read the psalm beneath the tall jungle trees in Malaysia, I spied a bundle of odd-looking figures loaded on top of one another, as the Chinese people threw their idols forward. 'Thou art great, and doest wondrous things, Thou art God alone' – never had the words had more meaning and or deeper implications. These people were giving away generations of family lineage: they had been brought up with this, and the idols had been handed down to them, this ancestral worship, this responsibility to their dead loved ones, to pray them out of their eternal suffering. They even had a responsibility to feed the wandering spirits; you will see a tiny altar with pieces of food on it at the door of many Chinese homes: they are making sure the dormant spirit of a dead family member is not going hungry!

To put all this behind them, and to burn the very memory of their closest family by putting away this affinity and loyalty – cutting off, it seemed, their very blood ties – is very hard, but love for God, obedience to the Holy Spirit and His Word, was what now was dominant to them. Unworthy traditions, idolatry, worthless, derogatory and invidious behaviour was ours to name and to follow after the true living God was their longing.

Soon the fire crackled, the idols burnt, the flame went up. We had to put cans of kerosene on the fire to finally exterminate them: those idols were hard objects!

Here was God in action changing lives after generations of perfidy, misery, tiredness, of vain, sad, grieving
existence. Jesus was joy to them, and miracles
happened. One child born paralysed, brain-damaged,
uncommunicating, was soon acting almost perfectly
normally, and when I passed that way a year later on
another missionary trip, she was *perfectly* normal!

Miracles flowed through the community, churches
sprang up – God did great works. The strenuous, heart-
rending act of breaking deeply with the past was the
open door to God acting, clearing the deck, sweeping in
upon us.

In Zululand, in KwaZulu-Natal out in the sticks, I
was preaching to thousands of these lovely people in a
huge tent. We had no electricity in the whole shanty
town. We had brought up a generator, which worked
by a petrol-driven engine, the huge cross lit up over the
door of the massive marquee. As I was preaching near
the end of my sermon on the merits and power of the
sacrifice of Christ on the Cross, people began to stream
out to the platform. Soon they were handing me
clothes, scarves, watches, laying down piles of saris,
shoes, pens (gold ones), books, and many other objects.

I stopped preaching. I thought this was the collection: they had no money so they were giving their best
possessions to God as an offering! I quietly spoke to the
tall Zulu interpreter, 'Can we have the offering *after* the
preaching, not in the middle of it?'

He laughed, he roared with guffaws, and he replied,
in between his lengthy chuckles, 'This is not the collection, these are things the people have stolen, and they
have been convicted about their sins through your

preaching of Christ's death. They want to bring back all their plunder!'

I was staggered beyond imagination, I looked down at the loot and shook my head. Faith is never surprised, I had often taught people in the UK, but I certainly was that day!

I thought of the brass serpent on the pole in the wilderness bringing miracle healing to thousands. Why? Because the brass was connected with omnipotence, a conductor of heavenly electricity! The Bible is truly the book of all books, bringing healing, quickening, strengthening, release of amazing, astounding power, comforting, purifying, I had seen it all in the space of a few weeks, in two remarkable revivals in two nations as different as chalk from cheese!

Back in England, I was preaching at a densely crammed service in one of our medium-sized towns. Many had been healed that afternoon, cripples trotting, blind beginning to see, deaf people throwing away expensive hearing aids, wheelchairs taken off for the scrap heap. A local reporter came and quizzed me, evidently moved by the genuineness of it all.

'What is this power?' he asked.

'Were you not in the service to hear my sermon and God's Word?' I asked in return.

He shuffled and blushed a bit. 'I was unavoidably held up,' he answered (they always come at the end of the service and try to miss my preaching).

'To answer your question,' I told him, 'it's simple – this power is the wounds, suffering, blood and sacrifice of Jesus Christ, the Son of God.'

Nothing whatsoever can make up for the Cross, no good can be done without it. It cheers the fainting hearts, comforts the mourners, humbles the proud, changes the dark, hard sinner's heart, rids the blight of disease from the sad and suffering.

Jane Austen said, 'The truest friend is hope.' The blood of Christ is our hope – it breaks upon you like a burst of glorious sunshine.

MAKING MUCH OF THE LINCHPIN

Another reporter, in another city, asked me, 'To get such power and results, where do you meditate?' He went on, 'Do you contemplate in the cosmos...?'

I replied, with a twinkle no doubt in my eye, 'No, I meditate a little higher up, in the heaven of heavens ... with the King of Glory!'

'I am not ashamed of the gospel of Christ, it is the power of God unto salvation.' Paul said, 'I want to know nothing among you but Christ crucified.' This is the pass key, the master key, the skeleton key: the red-covered tree of Calvary.

Bishop J. C. Ryle said, 'Without Christ crucified in her pulpits, a church is little better than a dead corpse, a well without water, a sleeping watchman, a silent trumpet, a speechless witness, an ambassador without credentials, a lighthouse with no power, a messenger with no good tidings. Such a church is a stumbling block to weak believers, a comfort to infidels, a hot-bed for formalism, a joy to the Devil, and an offence to God.'

An Indian in America told how a preacher came and told them there was a God. It did not move his people;

they said, 'We have many gods.' Another preacher came and told them they should not steal, tell lies, or get drunk with alcohol. But they did not accept the story; they said, 'We have tried in vain to reform many times.' Then another preacher came. He announced that he had only one theme – that God came to earth as a man, was born to a virgin, grew up, taught, helped, blessed and healed thousands. Finally he died on a rough-cut cross, bled to death, died after three hours, was taken down dead from the Cross and laid in a tomb. Three days later he burst out of that tomb, shattered death, won the victory that overcomes the world, and brought great glory to His Father and everlasting bliss and heaven to us.

The Indian people opened their hearts with faith and received great joy. All became Christians and are still believers to their third generation.

God on the Cross is God in action. I totally rely on this substitutionary death.

Two thousand years ago Christ, because He was God, had the capacity to see you in this new millennium – and blot out your modern iniquities and sins. Isaiah said, 'Cast all your sins behind His back.' Every church usually carries a cross outside or on its spire or inside on the wall or altar. I've seen the cross towering above buildings all over the world in 30 countries in four continents. Malaysia is a Muslim nation, yet a huge new Assembly of God Church in Kuala Lumpur carried a great cross on top – you could see it for miles around.

In Belgium on hillsides and even on corners of country roads, you see the crucifix. One old man years ago carried a cross all over the world, hundreds of thousands of miles. In East Anglia you see Jesus on a cross in villages, in town market places, in city centres. In the heart of Africa little mission churches in the wilds carry a cross on top of the hut. In the middle of 'Crocodile Dundee' country in the barren planes or outback of Australia, I saw a cross by a church. In the South Sea Islands, in Hawaii, Singapore, South East Asia, in Ireland, the bleak highlands of Scotland, the cross is everwhere.

The Cross is the symbol showing that Jesus died for us. Turn yourself over to Christ. The deaf can come, the blind can come, the black can come, the white can come, old people can come, children can come. This is the harvest time: there's going to be a glorious tomorrow. Spend eternity with Jesus.

Say, 'I want to change my way of living ... I want to be forgiven.' Jesus did it publicly, being nailed to a cross for you. You do it publicly ... and come to Him.

WE HAVE A CHOICE

Tozer rightly wrote, 'The will not the feelings determines moral direction.' A Turkish soldier gleefully beating a Christian till he was half dead, shouted, 'What can Christ do for you now?' The Christian replied, 'Give me strength to forgive you.' He made a great moral choice!

Look at the wrong choices, look at the mistakes made, learn from them, don't hide from them, but don't over-emphasize them either. Remember to forget them!

A verse shown me recently reads:

Look Behind You!
A doctor's mistake is buried.
A lawyer's mistake is imprisoned.
An accountant's mistake is jailed.
A dentist's mistake is pulled.
A pharmacist's mistake is dead.
A plumber's mistake is stopped.
An electrician's mistake is shocking.
A carpenter's mistake is sawdust.
A teacher's mistake is failed.
A printer's mistake is redone.
And yours?
Is remembered, repeated, distorted, remembered
    and repeated again.
FROM *Quote Unquote*, PUBLISHED
                    BY VICTOR BOOKS

Be prepared to leave your mistakes behind. Others may remember them, but God forgives them and gives you a fresh start.

That is the power of the blood of His Cross. 'He that taketh not his Cross and followeth after me, is not worthy of me' (Matthew 10:3). 'Take up the Cross ... follow me ... for whosoever will lose his life shall save it' (Matthew 16:24).

When David killed Goliath, the giant of a man and bitter enemy of God and his people, there was a striking victory. Although it is an Old Testament story, it is full of New Testament truth. Goliath, a picture of evil, satanic, anti-God power, was brought down with a single stone. David's catapult found its mark in Goliath's brain. He promptly cut off the head of the evil genius, the brain being the symbol of evil strategy, planning, scheming and power. 1 Samuel 54:17 tells us the head was taken to Jerusalem.

We hear no more in Scripture, but Jewish legend tells us about a very probable incident which happened after that. The head was paraded through the streets in triumph, and they had days of partying to celebrate their God-given victory. Finally the head was taken out of the city of Jerusalem and there buried with great ceremony on a small hill. From that time this place was renamed 'the place of a skull', or 'the hill of Goliath'. In Greek over hundreds of years this became known as the 'hill of Goliath' and finally the 'hill of Golgotha', where 1,000 years later, our blessed Saviour Jesus Christ died. He bled to death with His feet on Goliath's head! His feet were on Satan's head for ever, Scripture says: 'He shall bruise Satan under you' (Romans 16:20).

'Christ died for our sins.' 'God forbid that sin shall have dominion over you, sin abounds, but grace doth much more abound.' 'Greater is He that is in you [Christ], than he that is in the world [the man without Christ].' Jesus said, 'I give you power over all the power of the enemy.' 'Without me ye can do nothing.'

We have a choice to apply that anointing, to choose that triumph, to walk in that power. It is in our hands. As the people chose to burn their idols in Malaysia, so we have a choice that is the most vital key to seeing God in action.

– 22 –

ACTION IS CHANGE

When I was a boy travelling through Southampton to see my uncle, we would go on the tram. The old carriages lurched loudly, screeched as they passed through the cobbled streets. The conductor at the back would take the fares and shout the stops just coming up.

'The Odeon Picture House!' he'd call.

'Anyone for the cemetery?'

And then, when we got to the tram station, 'All change!'

God wants to change us all, change us from glory to Glory. Jesus Christ is the same yesterday today and forever. It is us who need to change. 'Change ... go up and make there an altar to God' (Genesis 35:2). 'Change ... the bad for good, and if he shall at all change ... then it therefore shall be holy...' (Leviticus 27:10). 'Wait till my change shall come, Thou shalt call and I will answer Thee. Thou shalt have a desire ... for Thou doest number my steps, and watch over my sins' (Job 14:14). 'They shall be changed ... Thou art the same, thy years shall have no end' (Psalm 102:20).

We don't want to change, however. Our trouble is God! We hinder ourselves. Jacob was set upon by an assailant, it tells us in Genesis 32:24–32:

So Jacob was left alone and a man wrestled with him till the break of day. When the man could see

*he could not overpower him, he touched the
socket of Jacob's hip, so that his hip was
wrenched as he wrestled with the man. Then the
man said, 'Let me go for it is daybreak.' But Jacob
said, 'I will not let you go till you bless me!' The
man answered, 'What is your name?' 'Jacob,' he
answered, then the man said, 'Your name will no
longer be Jacob, but Israel, because you have
struggled with God and with men and have overcome.' Jacob said, 'Please tell me your name.' But
he replied, 'Why do you ask my name?' Then
he blessed him there. So Jacob called the place
'Peniel', and he was limping because of his hip.
Therefore to this day the Israelites do not eat the
tendon attached to the socket of the hip because
the socket of Jacob's hip was touched near the
tendon.*

Note that a man wrestled with Jacob until the dawn.
Hosea says (Chapter 12) that it was 'an angel' – we
don't know who or what, but God was in it. What a
revolution in Jacob: his problems with God were over,
and he went from con man to prince, from the human
to the divine. Jacob was no longer wrestling with a
curse but with a blessing!

Some make so much of spiritual warfare, but it is
struggling with God which is harder and more vital.
Satan is nothing, Satan is a walkover. I find it's easier to
say 'no' to Satan, than to say 'yes' to God. Jacob got a
new name – 'Israel', a new ministry – he was never the
same again. The place got a new title also: the unknown
desert site was renamed 'Peniel' – 'The face of God'.

OUR DIFFICULTIES ARE WITH OUR GOD

Look at Job: his battle was not with the Devil – he disappeared in Chapter 2 out of 41 chapters! It is an action book with God; Satan is never referred to after that chapter. The whole book is about Job's problem with his Saviour. Augustine said, 'It was not Job who said, 'The Lord gave and the Devil took away.' Job battled with God through this book, but enemies are turned to servants, monsters are turned to ministers, by His attitude.

Too often we are 'enchanted but unchanged'. This phrase by Oswald Chambers is true. We have a power-less gospel in too many churches: a Cross with a Christ is a ritualism; a Christ without a Cross is a rationalism; but a Christ on a Cross is a redemption!

It is the miracle power and value of the Cross beamed forward 2,000 years into my services that bring forth the many cures, healings and miracles for so many sick people. Someone called one of my services recently, 'like a gigantic hospital ward!'

People go out well, uplifted, whole, healed, healthy again so often. I believe in the substitutionary atoning death of Jesus Christ, in the mighty resurrection miracle power of Jesus.

He, 'reconciled all things unto Himself, having made peace through the blood of His Cross' (Colossians 1:20). Jesus did a glorious, astounding work on that Calvary Cross. This wonderful truth changes us amazingly today. Here is a gospel of power, a gospel of Christ crucified. Here is a tumultuous, spirit-soaring climax as we see and prove the changing, utterly glorious picture of a mighty High Priest, interceding for sinners day and night, and transforming thousands today. This is God in action.

Ezekiel the prophet complained, 'Indeed to them you are nothing more than he who sings ... and plays well, they hear your words, but do not put them into practice' (Ezekiel 33:32). There must be a change in people or all is lost. The captivating beauty arrests the apathetic and hard-hearted, changing the seemingly indifferent with a magnetism that is divine.

Someone said to the atheist, David Hume, 'I thought you did not believe the gospel,' as he met him going early, at 5 o'clock one morning, to hear George Whitefield preach in the centre of Edinburgh. Hume replied, 'I don't believe, but he does!'

A gifted preacher said, 'I have failed if my preaching can charm but not change.' Ezekiel said in 33:33, the next verse, 'When it all comes true, and it surely will, then they will know that a prophet has been among them.' People are changed by the words of God.

I have loved my crusades among the South Sea Island people, New Zealand, the Samoans. One atheist European was speaking one day with a native on one of these tiny islands, where almost all were Christians, and churches packed. He pointed to the Bible he was carrying. 'We don't believe in that Bible any more!'

The local man replied, 'It's a good job we believe in it on this island, because before the missionaries came with the Bible we were all cannibals – we would have eaten you up long ago!' There was an atheist glad of the Bible.

The gospel tells us, 'His word was with power.' A tough Roman soldier cried, 'Speak the Word only and my servant will be healed.' It records, 'He sent His Word and it healed them.' Words of revelation, words of light, words of grace, words that change man from glory into glory.

WORDS KILL – WORDS GIVE LIFE

'The one who knows much says little, an understanding man remains calm. Even dunces who keep quiet are thought to be wise; as long as they keep their mouths shut they're smart ... Fools ... all they do is run off at the mouth ... many words rush along like rivers in flood ... the words of a fool start fights ... they are undone by their big mouths ... crushed by their words ... wise men are always listening ... words satisfy the mind as much as fruit the stomach, good talk is gratifying ... words kill, words give life, they're either poison or fruit – you choose ... [some] speak in soft supplications, [some] bark out answers' (Proverbs 17:27,28 and 19: 2,4,7,15,20,21,23 *The Message*).

A professor from Yale University was the after-dinner speaker at an academic banquet in England. 'As you know,' he began, 'I come from Yale, so I want to frame my speech around those four letters, Y - A - L - E.' His listeners waited eagerly for him to begin.

'The letter Y,' he said, 'stands for Youth...' and he spoke about Youth for 15 minutes. 'Now A,' he said, 'is for Ambition, the great American virtue...' The guests settled down as he spoke for 20 minutes on this subject. 'L stands for Learning,' he declared, and devoted 15 minutes to Learning. 'Finally, E is for that great institution, Education...' His listeners sank low in their seats as he finished with 20 minutes on Education.

As he sat down, he eagerly asked his neighbour, 'How did I do?'

'We enjoyed it very much,' was the faint reply, 'and we are all so glad that you are not from the Massachusetts Institute of Technology!'

Milton said, 'The measure of a man is the extent to which he can concentrate on words.' It is often said that something worth saying can be expressed in just a few words. I have heard hundreds of preachers all over the world during the four decades since I became a committed Christian. Some I cannot remember, and some I would like to forget! Some of the sermons were as much as two hours long, but some of the best I ever heard were the brief, snappy, sharp ones.

After all, the Lord's Prayer in the Authorized Version has only 65 words in it. The Ten Commandments are expressed in just 297 words, while the American Declaration of Independence comprises just 300 words. However, the Common Market's instructions on the import of caramel products run to some 26,911 words! What a waste of words!

Solomon advises us, 'Let your words be few' (Ecclesiastes 5:2). James tells us, 'Everyone should be quick to listen, slow to speak' (James 1:19). Jesus commanded us not to swear by anything and said, 'Simply let your "Yes" be "Yes", and your "No", "No"; anything beyond this comes from the evil one' (Matthew 5:37). We don't need to use a lot of impressive words to make a promise; a straightforward 'Yes' or 'No' should suffice.

Some politicians have a reputation for longwindedness – for using several words where one would do. A man was once taken out to a restaurant by a friend. When he had finished his steak and salad he went to the washroom. After washing his hands he went to the hand drier, and as he was about to push the button to make the warm air blow out he noticed with amusement that some joker had written next to it: 'Press this button for a tape-recorded message from the Prime Minister.' Too many people in politics are full of hot air!

But President Harry Truman was not a bit like that – he had a simple, no-nonsense approach to politics and indeed to life in general. When asked about the rigours of political life, instead of giving a lengthy reply, he would simply say, 'If you can't stand the heat, stay out of the kitchen!'

Somebody once asked President Woodrow Wilson how long it would take him to prepare a 10-minute speech. The President replied, 'Two weeks.' He was then asked how long it would take him to prepare a two-hour speech. 'I'm ready now,' answered Wilson. So we can see that the art of speaking or writing is not to say a lot but to say a lot in a few words. It is the *quality* of the words we say that counts, not their *quantity*.

Words are powerful. What we say can be an influence either for good or for evil. Our words should be few, careful and kind. When a family moved into a house they found that a few items had been left in the kitchen by the previous occupants. Pinned to the wall were a calendar, some recipes and this verse:

Every grouse shakes this house,
Every grumble makes it crumble,
But loving words
Will give it all the strength it needs.

The following comes from what seems a rather unlikely source – *600 Magazine*, a publication for machine tool manufacturers and engineers!

The six most important words in life are: '*I admit I made a mistake.*'
The five most important words in life are: '*You did a good job.*'
The four most important words in life are: '*What is your opinion?*'
The three most important words in life are: '*If you please.*'
The two most important words in life are: '*Thank you.*'
The least important word in life is '*I*'.

Recently I came across a list of nine words which express all that is best and worst in life:

The most bitter word is *Alone*.
The most tragic word is *Unloved*.
The most cruel word is *Revenge*.
The saddest word is *Forgotten*.
The coldest word is *Indifference*.
The warmest word is *Friendship*.
The most beloved word is *Mother*.
The most peaceful word is *Home*.
The most comforting word is *Faith*.

Words of faith can bring about a spiritual revolution in Britain, in Europe and across the world.

As Charles Wesley wrote, 'Inspire the living faith, the faith that conquers all.' Faith, Hebrews 2:6 tells us, 'Is being sure of what we hope for.' Its guidebook is the Bible, and the marks of a true man or woman of faith are a well-fed soul and a well-read Bible. 'The book of the law shall not depart from your mouth ... day [or] night.'

Mavis, 23 years paralysed, 13 long years in a wheelchair, bound, sad, sick, suddenly is set free: a miracle! She walks from one of my services, and is still free two years later, a testimony to hundreds of thousands of unsaved people in Yorkshire. Faith moves the hand of God today.

Wigglesworth said, 'We must get rid of our small measure of faith.' God honours faith – faith honours God.

Watching a little squirrel recently, bravely taking huge leaps across a tree, from one high branch to another, told me that to win *we must risk*, take the leap of faith into God's sure hands. Revival is in the air, the Spirit of faith is released in our land, I am seeing literally thousands born again and miraculously healed. Heaven is on our side, God is upon us in an awesome way. 'Nothing like this has ever been seen in our land before' (Matthew 9:33). Bible days are here again! Revival breakthrough and a re-birth of faith is on the way through words and demonstration of the Holy Spirit.

God calls for a change in us time and again. It is His command. Failure to see the blessing and power of God today, to see God's mighty movings, is chiefly due to this laxity: we will not change. He says in Holy Scripture,

'Put away strange Gods (false religious ideas, outward religion, your own unscriptural fanciful ideas), be clean, and change.' (Genesis 35:2)

'The change thereof in you shall be holy.' (Leviticus 27:33)

'I will awake till my change come, and thou shalt call and I will answer.' (Job 14:14)

'Shalt Thou change them, and they shall be changed.' (Psalm 102:26)

'But He will change them into cedars (strong structures, big people, sturdy, solid and upright people).' (Isaiah 9:10)

'Can the Ethiopian change his skin? Can the leopard change his spots? (Our personality is not changed, our colour, culture, ethnic, tribal background not changed, but as people we are changed, the person inside this outer man can be transformed).' (Jeremiah 13:23)

'Then shall his mind change and he shall pass over ... you have established them for correction.' (Habakkuk 1:7)

God says – 'I will change you.'

HINDU LORD MAYOR GOES HOME SINGING
CHARISMATIC SONGS

I was holding a large city-wide mission recently, in one of England's very old cities, not one of our largest, but historic for its Christian background, its noble writers, saints, religious history.

Hundreds filled the Assembly of God church to capacity. Not since the legendary Stephen Jeffries held a four-week revival in the 1920s had so many been born again and miraculously healed – so they told me, and that was 75 years before my visit!

The Lord Mayor and his wife and friends visited the crusade. He was the first Hindu Lord Mayor of this lovely city. There is a large immigrant Asian population in that community. But he was stirred by the worship, by God's effective, evident, glorious presence. Miracles took place, and nearly 50 people found Christ as Saviour in that one service alone. He left in the Rolls-Royce with his chauffeur, but later as I was leaving the venue very tired after praying with so many sick, disabled and pain-gripped people (including prayer for the mayoral party), his chauffeur, all dressed in a dark uniform and peaked cap, arrived back at the hall to thank me.

He commented, 'I've driven Lord Mayors to all sorts of religious services over the years, but this is the first time I've known the Mayor and Mayoress go home in the Rolls, singing gospel songs and hymns!' It seemed as if they had been so touched, changed, blessed, they sang the songs of Zion and of the Holy Spirit all the way home to the City Hall!

Recently I was holding a gospel-miracle crusade near to the small town of Olney, Buckinghamshire. I was taken by one of the organizers, a local Christian farmer, to the grave and church of John Newton, the great hymn writer. He penned majestic songs like 'How sweet the name of Jesus sounds' and 'Glorious things of Thee are spoken' and one of my mother's favourites, 'Amazing grace'. Changed from a life of atheism, drunkenness, debauchery and great financial gain from selling human slaves, Newton was miraculously changed. I noted the words in the stained-glass window dedicated to him in the church – 'He that doeth the truth cometh to the light.' Also on his grave were these words – 'He was restored, preserved, pardoned, by the mercy of our Saviour Jesus Christ. From an infidel to a preacher of the gospel and of the true faith for 44 years, which he once laboured to destroy.' He had been transformed by Christ.

THE CROSS CHANGES US

The Welsh preacher Eric Dando once said, 'It was the most unusual place that you could have expected God to meet the need of a dying, thirsty humanity.'

God could have used any way of redeeming us, but He chose the Cross. The Second World War poet, Alun Lewis, wrote, 'By what mysterious alchemy could God so fashion materials as this, to make them the pivot of his plans?' But the rough wood of the Cross, the piercing nails, were the emblems of Christ's greatness, His humility, obedience and love, materials transformed by the Father into glorious victory.

The Cross is the foundation stone of Christianity. When some Christian missionaries visited Mahatma Gandhi he asked them, before they left, to sing him one of their songs.

'Which one?' they asked, and Gandhi replied, 'Sing the one which best expresses what you believe.' They sang:

When I survey the wondrous cross
On which the prince of glory died,
My richest gain I count but loss,
And pour contempt on all my pride.

When we gaze at Calvary we see the very summit of Christ's greatness, the very purpose of His life, His glory, His magnificence, the proof of His love for us. John said, 'Jesus Christ ... loved us and washed us from our sins in His own blood' (Revelation 1:5). His love shone forth to the whole world.

A little boy who had come as an orphan to a Spurgeon's Children's Home was asked by the house-mother if he liked the chapel there. 'Yes, I do,' the child replied, 'I like that big kiss on the wall.' The cross is the symbol of God's love to a loveless world.

In Tibet the shepherds build small stone enclosures and each night place one small lamb inside. If a wolf comes at night it smells the lamb and, instead of attacking the main flock, squeezes into the enclosure to kill and eat it. But the wolf is trapped, it cannot get out, and in the morning it is killed by the shepherds. One lamb is sacrificed to save the other sheep. Jesus, the Lamb of God, died to save His sheep. 'We have redemption through His blood.'

The significance of this experience was that the ground of the Cross is level ground. All must kneel before the crucified Christ. At the foot of the Cross there is equality. There are no pretensions at the foot of the Cross. In the words of the old song, we must come:

Just as I am – without one plea
But that Thy blood was shed for me.

There is a story of a famous artist who met an old, ragged, filthy tramp, and asked him if he would model for him. He gave him the address of his studio and promised him a good fee. The next day the tramp turned up, but he had cleaned himself up, washed and shaved, and put on some decent clothes. The artist said, 'No, that won't do. I wanted you just as you were.' We cannot put on a veneer of cleanness, display our religion and righteousness, and try to prove our worthiness. We must come to the Cross just as we are, sinful and unworthy as we are. The Cross is sufficient to meet us.

CHANGED BY THE BLOOD – BY GOD'S ACTION!

In the Rocky Mountains there is a place called the Great Divide. Waters flow down the steep, rocky cliffsides into a deep ravine. Soon the fast-flowing stream becomes divided; the waters on one side flow across the country, eventually to empty into the warm waters of the Pacific, while the waters on the other side flow in the opposite direction towards the Atlantic. The Cross of

Christ is the great divide. We can accept it or reject it. We are either for it or against it, gathered to Him or scattered abroad, sheep or goats. We have a choice.

If we accept Christ's redemption, accept life instead of death, then we share in the glory that He won with His blood. Today we wait in the wings, but one day we shall take our place with our glorious Redeemer, in the full spotlight of His glory. That is the miracle of His Cross!

In the church of St Maria degli Angioli in Lugano, the wonderful frescoes of Bernardino Luini can be seen. The whole ceiling is covered with the representation of the Passion and right in the middle is the Cross, with Christ seeming to bear down upon the world, lifted high. One's overwhelming impression is that He is the pre-eminence – the central challenge – and one remembers His saying, 'I, if I be lifted up from the earth, will draw all men unto me' (John 12:32).

There is power enough in the blood shed on the Cross to cleanse the whole world of sin. The glorious work of Calvary is amazing in its effect on men and women. Noel Proctor, the prison chaplain who has seen so many miracles of Christ's redeeming power among hardened criminals in Strangeways Prison, told the story of one particularly hard and vicious man. He had been involved with the occult and was aggressive towards Noel, but one day he wandered into the prison chapel and saw the cross illuminated in the stained-glass window. He fell on his face beneath it, weeping. The very sight of the cross had broken one of the hardest of men. 'Christ died for the ungodly' (Romans 5:6); 'Who is he that condemneth? It is Christ that died' (Romans 8:34).

Calvary was the greatest sermon Jesus ever preached.

What can wash away my sin
Nothing but the blood of Jesus.

God wants us to be cleansed from evil and selfishness and dedicated to His will, filled with His love and power. He wants us to yield ourselves to the process of the Holy Spirit, whose work of dedication and sanctification produces inner peace in our lives, ends frustration, lifts burdens and doubts, frees us from striving and selfish personal ambition.

We cannot be holy, cannot be like Jesus, unless we know His character. St Augustine said, 'Who can call on Thee, not knowing Thee?' Spurgeon wrote, 'The highest science which can engage the attention of the child of God is the name, the nature, the person, the works, the doings ... of the great God.' Paul said, 'I count all things but loss for the excellency of the knowledge of Christ Jesus my Lord.'

It is wonderful, elevating, and joyful to know the character of Jesus and for that to become our own character. As a boy I remember singing at Salvation Army meetings:

Let the beauty of Jesus be seen in me,
All His wonderful power and purity.

God is the creator of harmony, beauty and truth, and can be satisfied with nothing less: 'As he which has called you is holy, so be ye holy' (1 Peter 1:15).

He wants to change you more and more! He calls us not only to make more people Christians – but to make the Christians more Christian!

A European King some years ago went missing, to walk among his people. He was asked not to do it due to the security risk, but he said, 'How can I rule my people if I don't know how they live?'

SUPERMARKET QUEEN IS BORN AGAIN

I was holding some revival meetings a short time ago in rural Shropshire, near to Telford. God came down with special blessing and glory. The June meetings were packed, people came from 45 villages and towns across the county. A local minister who had studied local church history over the past 500 years discovered that there had been no revival like it for 220 years since the visits of the legendary John Wesley. A great harvest of converts came in; 50 per cent of attenders were from outside the churches. It was not organization but agonization that brought this divine visitation.

One fine lady visited the tent, interested only in seeing the reported 'miracles' that had been noised about, having heard news of them carried in newspapers and BBC radio. This lady found a personal salvation; all she had dreamt about, longed for, in her heart for peace and presence of mind, fulfilment, purpose in life came to be born in her in that marquee, on the recreation ground at the foot of the Welsh mountains. When I was in further tent meetings near Shrewsbury a year later, I was introduced to Mary, the 'queen' of a supermarket chain. She was in charge of the building of all the new chainstores for this international company, a household name throughout the nation. Her job demanded much authority, responsibility, and contact with leading people in business, building industries, local and national government.

It meant much stress at times, niggling doubts about her inner self. Often in spite of great success in her career, her self-esteem fell, and feelings of much inadequacy and loneliness came over her. But she told how during the past year, since walking into that 'canvas cathedral' and being moved upon by the supernatural power of God, she had been totally and radically empowered, redeemed, changed, filled with purposeful confidence. God now reigned in her.

Scripture speaks of this inner experience in the heart:

'When he seeth Thee, he will be glad in his heart ... and I will be with his mouth and will teach (him).' (Exodus 4:14)

'Say not in thine heart ... who shall bring Christ again from the dead ... the Word is near you, in your mouth and in your heart, the word of faith.' (Romans 10:6)

'The spirit of the living God (is) not in stone, but in ... the heart, and such trust have we through Christ ... (for) we are not sufficient of ourselves ... but our sufficiency is of God ... not of the letter that killeth, but the spirit giveth life.' (2 Corinthians 3:3)

'With fear and trembling, in singleness of your heart, as unto Christ; not as men pleasers; but ... doing the will of God from the heart ... as to the Lord.' (Ephesians 6:5)

God is working in the heart, changing many people from every walk of life.

– 23 –

Miracles at Spurgeon's

I was preaching in Spurgeon's Chapel on the Northampton and Leicestershire border, the famed church, kept as it was 250 years ago. Fuller preached here, the great hymn writer of the noted tune 'Lynton'; the first missionaries to India, going out with Carey 200 years ago, worked from this great Bible centre. But the work had declined over the past 50 years. There had been no Sunday School for 35 years. A new young, lively, anointed minister, full of evangelizing vision, had seen half his church leave in a few months, as he stirred the status quo, and declared that things must change: 'We must recapture the biblical vision of winning the lost!'

I went there for a gospel healing crusade. The BBC carried it through the Midlands, newspapers gave half pages on it; congregations swelled with 80–90 per cent new, mostly unchurched, visitors – the first time for many in a place of worship. A hundred new people came to Christ, joy filled the pews, laughter came as sick people heard, lost pain, felt the healing of Christ. I was praying for a dear sickly lady, and her husband whispered to me, 'She has not walked at all for years!' Immediately she rose, walked at first weakly, gathered strength – then she walked on her own.

'Never has Spurgeon's seen such miracles,' the pastor declared. The media men who were present were staggered at the scenes of weeping husbands, as wives walked out pushing disabled chairs, as womenfolk jumped with delight at their partners' freedom from disease, panic and pain. God was in the old chapel, a new day had dawned. God visited us! A divine action was witnessed, it was precious. Soon counties around and hundreds of thousands of the population had read of the works of God. The chapel was built up with a revived interest, new converts, a growing new membership, love, care, hope for the hundreds of villages, towns, hamlets, in that wide rural district. God's actions stir communities. They want to see a God who works.

A friend of mine was preaching in rural Devon. He got up in the early hours, at about 3.00 a.m., to go out with the sheep farmer to see him deliver some lambs. After the delivery in a cold corner of a windy barn, the mother sheep licked his hand again and again, and the old farmer told his friend, 'I am there at her hour of need!' People are waiting to see God in action, to see faith work. This is their hour of need: many are waiting, Britain is ready, Europe is spiritually starving. This is the moment to show a mighty God.

Remember, God can work his works and actions through you! You are created in the image of God – 'crowned with glory and honour'.

I AM A PERSON

Created in God's image, fallen through sin and through choice, but you can become a child of God, an inheritor of the kingdom of God, saved by grace alone, redeemed by the blood of Christ. You are a person, you do have a choice. A person can choose: we are choice makers.

Everyone can change, we are not dominated by our genes, or by our chromosomes, or by our stars. You can change careers, you can choose your partner for life, the poor can become wealthy, the atheist can become a man of faith, you can change your mind, change your religion, change from dishonesty to honesty, from unreliable to totally firm as a rock; you can rebuild your life, you can go out reborn, remade, rehabilitated, renewed, restored, revitalized, ransomed, healed, restored, forgiven.

It means commitment; there is no change without commitment. You can channel your thoughts, energies, time, weaknesses, opportunities. God says you can manage your life, rather than your life managing you!

Believe God can do something through your life. 'God is my rock, in Him will I trust, He is my shield, my high tower, my refuge, my salvation' (2 Samuel 22:3). Bring prayer back into your life and home, be hungry to be something. Corrie ten Boom said, 'No person is too small for God's love, no problem too big for God's power.' Mother Teresa said, 'Aspire to be something to someone.'

People are starving in the UK – starving emotionally for spiritual hope, suffering from abuse, others committing suicide, turning to crime, grief-stricken through broken homes, hungry for love, for peace and presence of mind, hungry to be something, preoccupied with the things of earth, so much so that 3 million British mothers destroyed their own babies in abortion over the past 32 years. People are starving for life, for purpose, for the presence of God.

HUMBLE YOURSELF

In *Alice in Wonderland* Alice follows the White Rabbit. It goes through a very tiny door. Getting flat on her face, Alice tries to open the door, but it is far too small for her to squeeze through, then the door knob comes alive. It is the face of a bright old man, and she says to him, 'It's impossible to go through there.'

The old man in the doorknob replies, 'Nothing is impossible ... go and drink out of that cup on the top of that table.' But she looks up to find the table is six times higher than herself. She struggles, climbs, pulls at the table, and finally drinks of the cup and becomes tiny enough to enter the small door in her quest for the White Rabbit.

We must drink of the cup of humility, we must be lowly, modest, small at the feet of our Glorious Redeemer and Lord, who will open the doors of impossibility for us.

'The Lord knows the days of the upright.' Celsus, the pagan writer, noted about Christianity in his day: 'It turned nobodies into somebodies.' I like the old gospel song I sang in the Salvation Army as a boy:

When you are on your journey, stressed and tossed about,
Are you ever burdened with a load of care? Then ...
Count your blessings and every doubt will fly.

JESUS CHRIST CAN TURN YOU ABOUT

Each day I wake up with Jesus, among my first words after praising God and shouting 'Hallelujah' are: 'I'm fantastic ... *tomorrow never happened before*!'

When Philip came in from the streets, a drug addict, a heavy drinker, a criminal in and out of prison, remand homes, police custody and court for years, dirty and hopeless, God tapped him on the shoulder that night in our meeting in Wigan, Lancashire. As I prayed for him I said, 'You are a beautiful person.' He never forgot those words. Today, just out of Seminary (Bible School), he is preaching the gospel to the sick, disadvantaged and lost in society. He woke up to Jesus.

Perhaps you are angry, doubting, hopeless, disturbed, depressed, forgotten. For the first time you can see hope. God lives, God loves, God lifts, God listens. God labours, God leads.

A stranger asked a local the way in a new neighbourhood. 'How do you get to this road?' (showing a map).

'I don't know.'

'Which way to the main motorway?'

'I don't know.'

'How can I get to this junction, then?'

'I don't know.'

A bit impatient and exasperated, the driver added, 'You don't know much, do you?'

The local, smiling, replied, 'No I don't, but I'm not lost!'

Think, before you open your mouth, as someone said: 'Make sure your words are soft, as you may have to eat them later.'

Ask God to help you. This is the day the Lord has made, let us rejoice and be glad. Pray 'selfish' prayers: we can ask God to forgive us, a totally self-interested request. Pray. I fall asleep praying sometimes, I'm so earnest to get answers. Remember, when God answers – shut up! Don't keep on, accept the answer.

HEALING FORCES ARE AT WORK

I remember meeting a mighty man of God – he later wrote an introduction to my first book. As a young atheist, officially a Buddhist, this Korean was riding his bike one day, panting with bad, tuberculosis-ridden lungs. He cried out to God, if there was one, and the Lord heard. He healed him on his bike, and he has never suffered since. He found an Assemblies of God missionary, who led him to Christ. He was miraculously changed, and went on to win hundreds of thousands to Christ, and now pastors the world's largest church. His name? My good friend Dr David Yonggi Cho!

God wants you to find divine life. David Burns, an esteemed psychologist, said, 'The desperate need in the human mind is a human hunger for divine dignity.' We desperately desire to go somewhere, be what God plans for us.

Mother Teresa said, 'Be someone for somebody, do something beautiful for God, in the one life you have.' Don't waste it, don't throw it away, you can be someone, you can win! An old German labourer who was very poor left a note in his will: 'I leave my eldest son, my prize, my best tools, with which I carved the stones in Cologne Cathedral.'

I AM A PROBLEM

The problem with each of us is a three-letter word, 'S – I – N' – an old word, the ancient malady of the heart and mind, corruption, transgression, iniquity, sinfulness. Remember – sin is a condition before it's an action.

It may be lustfulness, unclean thoughts, money-grabbing, stealing or fiddling, the occult, being gay, cursing, alcohol abuse, adultery.

I was in an airport, buying a newspaper, when a man came up beside me, calling me by name. I had never seen him before, but apparently he recognized me. He said, 'You know, I prayed hard this morning that God would help me and now here you are.'

'What can I do for you?' I asked.

'How can I turn off this mass of disturbing thoughts that haunt me all the time?'

'What are your disturbing thoughts?'

'Fear, failure and futility! The three Fs, you might say. And they are pretty formidable.'

I thought for a moment, then answered, 'I have a friend by the name of Bill who writes wise statements that are printed in newspapers. One of them is this: "In adversity, some men break; others break records."'

He looked at me and replied, 'But it seems so impossible. I go to church every Sunday. I'm a member in my church. I'm on committees in my church. Why should I feel this way, when I'm so active?'

'How active in the Spirit are you?' I asked. 'You may be substituting an organization for the power of the Spirit. Maybe you'd better get less active in church and more active in the Spirit.' Then I added, 'If you get active in the Spirit, you will be doubly active in the church, because you'll have new power.'

'Have you a Bible text for me?' he asked.

'You might try this one. "Let the peace of God rule in your hearts" (Colossians 3:15). You're all upset and agitated. Let the peace of God rule in your heart. Another verse you might bear down on is Luke 18:27, which says, "The things which are impossible with men are possible with God."'

Say today, 'I have slipped, forgive me, Saviour.' Many try to do it by themselves – we cannot, we never will. Remember – to fail does not mean you're a failure!

I AM A POWER

Someone used to say to me, 'Melvin – may God use you without consulting you!' 'I may have many troubles, but you delivered me from them all' (Psalm 34:19). 'You are close to the broken-hearted, and you save those who are crushed in spirit' (Psalm 34:17,18). Smith Wigglesworth said, 'I'm a thousand times bigger on the inside than I am on the outside.'

'Those controlled by the flesh cannot please God ... the sinful mind is hostile to God ... If I live according to the flesh, I will die ... for I did not receive a spirit that makes me a slave again to fear ... there is now no condemnation for me ... I do not live according to the flesh...' (Romans 8:1–18).

Mencius, the Chinese philosopher, said, 'If others are unlovely, look into your own love ... if men are unruly, look into your own wisdom.' C. S. Lewis said, 'We only see ourselves truly alongside the crucified Jesus.'

It's the challenges, mountains, difficulties, that cause us to grow, move on and reach great achievements. Selwyn Hughes put it, 'When life hits a Christian on the chin, it tilts his face upwards to see the face of God.' 1 Peter 2:9 reads, 'We get knocked down, but we get up again and keep going.' A Sunday School teacher asked her class to list some of the virtues they should seek to follow on the Christian way. One little boy, however, put his hand up and piped up: 'You've missed one out, Miss, *the way to take things on the chin*!'

The preaching of the cross is the power of God unto salvation. In the Armenian earthquake, thousands lay buried. One mother with her child lay under the debris. To keep her alive she pricked her finger and let the child suck her blood. It saved the child: they were found and live today. Jesus gave His blood that we might suck life-giving power into our souls and minds and bodies. Jesus says, 'Let me help you, you are terrific ... in my hands you can do all things through Christ.' We can be nourished, fed, rejuvenated by Christ.

All that the Master has is ours. He said, 'As the Father sent me, so send I you.' Amazing! We are endowed, enclothed, cloaked about, covered by the same authority, love, graces, gifts, works, powers as Christ had!

Like many young children, I had a favourite book of nursery rhymes. I particularly remember Humpty Dumpty, pictured as a big, egg-shaped creature with a painted face and skinny arms and legs, perched happily on a wall. Then he fell and broke into countless pieces. As a child, I felt the hopelessness of the situation whenever I read that they 'couldn't put Humpty Dumpty together again'.

Since childhood I've come to know Christ as my Saviour and Lord. I've experienced Him as the great Potter, reshaping the shattered pieces of my life and the lives of others. I've had the joy of seeing many so-called hopeless drug addicts made new in Christ. As a result, I've added a line to the Humpty Dumpty nursery rhyme: 'What all the king's horses and all the king's men couldn't do, the King could!'

The King of Kings has all power, in heaven and on earth.

A LIVING FAITH IS A WORKING FAITH

Faith works as we are hemmed in, tied to the Father, as we go step in step with Him.

A group of scientists and botanists were exploring remote regions of the Alps in search of new species of flowers. One day they noticed through binoculars a flower of such rarity and beauty that its value to science was incalculable. But it lay deep in a ravine with cliffs on both sides. To get the flower someone had to be lowered over the cliff on a rope.

A curious young boy was watching nearby, and the scientists told him they would pay him well if he would agree to be lowered over the cliff to retrieve the flower below. The boy took one long look down the steep, dizzy depths and said, 'I'll be back in a minute.' A short time later he returned, followed by a gray-haired man. Approaching the botanist, the boy said, 'I'll go over that cliff and get that flower for you if this man holds the rope. He's my dad.'

Oh, that God might give us the faith of that boy!

Have you learned to trust the Lord like that, my friend? If anyone else holds the rope, I dare not go. But since Jesus is holding me fast, I can never doubt. Are you willing to say, 'If my Father holds the rope, I shall not fear'?

'Your faith shall not stand in the wisdom of men, but in the power of GOD' (1 Corinthians 2:1–5). Faith brings in the power; but the majesty and might of God brings in faith; both work frontways and backways ... to produce the greatest force known to man, the power that shakes the nation, the power of a believing soul of simple faith in you and me.

Rev. A. Smith's lines tell us:

He holds my hand, this wonderful Saviour
And He is mine;
So why should I fear when I know He's so near,
And I know that His hand holds mine?

The noted preacher of last century, George MacDonald, was talking to his son about the glorious future of those who had growing faith, and all the blessings of our loving Father. 'Daddy,' said his son, 'it seems too good to be true!'

His father replied, 'No, lad, it's just so good it must be true!'

FAITH UNDER PRESSURE

James wrote in his epistle, 'Know that under pressure your faith-life is forced into the open and shows its true colours ... ask boldly, believingly, without a second thought ... don't think you're going to get anything from the Master ... adrift ... keeping all your options open...' (1:1–7 *The Message*).

Keep faith, don't pull away, don't go in a wrong direction. The story is told that two men had been out deep-sea fishing when night began to fall. As they headed back towards land, the more experienced seaman got sleepy and turned the helm over to his friend. The veteran sailor pointed out the North Star and said, 'Just keep the boat going in that direction.'

The man had not been at his task very long before he, too, fell asleep. When he awoke he was thoroughly confused. He shook his friend frantically and shouted, 'Wake up and show me another star! I've run clean past that first one!'

Don't miss that guiding word! Act on His words, keep to His Word, even under pressures hold on, don't give up. 'Let's keep a firm grip on the promises that keep us going for .. if we give up and turn our backs on all we've learned and been given ... we are left on our own' (Hebrews 10:9–11).

God's Word is the compass that keeps you on course. Knowing the Bible is vital to knowing the God of the Bible. When the going gets rough, still keep on.

BELIEVING WITHOUT SEEING

A small child named Pat lost her leg in an accident and bled profusely. At the hospital she overheard a doctor tell her mother, 'She won't last until morning.' A short time later, Pat felt a gentle hand on her forehead and heard someone say, 'Go to sleep, Pat. When you wake up, you'll be better.'

Her mother, only a few feet from the bed, heard and saw nothing. But that night Pat slept soundly, and the next morning she was much better. Today, Pat is convinced that it was an angel who touched her and spoke to her. 'Blessed are those who have not seen and yet have believed' (John 20:29).

> God, give me the faith of a little child
> Who trusts so implicitly,
> Who simply and gladly believes Thy Word,
> And never would question Thee.

NO SUCH WORD AS IMPOSSIBLE

Jesus prayed for us all, for a great fact: 'that our faith faileth not' (Matthew 22:32). The word 'impossible' is not in the Christian's dictionary; there is no such word. Look up with faith; God has outnumbered your enemies.

'Do not fear, for those that be for you are more than they that be with them' (2 Kings 6:16). Don't quit, your faith will see you through.

There is a constant stream, an always-flowing river, of mercy and might and matchless love and strength, for the believer – open through the doorway and path of faith. 'He who believes in Me, as the Scripture has said, out of his heart will flow rivers of living water' (John 7:38).

The Scripture tells us, 'O Lord of Hosts, blessed is the man who trusts in you' (Psalm 84:12).

God wants us to give every ounce of faith to reach His goals. 'The Lord takes pleasure in His people, He adorns the humble with victory' (Psalm 149:4).

God's living Word is the only hope for a dying world. The Word of God in us produces faith. Dean Inge said, 'He who marries the spirit of the age will find himself a widower.' The spirit of Anti-Christ is in the world. True faith obeys without delay or doubt. 'Your Word have I hidden in my heart that I might not sin against you.' Faith is not of this world.

Psalm 84:10,11 says, 'No good thing will God withhold from those who walk in His ways.' Many people say, 'I hope this may happen,' or, 'This is what I'm praying for, I hope it's answered,' or, 'Are you believing in God? I hope so.'

Yet hope is one of the mightiest of virtues and gifts in the Bible. Paul cried, 'According to my earnest hope ... I continue with the joy of faith.' Hope is linked to faith, it's not the weak, wavering cousin of it.

John Calvin said, 'Hope is nothing else but the constancy of faith.'

Hope is the fore-longing of God's promises and precepts; faith is the actual evidence of those things hoped for! Paul's faith in God's promises brought hope even to 270 unsaved sinners on the doomed sinking ship in Acts 27:23–41, inspiring the whole shipload that they would be saved. Hope came to them, and not one was lost, all being shipwrecked on the Island of Malta.

As we bring Christ we bring hope – as the godly Richard Baxter of Kidderminster wrote: 'If we teach Christ to our people, we teach them all!'

May faith, hope, love fill your hearts. In the greatest chapter after John 3:16 in the Bible, that is 1

Corinthians 13, it tells us that there is nothing greater in the world, in all our lives than faith, hope and love. Love is the greatest, but close to it are faith and hope!

HOPE THOU IN GOD

It is mentioned in 29 books of the Bible, almost half of the books.

- 'Because of their hope they shall take rest in safety' (Job 11:18).
- 'Hope has said – "Thou are my confidence"' (Job 3:24).
- 'He rests in hope for Thou wilt not leave my soul in hell' (Psalm 16:9).
- 'He shall strengthen your heart, you that hope in the Lord' (Psalm 31:24).
- 'They that hope in His mercy shall be delivered from death' (Psalm 33:8).
- 'In Thee O Lord I hope, then Thou will hear me' (Psalm 38:15).

Say today with the psalm-writer in 39:7: 'My hope is in Thee, deliver me from all my transgressions.'

We live in a storm-tossed world – the dark night of the rule of the Anti-Christ will soon begin, this terror is soon to engulf the world. But by hope and faith in the Lord of the other world – you can be more than conquerors. John said, 'The world is passing away and the lusts thereof.' But to have hope and faith is to beat the worldliness, despair, defeatism, sadness and decadence and be lifted into the dazzling heights of glory with our majestic, fabulous, beautiful Lord Jesus Christ forever.

Faith is resting on what Christ is rather than on what He has done. Hope and faith are not flashing emotions or sentiments, not great sensationalisms, not mere feelings. There is no horizon to hope, and none to the vision of faith either.

Hope and faith invite Jesus into your life and they invite heaven too!

The poet had hope when he penned the noble lines:

Earth's crammed with heaven
And every common bush afire with God.

Life is no longer dreary, but thrilling, exciting, bright with the promises of God, radiant, sparkling, brimming full with joy!

Preaching from a soap-box in a public square in Kentucky, the speaker asked an inebriated man standing in front of him: 'Do you want to be converted?'

He replied: 'I'm drunk.'

'God can save you, drunk or not drunk,' he retorted.

'If you say so it must be so,' conceded the man as he knelt in prayer. Suddenly he opened his eyes, looked around in surprise and exclaimed: 'Why, He has saved me, and I'm drunk too.' Soon he was completely sober. God saved him and sobered him in minutes. How much more dramatic than that can you get?

Maybe you were not saved from such a debauched life, but as one religious and devout man testified, 'I was not saved from drugs, womanizing, alcoholism, debt, or being gay, but Christ saved me from an easy armchair!' Apathy, indifference, pride, contempt, cynicism, secularism are just as deadly destroyers as the other sins. The dear man was right and had an equally glorious, transforming friendship through Christ our Lord. Rise in hope.

Look up in faith, reader, this is your day. It is not too late, no matter what your past, your wasted years, no matter what your frustrations, your weaknesses, your lost ideals. This is the day of the ordinary believer, who through hope and faith, becomes an extraordinary man or woman of God.

God is unfailing, He is constant, He will never run out of resources, joys, blessings, spiritual sustenance, to match and keep us. The river of God's love runs as vigorously as ever! It will never, never, run dry.

I have seen hundreds of thousands of people who have found that by faith, tapping into God's mighty river, that sooner or later, if they don't give up, the crowning phase of faith comes. They reach the crest of the wave and ... the mountain top is scaled, success is achieved! A habit is broken, the court case is won. The chains are loosed, the bones are healed. The doctor tells you you can go home now. You walk back into the sunshine. A broken relationship is healed. The emptiness and loneliness of life is filled with a new friend and loved one. Heaven bends low, revival comes, the church grows, prosperity, peace, comfort and hope are reborn!

I often say – Please be patient – God isn't finished with me yet!

My wife Lilian, often says: Whenever I go to the hairdressers I must be prepared, oddly enough, to look anything but beautiful – at least to start with.

Sitting beneath an unflattering waterproof cape, I permit someone to work on my straggly hair. As it gets drastically cut, soaked with smelly solution, wrapped around tiny curlers, and then encased in a piece of plastic until it 'takes', I steal a glance in the mirror. Horrified, I invariably ask myself, 'Why am I *paying* someone to do this to me?' The satisfying answer is always the same: I hope to walk out of there looking fantastic.

That's the way it is in our Christian walk. This world is God's workshop. He skilfully changes our lives through trials of faith to make us more like Christ.

'We do not look at the things which are seen, but at the things which are not seen' (2 Corinthians 4:18). We are God's product – God's fruit.

– 24 –

MIRACLES IN VICELAND

SOHO SHAKEN BY THE MIRACLES OF GOD

In the night-clubs, the cellar drinking bars, in red-light ghettos, in gay clubs, in the thronging Chinese restaurants, in back streets and blazingly lit fronts of peep shows and topless pubs, we were amazed to hear that posters telling of the miracles of God had been gladly put up in most of these places, advertising my visit – the first ever miracle explosion crusade to Soho.

Hundreds of Christians were praying, in Holland and Belgium, in London, round the UK and elsewhere. God was about to shake the Gold Square Mile of Vice like never before. Billy Graham, the last evangelist to seek to penetrate this sordid area, was mobbed and could not move as he spoke from the top of a van with a loudspeaker. This time things were different!

'Everyone who preaches speaks to men for strengthening, encouragement and comfort' (1 Corinthians 14:3). J. R. Parker said, 'Preach to broken hearts and you will never lack a crowd.' 'It is the anointing of God that breaks the yoke' (the burden or chains of sin, guilt, curses, poverty, grief, habits, fears, obsessions, worry). People's minds are like sewers today in our society; as Lady Macbeth said to the King, 'You look the innocent flower, but see the serpent beneath it!'

Jesus drew strange people to him – the sceptics, the irreligious, street women, tax fiddlers, the local Mafia

(Zacchaeus), the religious theologians (Nicodemus and
Saul), the rich and the poor, the winebibbers, the good
and bad, a motley crew. My meetings draw together the
widest of society: in past weeks I've seen from mobsters
and their women to royalty, from the winner of an
Oscar in Hollywood to prostitutes; from the Lord
Mayor of the city to members of the local gay club!
From the most irreligious to monks, priests and nuns.
The highest and the lowest of society. From a multi-
millionaire to a low-incomed old-aged pensioner on
benefits. All have been equally welcome; I can honestly
say I've spent no more time praying with the very
wealthy than with the heroin addict. No more time
with the royal figure or the top film star than with the
homeless street people. All are given the same believing,
anointed prayer, faith and counselling. I don't have
special seats for members of the Government, or VIPs,
or well-known stars, as some evangelists do from overseas. All seats are free and the famous have to sit down
with the poor!

LET THE CHIPS LIE WHERE THEY FALL!

P. T. Forsythe, my favourite theologian, put it: 'The
Christian mission cannot live on improving pagans and
heathens, but only on passing them from death to life.'
Or, as Spurgeon wrote, 'The mystery of the spiritual
anointing ... we cannot tell to others what it is ... you
cannot manufacture it ... it is priceless if you would
edify believers and bring sinners to Christ.'

One young lady missionary had been working on
the streets of Soho for three years, often meeting with

resistance, apathy, abuse. But she prayed, showed kindness, a listening ear, and made many contacts. When I came for the crusade, she said that these folk just did not want to come to meetings. To get one into a service was three months' hard work. But as soon as the leaflets were given out about the supernatural power of God, about miracles – modern, amazing signs of God – they showed the greatest possible interest, the first time ever in three years! She invited me to meet some of them prior to my meeting. I went along to her flat behind the Windmill Theatre, squeezed between a gay bar, a disco and a striptease peep show!

Fourteen folk had gathered, crammed in her tiny rooms. A few men, almost all women, some youngish, others older. We ate together, talked about ordinary things. They were expecting a bald-headed monk with his face painted and ashes on his head instead of an ordinary, plain-faced, smiling, off-the-cuff evangelist. They all laughed, joked, talked together. As I stood up later on to speak in the revival rally, I saw that every one of them had come. Almost all of them gave their hearts to our Lord Jesus Christ, repented of their sins, began a new life.

FALSE SECT ALL RESCUED IN STARTLING REVIVAL

Over 20 years ago there was a well-known 'healer' in Germany, who had much success in people being cured of various types of ailments. Quite elderly, he lay on his deathbed. He had been a good Christian man, his powers he claimed came from Christ. But jokingly, as he talked to his family about the great things they had seen in healing over the years, he (unwisely) said, 'If you don't get many results when I'm gone, then call on me and I will come back and help you!'

He died and was buried. One day some months later, his wife recalled his words, and the little group began to wait quietly in a room, hands in the air, requesting his help. Strange events happened and people began to be cured again, some quite astonishingly. This group grew, and they formed eventually a society called 'The Friends of Jon Bom' and it spread over the following 20 years all over Europe.

Scores upon scores of groups have been planted and thousands of followers joined. But it had become a cult. One day last year, 25 members of one of these groups turned up at a revival meeting, seeing the advertisements, hearing of miracles, 'wanting stronger powers', they came to seek. Indeed their 'pastoral' letter encouraged them to visit churches where 'Jesus is strongly proclaimed and where healings are encouraged'. They all turned up, quietly sitting in rows, lifted their hands up, looking towards the ceiling, sometimes eyes closed, or with a glassy stare. The band struck up and nearly blew them out of their seats! It was the explosion of a bomb! They did not know what had hit them! We thought they would all walk out, but no, they stuck in there, waiting for the 'cures' to begin. I preached away at them about the 'Blood of the everlasting covenant', Christ dying for all mankind, the One who was crucified, resurrected, ascended, glorified, and now interceding for us.

When I made a challenge for people to 'weep before God, seek the one way to redemption through Christ alone by His mercy and grace', when I called upon everyone to see the 'spiritual relationship with God as more important than any physical relationship', these people rushed to the altar to repent. It was staggering: one whole cult group was getting born again! That night they changed, they found true peace, their hearts were cleansed. Their doctrine was weird, but perhaps because originally it came from a Christian minister with some truth (although it was now screwed up, off track), in deep darkness there was still hope. It took months, a whole year at least to straighten those people out, with deliverance, praying, fasting, intercessions, long hours with God's Word, putting divine truth into them. But the time spent paid off. By God's biblical proclamation, by solid doctrine, they are being changed.

ARE WE NEVER SURPRISED BY GOD?

Faith certainly has some cards up her sleeves! Just when I was tired, my finances low, the demands from all over the world to preach the gospel pressing in on me, hundreds of orphans to feed, thousands of Bibles to go to Egypt, Sudan and Mozambique, hundreds of crusades being planned across Europe, TV and radio invitations flooding in, journalists from newspapers ringing me – I went to that meeting that night, and God springs such a surprise on me – the sudden conversion of those cult members!

God is full of exciting plans for us. Those people are now bringing in dozens of their old sect followers, they are telling of Jesus everywhere. People are finding Jesus Christ weekly through this group. That church has boomeranged, and will soon have to be extending its premises! God is surely in action as we begin the new millennium!

– 25 –

IN TOUGH TIMES

A friend told me that so often, 'the walls of joy are built with the spade of sorrow'. 'Anyone signing up for the kingdom of God has to go through plenty of hard times' (Acts 14:22). Or in the NIV translation, 'We must go through many hardships to enter God's Kingdom.'

A man came to a pastor I know and was really down. 'I'm in a bad way,' he said.

The minister enquired, 'How bad?'

'So bad, all I have left in life is God!'

The pastor got excited. 'I'm so happy that all you have left is God, *that's more than enough for victory*!'

God's actions are seen in our tough days. See your Goliaths as a challenge not a problem.

One man said, 'I can't stand much more, how much longer must this trouble go on? Why this storm?' But from John the Baptist to William Tyndale, the same question and difficulties have beset believers. From the puritan Fathers to Madame Guyon, from Bunyan to Bonhoeffer, till our people in North Korea, Sudan, Iran and China today. And even closer at home in our own lives, if we are on fire, if we mean business with God, there is a fight on our hands.

Develop an excellent spirit in your tough times. The storm is better than stardom. Through the storm you are marooned but not drowned! More mature in grace, ever stronger in purpose, and faith more vital. 'Many are those who say there is no help for me; but you, O God, you are a shield, for me, the glorious lifter of my head' (Psalm 3:23).

No real satisfaction can come to anybody's life without obstacles. Jan, a church music director, had led her combined choirs and orchestra in a stirring but difficult cantata. Rehearsals had not gone well, especially for the string section. Following the performance, one of the violinists snapped at Jan angrily, 'We should have practised more for this programme so we could have done it right!'

Jan was devastated. This was, after all, a volunteer effort for a church audience. No admission was charged. Many of the musicians were not trained, but they were willing to give their talent to the Lord. They had done well, and people were uplifted.

As Jan drove home, she prayed with tears streaming down her face. Then the Lord spoke to her heart, reminding her that He accepted her efforts. This gave her peace.

Don't let unjust criticism about your ministry get you down. Keep serving Christ fervently (Romans 12:11). The Lord is pleased by service done from a willing heart and a desire to honour Him. What God knows about us is more important than what other people think about us.

If we keep doing what is right
And serving Christ each day,
We need not fear what others think
Nor what the critics say.

TURN YOUR TROUBLES FROM LOSS TO GAIN

The book *In His Steps* may have earned less money for its author than any other best-seller in history. Charles M. Sheldon wrote it in 1896, and it was first published by a religious weekly magazine. The magazine's publisher failed to meet copyright regulations, so Sheldon lost legal ownership of the book. Scores of publishers then sold millions of copies, and the author couldn't claim any royalties.

Forty years after Charles Sheldon 'lost' his book, he said, 'I am very thankful that owing to the defective copyright, the book has had a larger reading on account of the great number of publishers.'

> Although I may not understand
> The path You've laid for me,
> Complete surrender to Your will –
> Lord, this my prayer shall be.
> SHERBERT

When you grasp, you lose; when you yield to God, you gain. Vera Lynn, the great entertainer, singer, inspirer of millions during the dark days of the Second World War, used to sing a song at that time, which I remember as a small boy. It went something like this: 'When you're up to your neck in hot water, be like the kettle and sing!' Don't let the trouble get you down. De Gaulle used to say, 'Only the vanquished accept defeat.' Booker Washington wrote, 'I have learnt that success is to be measured not so much by the position one has reached in life, as by the obstacles which one has overcome while trying to succeed.' A tea bag will not release its flavour until it goes through hot water.

God brings beauty out of ugly situations. Rather than complain about the thorns on the roses, be thankful for the roses among the thorns! Turn your scars to stars! Catastrophe leads to character.

I like the sermon title of a well-known American preacher: 'What do good people do when bad things happen to them – they get better!' 'You meant it for evil; but God meant it for good' (Genesis 50:20).

G. K. Chesterton wrote, 'I like to get into hot water, it keeps me clean!'

GOD HAS MADE HIMSELF AVAILABLE

I like Overton's verse:

> There's so much now I cannot see,
> My eyesight's far too dim;
> But come what may, I'll simply trust
> And leave it all to Him.

When you are swept off your feet, slip down to your knees.

One of today's most successful corporations began in 1916 as a carpenter's shop in Denmark. When the housing market collapsed during the Great Depression, the shop was converted to manufacture toys. When the wooden toy department burned down in 1960, the company staked its future on the little interlocking plastic bricks it had been making. Today we know the company as Lego, the fifth-largest toymaker in the world, with annual sales of $1 billion.

Joseph too rose to prominence after encountering a number of calamities along the way. He was sold into slavery by his own brothers (Genesis 37:23–28), falsely accused of sexual assault and imprisoned (39:6–20), and forgotten there by a man who had promised to help him gain his release (40:6–23). In spite of all these obstacles, Joseph became second in command to Pharaoh, saved many lives (45:4–7), and freely forgave his brothers (50:19–21).

We tend to look at success and forget the difficulties and delays that preceded it. There are events we cannot control – the unfair employer, the illness or injury, the unfaithful friend. But we can choose our response.

Are you dealing with a difficult situation today? Ask God for guidance. Then leave the outcome to Him. 'Every branch that bears fruit He prunes, that it may bear more fruit' (John 15:2).

Jarvis wrote:

God has a purpose in our heartaches,
The Saviour always knows what's best;
We learn so many precious lessons
In each sorrow, trial, and test.

When Alexander Whyte (1837–1921), the great Scottish preacher, was a boy, he badly injured his arm in a threshing machine. Instead of going to a hospital for almost certain amputation, he was treated at home by a neighbour. When the boy complained of his suffering, she simply said to him, 'I like the pain. I like the pain.' She knew it was the first step to recovery.

Years later, when people complained that Whyte's sermons were too critically soul-searching, he would reply, 'I like the pain. I like the pain.' He believed that conviction of sin was needed for their spiritual healing.

Pain may be discipline from God for disobedience to His Word. But sometimes when we suffer pain, we wrongly interpret God's purpose in it. While prayerfully examining our lives to detect disobedience, we ought to consider another possible reason for our affliction. Pain may be God's pruning of our already fruitful lives to make us more spiritually productive (John 15:2).

Great faith is often built during great trials 'Endure hardship as a good soldier of Jesus Christ' (2 Timothy 2:3).

Is faith an escape?

Travel to the moon is no longer a fantasy. Human beings have walked on its surface. But years ago, when the Hayden Planetarium in New York advertised (merely in jest) that it would take reservations for that lunar trip of 240,000 miles, 18,000 people applied within a few days.

A psychologist who studied their letters concluded that most of them were eager to escape from their responsibilities and problems. One woman wrote, 'It would be heaven to get away from this busy earth ... and just go somewhere that's nice and peaceful, good, safe and secure.'

But we cannot run away from our problems. We find God's realities, God's actions, God's grace and might in trouble and testings. The German poet Goethe told a fable about a poor fisherman's crude hut. When a lighted silver lamp was placed inside, the entire cabin was transformed into silver – the flooring, the logs that formed the walls, the roof, even the furniture.

This is a beautiful picture of what happens in a home when the Lord Jesus is allowed to reign supreme. Where bitterness, hatred, and ill will once prevailed, now the brightness of His holiness and the warmth of His love are enthroned. Out of the rough comes smooth; out of the bitter comes the sweet.

Silencing the preachers

More and more Full Gospel preachers are being arrested in western countries for preaching the gospel. Fourteen young evangelists were recently grabbed and bundled into a black Maria in Bradford after conducting street open air services. My son was arrested in London for standing in the street proclaiming in a sane, quiet, clear way the gospel message. The judge later cleared him.

Roland Parson, the famous Gloucester 'city preacher', has been featured many times in the county papers for his fearsome gospel preaching. He is again being charged by the Gloucester constabulary – what for? For reading a passage of the Bible without an amplifier or loudspeaker, in the city centre there! This is the home city of Rakes, who pioneered Sunday schools, of Tyndale, who translated the Bible into English, of George Whitefield, the great revivalist.

Now in the 1990s and at the start of the twenty-first century, the Christian tradition is being banned, and the

British police are rigorously enforcing against religious freedom.

Freddy Galliochan, who was charged with a £20,000 fine in Bristol, refused to back down, but received overwhelming support from the general public. There was such great interest, the world-wide media services and programmes featured it, BBC, ITV, America's NBC, Canada, Australia, Sky TV, all the national newspapers, the age-old right of Christians to be able to preach Christ publicly. I know Freddy and his family, they sang at my crusades a few years ago, they have been on holiday Bible weeks we have run. Their characters are good, sound, sane, godly, but they were under vicious attack by the Bristol City Council. We fought hard with petitions, letters, prayer, media presentation, and finally the Council withdrew at the last court appearance, even giving some money for Freddy's legal costs. But it was a hell of a fight for five months! Some might say – what's the use, all the stress? It's no good!

Over 70 years ago Murray Spangler was stricken with asthma. He had to give up his work as an engineer and took a job as a janitor. But the dusting and cleaning brought on more spasms. He knew he had to find some way of cutting down the dust which was aggravating his asthma.

He found a small electric motor, and with a wooden box, length of hose and a broom handle, he rigged up a floor cleaner that sucked up the dust. He took this odd-looking gadget to a friend called Hoover, and they started to manufacture the vacuum cleaners which have been a boon to households all over the world.

Spangler died quite young – from asthma – but I like to think that he lived to see something of the blessing he brought to millions of homes. Out of loss and trouble and a hopeless position came a blessing to the world.

God was on the scene! God was in charge.

I suppose most of us have periods when worries tend to keep us awake at night. When I have that experience I try to remember the American Bishop, William Quayle, who said that one night when he was pacing his bedroom, worried and sleepless, God said to him, 'Quayle, you go to bed. I'll sit up the rest of the night!'

Whimsical? Slightly irreverent, even? Well, perhaps so. But what a great point it makes ... the God who 'shall neither slumber nor sleep', who 'guardeth our sleeping and our waking', will watch over us. What lessons we can learn from this, with our daily stresses, to learn to appreciate and understand the God who guards and takes care of our highest interests.

I love the story of Jonah. He is my favourite evangelist. In my own crusades I have seen 10–15 per cent of Irish and some English towns turn out to attend my gospel miracle healing crusades. In some border towns along the Irish Republic with the North of Ireland, sometimes 60 per cent of the population have come to hear the gospel and be healed of their sicknesses and diseases.

But Jonah was the most successful of all time. He had failed, but God gave him a second chance, and he won 100 per cent of the city of Nineveh to God. What a revival! I thought I had seen revival, 60 per cent of a town hearing the gospel, but this man wins every child, boy, girl, old person, sick and healthy, young and old, black and white, every man and woman and family, the entire city, was won to God, to faith, to the Ten Commandments! What a ministry! What a visitation of God!

Jonah Chapter 3 tells us: God gives us a second chance (v. 4), 'and the word of the Lord came to Jonah the second time'. How much easier it is to answer His call first time (v. 2), 'Arise, go unto Nineveh ... preach unto it ... [what] I have bid Thee'. He goes through the streets calling on them, but he is not changed in his heart, there is no mercy in his voice (4:1–3). The ordinary people flocked to him; they repented first, then the high-ups. (This has always been so – I have found, like our Lord, 'the common people heard Him gladly'.) Here is a miracle of the ages, a whole city turns to God in a day. Think of Birmingham repenting and finding Christ in one 24 hours of preaching. Staggering!

There is universal fasting, mourning, weeping, crying to God, even the King mourns, there is a royal proclamation, fasting commanded nationally, a petition to God for the nation, hope is declared ... what a successful evangelist! I have seen whole towns shaken, the Maoris received me, leading citizens attending my preaching, vast crowds, sometimes 10–15 per cent of the town came out to hear the gospel, the largest auditorium packed, thousands saved ... yet I have never seen a whole city repent in a few hours, and a whole nation move towards God in a day or two (vv. 5–9).

GOD RESPONDS

Genuine repentance secures remission of judgement and hope and peace for hundreds of thousands of people. Every day God puts off the judgement of the nations. He gives a further breathing space to repent, yet churches are cold hearted, there is little passion for soul winning in the hearts of many ministers and Christian people, many sleep as the Devil makes hay of the poor, lost world.

We must shake ourselves. The Church has failed. False religions and cults, materialistic gods, occultish powers are at the gates, *O Zion awake* ... evangelize, repent, win the lost, you have lost your first love, restore yourself, seek the Lord, return unto His Holiness ... change your ways.

It is unbearable almost to see a child of God lose their abundant joy, excitement for Christ; their enthusiasm abates, fear increases, hope vanishes, they soon become moody, sulky, petty, small-minded. It is terrible when a servant of God loses his hope, his joy becomes merely professional and he becomes bitter. As President Theodore Roosevelt said, 'The poorest way to face life is with a sneer.' How much better to keep a sense of wonder of the calling and responsibility and a real feeling of the glory of the Lord. Like King Lear in Shakespeare's play: 'I shall do great things ... they shall be the wonder of the earth.' Let us have hope, possessiveness, wonder at our calling as preachers, laymen, church workers, elders, deacons, the mighty ministry committed to us. As a mayor who was welcoming me to a certain suburb of London a few years ago for a large crusade said, 'It must be an awful responsibility to take your message to all those people out there.' She had it right.

Have you forgotten love? On his eightieth birthday, Bertrand Russell told us what it was. He said, 'The root of the matter is a very simple, old-fashioned thing ... the thing I mean – please forgive me for mentioning it – is love, Christian love.' He added, 'If you love, you have a motive for existence, a reason for courage, an imperative necessity for intellectual honesty.'

Christ himself said it long before Bertrand Russell: 'Love God – and your neighbour as yourself.' If only many had known the verse. *Don't you forget it*!

> If you can mend a broken heart,
> Now full of care – run, mend it!
> If you can lend a helping hand
> Sometime, somewhere, please lend it.
> If you've a worthwhile job to do,
> Scorn all delay, and do it,
> For those who might have served but failed
> Will come one day to rue it.

When Jonah was running away from God, God showed He cared! He had prepared a big fish to save Jonah, He prepared a large gourd, a tree-like plant to protect him, He prepared a worm to remove it when He wants to guide him out of his misery into a blessed place, He prepares a wind to aid him.

Sir William Osler, the famous Canadian physician and professor of medicine, always had his lectures crowded with students eager to share his skill and knowledge. But one of them, who later became a prominent physician, said that the greatest lesson he ever learned from Osler was from the opening words of one of his lectures: 'Gentlemen,' he said, 'the first requisite in the care of a patient is to care!'

God cares for us His people. A church in the south of England, very close to revival, confessed that their congregation had been uncaring, flippant and unloving for years. A young woman attending their church committed suicide; she left a note found near her body at the bottom of the cliffs, 'Nobody cares'. She was pregnant and unmarried. This drove the church into prayer, gathering together and weeping and asking themselves – do we care? God broke them down, they responded with contrition. Today they are one of the kindest, most caring, warmest, most effective churches in the whole of the UK.

Dr Clyde Narramore said, 'Everyone is worth understanding and caring for.'

GOD CARES

Jonah faints and desires to die ... God vindicates himself and spares the city of Nineveh. His words are touching: 'I feel sorry for Nineveh and its 120,000 people under utter darkness' (4:10 *Living Bible*). What an amazing, marvellous, personal God we have. That is the miracle of the book of Jonah. We see the Church calling today in this small, but influential and heart-touching book. We see a God acting miraculously.

Jonah was brought low but taken high! When you have been through it, failed, fallen, weak, disobedient, critical, lazy, boneless, apathetic, *then let God wake you up*!

We see:

- Jonah was called to world mission – so is the Church failing in this task.
- Jonah refused to fulfil his calling – so is the Church failing in this task.
- Jonah was punished by falling into the sea – the Church has been scattered, persecuted, scandalized in and by the world.
- Jonah was preserved although undeserving – the Church has been miraculously preserved, although totally unworthy.
- Jonah repented and was restored – the Church needs and is begging to be restored – it needs more brokenness and repentance today.
- Jonah, obedient to God, went on his calling to witness – the Church is returning gradually to this task, although many Christians are still slack and indolent.
- Jonah was blessed in Nineveh and it was brought to God's salvation – the Church will be blessed in the last days in bringing the gospel to the whole world (although not all will receive it) – and the earth will be filled with the Glory of God.

At church we sang that great hymn of triumph, 'Crown Him with many crowns'. As we sang I couldn't help thinking of a boy born 180 years ago who loved to sing. His name was George Elvey. He lived in Canterbury, where he and his brother were in the cathedral choir.

Nothing thrilled George so much as the wondrous music that pealed forth from the great pipe organ. Perhaps it was as he sat listening to it that he made up his mind he would one day be a great organist. Such were his gifts that, by the time he was 19, Queen Victoria appointed him to the Royal Chapel at Windsor Castle.

Yet, despite his shining success, George's life was almost unbelievably tragic. He lost his young wife after 15 happy years. He married again, and nine years later his second wife died. Then his beloved son, a young man of 24, died – and, as if all this was not enough, his third wife also died.

How strange it is that George, who knew so much sorrow, should have given us one of the most victorious and joyful of tunes – for it was he who wrote the matchless music for the verses we sang:

Crown Him with many crowns,
The Lamb upon the throne;
Hark, how the heavenly anthem drowns
All music but its own...

The old verse says:

The going's never easy when one has secret fears,
It's hard beyond all telling to hold back scalding tears.
But how the *gallant spirit* sings
If we can smile at bitter things.

Years ago, Mr and Mrs Robert Simpson of Grangemouth, learned that their only boy, Robbie, would never be able to leave his bed. What suffering – he was only a lad of 10, and you can understand the heartache this verdict meant to his parents. But they made up their minds his life should be as full and happy as they could possibly make it.

One difficulty was that his bedroom had to be upstairs and there were times when Robbie felt cut off from the family life in the kitchen just below – lonely, sad, hurt. Then Mr Simpson cut a hole in Robbie's bedroom floor and fitted a pane of glass into it, and now Robbie can see into the kitchen and when his father and mother are having their meals he almost feels he's at the table too. At night, if his own room is in darkness, the light from the kitchen shines up by the side of his bed. Great suffering, but great comfort. It was a simple idea – yet what a blessing to Robbie, whose life is bounded by four walls, but whose interest never flags from morning to night.

There is always a way through. God always wants to lift the strain of work for us!

As soon as he graduated from university, Dr John Smith sailed for Africa as a missionary. For years he laboured among the people, wearing himself out in their service. Then he fell ill. 'You must give up your work and return home at once,' the doctor said. 'If you don't, you'll be dead within six months.'

Sadly, John Smith packed his bags, bade farewell to his friends, and sailed out to the liner waiting in the bay. He turned for a last look back – and, lining the shore, he saw hundreds of black faces, tears running down their cheeks.

For a long moment he gazed at them. Then he turned to the captain and said, 'I'm sorry. I won't be going with you. I must stay here.'

Six months later the Africans were weeping again as they laid their beloved friend to rest and placed a wooden cross over his grave which bore these words: 'Greater love hath no man than this...' Can we ever rest with the example of men like John Smith to challenge us? What pure, sacrificing love.

GOD IN CHARGE

He does not have to explain everything to us, why this happens, why this is done, why that tragedy was not averted. He is a God of wonders, a many splendoured Lord, who reigns, who knows all things. If we knew everything about Him, as the old Welsh evangelist Howell Harris used to say, 'We would be God'. It is good that there are mysteries. If it was rational and could be explained, what point God, the wonder, awe, mystery, 'the hidden things of God', Scripture calls them?

Job 1:15–19 tells us, 'The fire of God is fallen ... there came a great wind and smote ... the house ... and it fell on the young men and they died...' Remember God initiated the whole drama, He was in charge. There are many tragedies. God does not send them all, many are from man's evil, natural disasters, human errors – the Sudan famine, the Bangladesh floods, the London bombs, Dunblane, cruel hijacks, the IRA murders, the rape and killing of little children. God seems to get the blame for it all, instead of the real culprit, the evil one who has caused all the chaos.

The Devil's one ambition is to undermine our confidence in God's promises and will and Word; he wants to turn us away from the Living God. He strikes hard at the holiest and best of the believers. Through holding on, walking in faith and victory, untold millions can be blessed. God wants to bring you through the afflictions, heal you, He can, He will, He is able to do all things. Sometimes He gives folk great grace.

We need to learn to listen. A teenager said that her parents never had time to sit and listen for a few minutes – how sad! Solomon said, 'To draw near and listen is better than ... sacrifice' (Ecclesiastes 5:1 RSV). Pascal said that 'all men's miseries derive from not being able to sit still in a room quietly and listen.'

I remember as a small boy crouching in the darkness of our little cottage in Chippenham, Wiltshire, lit by the dim gaslight and the warm coal fire. Bombers thundered overhead; I would only have been about three or four years old, crouching around the old wireless, crackling and almost inaudible. Mum said (Father was away in the war), 'Listen carefully, my son,' and after some time an oldish, growling voice came through, as I put my ear to the wireless: 'We shall fight on the beaches, we shall fight on the landing grounds, we shall fight ... in the streets ... we shall never surrender...' I listened to a voice I will not forget, the voice of a great man, Winston Churchill.

Listen to God. You will never forget what He says – no matter what the critics say, no matter what the 'Job's comforters' say.

GOD CAN ACT

Faith may come with the spring flowers, but faith comes too when the wind howls and it is cold. Faith may come when our world is collapsing and the prospects seem dreary. It is strange, but true, that at those very times we can still sing,

> Then with my waking thoughts
> Bright with Thy praise,
> Out of my stony griefs
> Bethel I'll raise,
> So by my woes to be
> Nearer, my God, to Thee,
> Nearer to Thee!

A neighbour was telling the cynic and I about her son, Frank, who left school a few months ago. 'He's got a job at the printing works,' she said with just a touch of pardonable pride, 'and they seem to like him very much – but, of course, he's a nice boy, although I say it myself. He's so fond of his job that he often gets to work before time, and he went back after only half an hour for dinner last Thursday – there was something wrong with a machine and he wanted to see it taken to pieces, you know ... he's awfully keen.'

The cynic nodded his head. 'He'll soon learn it doesn't pay to make a fool of yourself that way.'

How sorry I felt for that middle-aged, disillusioned man with a sneer.

TALK TO GOD

The next time you feel down, don't hide those feelings. Do as Job did, and talk to God about them. 'Why are you downcast, O my soul? Why so disturbed within me? Put your hope in God, for I will yet praise Him, my

Saviour and my God' (Psalm 42:5 NIV). The old-fashioned saying goes, 'The answer to prayer is already on its way when we say, "Please, God, help me to answer my own prayers."'

I have just been re-reading one of H. V. Morton's famous travel books, *In Search of Ireland*. 'Then, as they parted at the gates of the monastery the lay-brother said, "Pray for me tonight and I will pray for you. If all the world did that how different it might be."'

It is said that when Stanley Baldwin was elected Prime Minister, his friends gathered round to congratulate him, but he said to them quietly, 'It is not your congratulations I need, but your prayers.'

After a snowstorm that closed all the local schools, the teacher asked one small boy if he had used his time constructively while he had been off. 'Yes, Miss,' he replied. 'I prayed for more snow.'

Five-year-old Philip was travelling with his mother in a car when it broke down. Mum got out and examined the engine, then got back in to try it again. She found Philip with his eyes shut, deep in prayer, and was just in time to overhear him say, 'Please God, help Mum to start this car and if You can't come, send my Dad.'

I am happy to tell you that the car started without any more bother, so Dad was not needed after all! Some think God cannot do it Himself. *Pray – do your best – and leave the rest with God.*

In the times when the Bible was written, people had a severe idea of God. In those days, as many still think today, people believed that all suffering was God punishing sin – 'Who ever perished being innocent?' (Job 4:7). God rightly answers this with outstandingly powerful words. James said, 'Count it all joy when ye fall into temptation, knowing this, that the trying of your faith worketh patience' (James 1:2,3).

Our whole life is to please God and glorify Him. Even Jesus set this example: 'even Christ pleased not Himself' (Romans 15:3).

The Westminster Confession tells us that the 'chief aim of man is to glory God'. Jesus came to glorify the Father. Out of Job's sufferings this happened too. God dealt with Job.

1. He was broken (17:11).
2. He was melted (23:10).
3. He was softened (19:21 and 23:16) – 'God maketh my heart soft'.

God broke him down. We used to sing when I was a boy in the Salvation Army,

Spirit of the Living God,
fall afresh on me,
melt me, mould me,
break me, fill me...
Spirit of the Living God,
fall afresh on me.

God said to Job, 'I will lay my hands on thy mouth.' Job, finally yielding, cries, 'I uttered ... things too wonderful for me ... now mine eyes hath seen Thee ... I abhor myself and repent in the dust' (Job 42:3–6). He is broken but triumphant.

The fact that God let him suffer does not mean

dereliction: Jesus suffered alone in Gethsemane and on the Cross, but He did not sin. 'God will not cast away a perfect man.' In other words, if you're good, you only ever have good in your life all the way through. If you're bad it will be all bad. This is not righteous. The Word says that God let Jesus suffer all the way to the Cross, yet He was the perfect man! There *is* suffering in this life. But *God has given us the way to stand it and rise above it.*

Walking home one afternoon with a minister, I happened to look up at a row of TV aerials. On one aerial sat no fewer than seven little birds. The minister remarked, 'That reminds me of a little sermon I found one very windy day. I noticed a TV aerial that was evidently coming adrift. What amused me was the little bird sitting on the horizontal bar ... rather enjoying himself as he swayed. And then, even as I watched, the aerial swung back and crashed down on the roof.'

'And the little bird?' I asked quickly.

'When the aerial fell he just spread his wings and flew off safely. And that's where I got the theme of my sermon. When storms assail us, you and I are bound to fall unless we, too, can spread our wings – the wings of faith – and rise triumphant over all our troubles.'

Job 9:32,33 says, 'There is no umpire between us, who might lay his hand upon us both.' Job looks for an umpire, a mediator, a friend who is true, but cannot find any: they are tainted with the easy-going, black-and-white theology of the age, and that aspiration was only finally met in the one mediator between God and man ... who came later, the man Christ Jesus. *If we have great need of Christ, we have a great Christ to meet our needs.* He is our true friend, the faithful one, who sticks closer than a brother.

Calvin said, 'Afflictions ought always to be estimated by their end.' When the trials are over you will assess and see what you have learned. You will soon see you have learned far more through the trial than through the easy, soft, comfortable times. Job says, 'My soul is weary of my life.'

Out of the worst times and experiences can come so much good. I know of a businessman who went bankrupt in the recession of the 1980s. The experience really flattened him, but it brought him into contact with so many other people in business who had gone under, some to suicide, nervous breakdown, home and family collapse, etc. He wondered and thought, 'Something must be done to salvage such brains, potential and fine, unique men and women.' Gradually he found opportunities presenting themselves to assist and help such people in financial disasters and trouble, and he became known as a good counsellor to such need. Today he has an outstanding agency, counselling and encouraging work for business people, that is in great demand. Out of bitterness came sweetness and demonstrated Job's experience; good came out of ill. As Paul put it later in Romans 8:28, 'We know in everything God works for good, with those who love Him, who are called to His purpose.' Charles de Gaulle said, 'Difficulties attract the man of character because ... in it he realizes himself.'

Our glorious God

In Job Chapter 12, what magnificent pictures are painted here, the whole earth, sky and creation, speaks of the awe and wonder of our God. '...birds and animals ... the creatures of earth and sea ... It is God who directs the lives of His creatures, God has insight and power to act ... drought comes when God withholds rain ... floods when he turns water loose, God is strong and always victorious ... He takes away the wisdom of rulers ... dethrones Kings and makes them prisoner ... humbles priests ... He silences men ... He disgraces those in power ... He sends light to places of darkness ... He makes nations strong and then defeats them ... a God who is totally in charge and all-powerful in every direction...' (Job 12:7–10 and 13:22, GNB).

In one of her books, Rita F. Snowden tells of a visit she paid to a tiny village school in the Yorkshire Dales, where she was able to examine the school's logbook going back for nearly 100 years.

Fascinated, she turned over the pages, reading about the children, their activities, the books they read and poems they learned, the weather, visits into the surrounding countryside, and much else besides. Then came a change of teacher, and over and over again the pages simply bore the words, 'Nothing worthy of notice this week.' But of course, it couldn't be true. It wasn't that nothing happened. It was that the teacher didn't notice it!

It is sad what so many miss in this world in which God is so glorious, filled with such diversities, changes, a world of great wonders. Einstein said, 'He who can no longer wonder and stand in rapt awe is as good as dead.' James Watt sat as a boy watching his mother's kettle boil and in that wonder the miracle of locomotion was born. One poet put wonder and change in this way:

Yesterday the twig was brown and bare
Today the glint of green is there
Tomorrow will be leaflets spare...
I wonder what will next be there?

The Christian faith is full of wonder. Once that sense of glory is gone, all is lost. St Francis walked starry-eyed all his days and lifted multitudes of the poor – he saw it as a gift to God. For the modern missionary teaching the primitive tribal people in the New Guinea highlands, or the Amazon Basin, filled with love, gripped by a sense of wonder, everything about the Christian life has a glow of awe. The early disciples learned this as they met the Risen Christ: 'they yet believed not for joy and wondered' (Luke 24:41).

I love God's wonder in a child; it is sometimes exciting, to have a glimpse, however brief, into a child's world. I have just heard of a little girl who told her equally tiny friend next door, 'It's Mum's birthday. She's 26.'

'Gosh,' exclaimed the little friend. 'She's getting old!'

'She sure is,' agreed the girl. 'And do you know, she can still ride a bicycle!'

I remember standing at the grave of the great Welsh writer and poet Dylan Thomas at Laughan cemetery near Carmarthen, West Wales. The agnostic, of course, did not have assurance of the next life. He wrote of death, 'Do not go gently into that dark night' – in other words, fight it, cry, curse it. I have to laugh. Thousands visit the grave, including multitudes of Americans in the summer; the path is worn thin to the brown earth, where folks go and stand and read his poetry at the simple white wooden cross on the hillside. But straight behind there is a large white stone in memory of a Christian, who no doubt had purchased the ground just after, and when he died he made sure the large stone was put up with a huge text on it. Job's words here are a witness to the tens of thousands who have stood at that place through the years and to millions through the centuries: the words on the stone are from Job 19:25: 'FOR I KNOW THAT MY REDEEMER LIVETH.'

One day Elihu comes to Job; he perhaps gives some spiritual advice, he cannot be numbered with the faint-hearted, weak, spiritually deceived comforters – he is different. He advises, 'O Job, stand still and consider the wondrous works of God' (37:14).

I always set off for my services very early, arriving often one hour or more before the meeting starts. I want to sit and be still, ready in the quietness to hear God's voice. Walk in the country, read a book quietly in your armchair, head off out of the office into a quiet corner and meditate, or to that favourite little corner café for the hot chocolate, crumpet and cheese! Sit in the garden with the dahlias, daffodils, the pansies, the green grass, the rich colours. I love to lie on Roundway down on the edge of Salisbury Plain and rest awhile, watch the birds, the scenes of nestling, peaceful Wiltshire villages miles across the magnificent terrain.

It is good just as Elihu suggested to *stand still* ... in this modern life of noise, hurry, harassed by crowds, trapped in the vortex of rushed living, to bring our fragmented minds and be still. Recently I was trying to find my way to a certain church in Nottingham when, as the dusk came down, I saw a jogger coming along the road. I hailed him, he stopped and was most helpful giving me directions and showing me the way, but I noticed he was still jogging – although stationary he was still moving his legs even in his standing position and I realized how hard it is to stop! People seem to have no time for anything worthwhile today. Kleiser put it in his famous verse,

> Hadn't time to sing a song
> Hadn't time to right a wrong
> Hadn't time to send a gift
> Hadn't time to practise thrift
> Hadn't time to see a joke
> Hadn't time to see his folk
> Hadn't time to study poise
> Hadn't time to repress noise
> Hadn't time to lend or give
> Hadn't time to really live
> Hadn't time to read this verse
> Hadn't time ... he's in a hearse
> HE'S DEAD!

The Psalmist said, 'I have quietened myself' (Psalm 131:2). I like Faber's words:

Only to sit and think of God
Oh what joy it is!
To think the thought, to breathe the Name
Earth has no higher bliss!

'For my thoughts are not your thoughts, neither are your ways my ways', declares the Lord. 'As the heavens are higher than the earth, so are my ways higher than your ways and my thoughts than your thoughts' (Isaiah 55:8,9 NIV).

The old proverbs say: 'Don't give up when the clouds surround you. It can be a sign that you're climbing higher.' 'When you come to the end of your tether, remember that God is at the other end.'

The toughest circumstances and experiences can work out for the best. It is there so often we meet God, prove Him at His greatest, as Spurgeon said: 'God gets His best soldiers out of the highlands of affliction.'

Job 42:1–6 tells how Job had demanded to meet God face to face so that he could argue his case (23:3–7) – but now that he meets Him, he humbly repents and acknowledges that had he known what he was talking about, he would never have presumed to question the ways of the Almighty. His conclusion is that if God does not work in the way that Job thinks He ought to, then there is a good and just reason for it – even though it may be hidden from Job's understanding. The God who was such a delightful reality to Job in the days of his prosperity had not ceased to be. Job realized that the Almighty, though unseen, unfelt and unrecognized, and veiled by tragedy, still cared for him. This conviction brings him through the fog of confusion to renewed confidence. How vital it is to turn heartbreak and sorrow to joy, to look at it in positive faith, humorously.

A friend was telling me about a break-in which had taken place at an old lady's house. She lived all alone. Not long ago she had a small shop. When she gave up business, the tale was that she had sold out for a big price. It was probably because of this rumour that her place was burgled. My friend went along the very next morning to express his sympathy and offer any help he could. To his astonishment he found this 'unfortunate' lady simply doubled up with laughter. 'What's so funny about this?' he asked.

'Do you remember,' she answered, 'how I always told people that I didn't have any money, and how nobody would believe me?'

'That's very true,' he said.

'Well,' she told him, 'at least there's someone who believes me now!'

Job 42:7–17 describes how Job's trials are now over and Satan has lost a battle (later through Christ, he was to lose the war!). Job's full restoration begins when he turns from focusing on his own troubles and problems to intercede for his friends. His acquaintances, friends and family gather around and give him comfort and consolation, but the greatest blessings come directly from God. The Lord's blessing upon Job is even greater than he knew in the earlier part of his life, and he is blessed with 10 children (seven sons and three daughters), a tremendous amount of livestock, and he lives for another 140 years. Job died at a ripe old age, full of joy and honour. He received healing and prosperity – seven times more than he had before!

PRAY FOR OTHERS, FORGET YOURSELF

Why was it that when Job prayed for his friends, God suddenly turned the spiritual tide in his favour? Some think Job was angry with his friends, and the moment he gave up his anger, God was able to move mightily in his life. Are you angry with anyone today? Then pray for that person – now.

At one of the first meetings of the newly elected Senate of the United States, a boy called Johnny Jones was present, accompanied by his father. From his place in the gallery, Johnny observed an elderly man rise before the opening of the session. Pointing him out to Johnny, his father explained that he was the Chaplain.

'Oh,' said the boy. 'He prays for the Senate, doesn't he?'

'Well, no,' replied his father, 'not exactly. He gets up, has a good look at the Senate, and after that he turns round and prays for the country!'

Learn to pray – sincerely – for others! The old Scottish verse goes:

Nobody knows what a prayer can do
When somebody, somewhere, prays for you ...
Clearing a path through the tangled track,
Easing the strain on the breaking back.
When hope fades away and is lost to view –
Nobody knows what a prayer will do.

During a Gentlemen versus Players cricket match some years ago, batsman Peter Parfitt was caught out by the Rev. David Sheppard, now Bishop of Liverpool, who was then a member of the England team. Returning to the dressing room, the batsman apologized to his captain, Freddie Trueman.

'That's all right, Peter,' declared Freddie. 'When the Reverend puts his two hands together, he stands a better chance than most of us!'

The angels are dumbfounded that we pray so little – we can change the destiny of nations by *our* prayers. The one who prays is one million light years ahead of the one who does not *believe* in prayer.

The God of power acts for those who have learnt to pray through the tough, hard times. I pray on trains, in cars, usually laid out on the back seat while my assistant evangelist drives the car hundreds of miles up and down Britain's motorways to our crusades. I pray on planes – in fact, it's one of the most successful prayer-places, on a jumbo jet at 30,000 feet. Especially over India in a tornado, when the great aircraft drops a mile in 10 seconds. Everyone wants to repent – I have 300 instant converts on my hands! When I boarded the plane, no one was interested in my prayers, but when it hits that tornado and falls out of the sky, I'm the most successful evangelist since Jonah: everyone wants to repent – the whole lot want to start praying!

I pray all night sometimes; I fast and pray for days on end; I pray on my bike when riding in the country; I pray when I'm jogging over the Wiltshire plain; I pray when I'm happy; I pray when I'm sad; I pray when I don't feel a thing!

PRAYER MOVES GOD'S HAND

Prayer moves the hand that moves the world. 'I have seen the affliction of my people and heard their cry' (Exodus 3:7,8). 'He feared and sought the Lord, and set a fast, and they gathered to ask help of the Lord, even out of all the cities, they came to seek the Lord' (2 Chronicles 20:1–4).

I urge you to pray till the Devil has a nervous breakdown! Prayer brings us close to God's heart. Prayer makes us hear His heartbeat. It exposes the darkness and dangers that may await us.

Prayer is a mind full of rich minerals. If we don't pray, we can't tap that mineral resource. Prayer is unruffled by storms. Prayer is the mother of a thousand blessings. Prayer results in supernatural breakthrough.

Jesus prayed in the morning hour, at noon, in the evening. *Prayer will help you to win*. Every new move I have experienced, every new step, every new venture, is by prayer.

Through our personal loss, disasters, tough times, discouragements, setbacks, heartaches, griefs, upsets – can come more prayer, more consecration, more love, more wonder, more waiting upon God, more challenges – and as a result more victories for us and for our beloved, precious Lord and God.

With prayer, we are filling the land with the glory of God.

– 26 –

HEROIN ADDICTS FIND NEW LIFE

David and Philip recently worked with me in a thriving church near Anfield football ground in Liverpool. Both are only barely two and a half years old spiritually, before that they lived on the street, homeless, high on drugs. They were criminals well known to the police and courts in the Wigan/Lancashire area. David spent 10 years in and out of prison, having been brought up as a child in a dozen foster homes. He was crying out for love, broken, lost at the bottom of the scrapheap, when he was delivered in a moment in a great gospel crusade in Wigan town. He was washed, redeemed, reborn, totally rehabilitated. David and Philip have both now been through Bible School and have come into the ministry as preachers. They are mighty miracles showing God in action, helping broken humanity. What a wonderful Lord!

GETTING CHANGED AND STAYING CHANGED

Micah the prophet said, 'I am filled with the spirit of the Lord to declare with power justice, righteousness...' Sometimes oppositions build up when revival fire comes. Often we experience antipathy, misunderstanding, direct counter-attacks, as we are granted the workings of God.

Roger Forster has said, 'The warfaring church is not always a respectable church.' Jesus said, 'Beware when all men speak well of you.'

Paul spoke of the 'fellowship of his sufferings', and again, 'I know how to be abased'. God works and the Devil works. God moves and all hell is shaken. Give the Devil a hard time and he will hit back. God's actions and movings cause many currents.

I had a very good friend in a Third World country, a Rhodes Scholar, an absolutely brilliant man. He was the pastor of the largest church of his denomination. I remember he once debated with a leading political figure on national television on the issue of legalized lotteries and gambling. He totally routed him. It was a national humiliation for that dignitary. My young pastor friend was particularly concerned that the people of his homeland were not listening to the Word of the Lord. As long as he told them what they wanted to hear it was great. As long as he preached that all was good and bright, that they would be prosperous and peaceful, that was super. But the young pastor was convinced that things were bad in his country and something needed to be done about it. People needed to be brought to repentance and to take God seriously.

He felt as if he had been hammering his head against a brick wall. So one day he came into church late for the Sunday morning service, to get the people's attention. He came in the back door instead of the front. That also aroused their attention. Instead of wearing his pulpit gown, he dressed himself in sackcloth and covered himself with ashes. Instead of carrying a Bible he carried a bell, and he came in ringing it. As a result, they fired him as their pastor and put him in a home for the mentally unstable. One day I talked to him and asked, 'Did you have a nervous breakdown?'

'No,' he said. 'They decided that was what I had, but in actual fact I was trying hard to get their attention. I got it,' he went on, 'and when they gave me their full attention, they locked me up. They didn't want to know.'

Such has always been the lot of the prophet. The person who tells people what is really happening in the world is not always welcome. Indeed, as Jesus said, 'A prophet is not without honour, *but* in his own country...'

Act with God – and they will call you mad or glad! It's not suffering *or* victory. No, it's *victory through suffering*! It's Calvary Blood that is our power. After a night of true miracles, healings, conversions, a worldly-wise newspaper man asked me, 'Where is this power from?' I replied, 'It's the red bleeding hands of the cruci-fied but now risen Son of God.'

A noted preacher, J. J. Hall, put it, 'The church has permitted its message to be filtered through the sieve of worldly glory.' The true power of our faith is power that the world calls weakness, and the victory of our faith is victory that the world calls failure.

The Christ we profess to follow was made 'perfect through suffering' (Hebrews 2:10). We prefer to be made perfect through success. But grace will not do for us what it did not do for Christ – exempt us from suffering. Jesus was brutally honest. He never left His followers in doubt as to what awaited them; He did not dazzle them with promises of riches and honour and power. Rather, He spoke of carrying a cross and denying self, of persecution and ridicule, of losing in order to find, of dying in order to live. In short, He never promised them a rose garden.

Let's listen to Jesus as He renews His call to Simon Peter in John 21. The resurrected Lord has dined with His disciples on bread and fish that He Himself prepared. After dinner Jesus invites Peter to take a walk with Him. As they walk, Jesus suddenly says, 'Simon son of John, do you truly love me more than these?' (v. 15).

And Peter answers, 'Yes, Lord ... You know that I love you.'

Jesus said, 'Feed my lambs' (v. 15).

This is done three times and then Jesus gets to the bottom line: 'I tell you the truth,' He says to Peter, 'when you were younger you dressed yourself and went where you wanted; but when you are old you will stretch out your hands, and someone else will dress you and lead you to where you do not want to go' (v. 18).

He said this, John tells us, 'to indicate the kind of death by which Peter would glorify God' (v. 19).

And then, after describing what will happen if Peter follows Jesus, the Lord says, 'Follow me!'

But that's a poor sales pitch and bad psychology. Jesus could have said, 'Peter, if you follow me you will become famous, you will preach the Pentecostal sermon, you'll write part of the Bible, and a lot of people will call you the first pope.' Now *that's* a sales pitch. But the only thing Jesus promised was a martyr's death.

Several years ago a denomination revised its hymn book, putting in some new songs and taking out some old ones. And they took out one of my all-time favourites: 'Jesus, I My Cross Have Taken'. Are you familiar with it? The first verse goes like this:

Jesus, I my cross have taken,
All to leave and follow Thee;
Destitute, despised, forsaken,
Thou from hence my all shalt be:
Perish every fond ambition,
All I've sought, and hoped and known;
Yet how rich is my condition,
God and heav'n are still my own.

And it has other verses, too, with phrases like 'Let the world despise and leave me', and 'Foes may hate and friends may shun me'.

I sought out a member of the review board and asked him why they removed that hymn. His answer?

'We felt that it portrayed a poor self-image and might contribute to a low self-esteem.' In other words, it's bad psychology. But listen to this: 'I consider that our present sufferings are not worth comparing with the glory that will be revealed in us' (Paul, Romans 8:18 NIV).

The story goes of a preacher who commenced his ministry in a new church. He spoke one Sunday morning on 'the dangers of smoking'. After the sermon a head deacon came and challenged the preacher by telling him that one-third of the congregation smoked. 'This will greatly offend them!'

The following week he spoke on 'the dangers of gambling', and the deacon came again after the service and told him that this would not do, as 25 per cent of the congregation were racing horse breeders.

The next Sunday came and he spoke on 'the dangers of alcohol abuse', and again the deacon came frantically upon him, pointing out that another quarter of the church members were hop-growers, and lived from the sale of alcohol!

Finally, on the fourth Sunday he found a subject that pleased everyone: he gave them 'the dangers of deep-sea fishing in Atlantic waters'! All was very peaceful. But do not compromise your message like this, *or you will finish with no message at all*!

Cost, sacrifice, challenge, suffering, opposition, are always my lot through the years, as I have gone in faith to see God's glorious movings. I have found that the way of God's actions, of revival, of Holy Spirit manifestation, of great conversions, noted church growth, of miracles that stir cities and nations, costs everything. It's a pathway of suffering at times. It's no easy road.

I like the Bishop's words to King Richard III in William Shakespeare's play: 'Those who stand high hath many blasts to shake them.' When we come to Christ, we have a great transformation in our experience and there is a watershed in our life. Nothing so worthwhile as this, nothing so real, such a prize of life, so rich as this discovery of divine life, nothing like this can be achieved without its costs and responsibilities. *Great grace, great love – great demands*!

The challenges will be varied, the road not always smooth. David, the ex-addict and criminal, is not finding it easy studying for the ministry. He thought it might be heaven on earth at the Bible School, but he found the Devil in there also!

Many are the battles, but great are the victories; many are the miraculous happenings, when we have to fight our way through.

No easy ride

But God is the God of the unstable road as well as the straight, sure grass turf. A young lady I heard of years ago was a new convert and very enthusiastic. She worked in a factory with a load of nicotine-smoking, cursing, dirty talking young girls. They laughed at her, made mockery of her, played tricks on her, tempted her with all sorts of sinful methods, but she grew strong in faith, gave good answers, and shone for Jesus. She became a good character, beaming, happy, reliable, honest, and her workmates really grew to love her, admire her – and some even followed her.

But then she left the factory, to go and work at the Salvation Army headquarters, all among Christians. But after a little period, she fell away and backslid. She withered and died in the hothouse, but she thrived and grew in the hell-house!

Pub regulars welcome gospel

So many people crowded into the Church of England parish church in Bow. The news soon spread of sick being carried in and then running out, the blind seeing, people suffering years with a malady were going home to their husbands fit and well, no longer crawling along to the shops, no longer taking an hour to get out of bed in the morning with the pain so immense. Soon the talk of the many public houses of Bow's East End was the miracles of Christ.

The vicar, a lady, who had hired out her large, empty Anglican sanctuary to the Black Pentecostal church and pastor, looked out of the manse window. Instead of the normal four or five coming along at the last minute in a church seating 250–400, large crowds were queuing up to get in. This was unknown in a tough East End parish. Fits of jealousy overcame her. The evil one called Satan took advantage of her fleshly outlook on the matter. Suddenly, after three days of revival that was the talk of public houses, of the huge tenement flats, of the docks and of the working class population, she suddenly cancelled the hall hiring, withdrew the keys, and was prepared to leave the evangelist, his team, the good Pentecostal members who had paid for the hall and worked so hard and prayed for many nights over the preceding months, she was prepared to leave us all, plus hundreds of sinners struggling to get into the church to hear the gospel, outside on the road, with nothing!

It was unbelievable; it was heartless – but that is how some of the clergy and some of the Christian Church are in UK today!

I set out to walk around the pubs. Everywhere men shook my hands, gratitude was overflowing for the many children, adults and old people miraculously healed by Jesus in the revival that had broken out. Every publican who had premises spacious enough offered us room to bring the people and hold a service! As on the day Christ came from glory, the Church had pushed Him outside to be born in an inn – in a pub! They were turning Him away again. But even if we had two or three services, the biggest pub guest room or billiards room would not take the numbers. But how gratifying that pub regulars were welcoming Christ and His gospel!

Finally we made a phone call to the Archbishop's Palace, and I warned the church dignitary of the dire consequences of such a move by the local vicar to deny the preaching of the gospel, also the legal implications. Soon an urgent call came from the Bishop of Stepney's solicitor, saying that the Palace was very sorry for what had happened, but we had a legal right, seeing the church building fee had been paid for, to be housed by the church. They had reached a compromise: we could use the spacious, empty church hall instead!

I replied, 'You've put Christ out of the sanctuary into market place!'

I accepted the offer, nervously but with relief. The church solicitor said, 'You know, you could have sued us for up to £10,000, but you made no threats, and acted only with the greatest grace!'

'God does not pay His debts always with money,' I said. 'I know our rights, but mercy is better than sacrifice.'

The vicar lost everything including God's blessing and peace. But a revival of great proportions hit that district, which is still having an impact. In blessing is opposition, but in opposition we find many new friends.

CHANGE IN LIFESTYLE

I was sitting on the veranda in the 75° heat in Cyprus, the table laden with delicious pomegranates, figs, myrtleberries, water melon and papaya, in my hand my favourite herb tea mixed with rosemary. The small, dark-skinned Greek businessman across the table shook gently and nervously. I had been invited to speak to this young man whose businesses had shot up across the island, who had made so much money working day and night. 'If I become a Christian it means I cannot cut corners, I cannot give bribes to get work. What would happen to my business...?'

I said to him, studying his open face and longing gaze, 'What difference do you find in your two friends here?' (they were the devout believers who had introduced me to this gentleman).

He looked at them. 'There is no one in Cyprus I would trust but them, no one would I put confidence in. Most would stab me in the back, but this man I know, his faith works.' A godly character, a truly honest lifestyle, had taken root and made impact on many lives.

I quoted the words of Jesus, 'Seek ye first the kingdom of God and all other things will be given you. You are searching, you are close at hand, don't miss it, ask Christ to be the first person in your life. He will change you from glory into glory.'

So that man was impacted and converted, like others, including some who were marvellously healed, through our mission in Cyprus.

IT'S A FIGHT TO SEE GOD IN ACTION AT TIMES

You take care of your character and God will take care of your reputation. As we call hungry people to eat and thirsty people to drink, there is a pull, a tug in our own hearts. On the noticeboard of a Bible College the words of a text urged the students to 'Give yourself as a living sacrifice.' Someone added a note: 'The only thing with a living sacrifice is you have to keep it from crawling off the altar!'

Go for God, be ready for the slurs, hits, kicks, stumblings, failings of others, the cat-calls. God is changing you, let nothing take your eyes from Jesus. We all have failings, plenty will point them out to us.

Press ahead, be willing to change. Mobsters, gangsters, Oscar-winning film stars, royalty, doctors, university professors, actors, chiefs of police, people from every walk of life are presenting themselves at our meetings, or asking for private audience, to hear the good news of our Lord Jesus Christ, because of the miracle changes in so many who flock to the revivals.

Say with God's Word, 'I love your commandments more than gold' (Acts 7:48). Again, 'Your promises have been well tested.'

God is changing us. The initiative is with God. Be ready for a fight, for as He does bless and purge and remake us, be sure there will be plenty of upset, obstacles, enflamers that stand in our way. Everything worth living for that is of such pure gold and incredible joy, is bound to be opposed.

– Epilogue –

GET UP AND GO

A Dutch clockmaker had just finished making two identical grandfather clocks. One of the clocks asked its maker how hard it would have to work and how many times it would have to tick during its life. The clockmaker replied that with 1,800 ticks per hour, the total number of ticks would be many millions. The clock thought about this, then worried about it for a long time, and then died of anxiety, coming to a complete stop! The other clock decided not to ask too many questions and not to look too far ahead. Instead it would live one day at a time and just tick away quietly, facing the minutes and hours as they came. The clock lasted for hundreds of years, keeping perfect time!

The well-known gospel song goes:

> One day at a time, sweet Jesus ...
> That's all I'm asking of You ...
> Just give me the strength to do every day
> What I have to do.

To know God's action – God's miracles, to climb mountains, bring down giants, achieve the incredible, you must – *start and stick at it*!

BEGIN!

In the first verse of the Acts of the Apostles Luke writes, 'In my former book, Theophilus, I wrote about all that Jesus began to do and to teach...' Jesus *began* His great mission and task, and He *carried it through* to completion on the Cross. How often we talk about doing some task or project without ever actually beginning it.

John Masefield, a former British Poet Laureate, wrote:

> Sitting still and wishing
> Makes no person great;
> The good Lord sends the fishing,
> But you must dig the bait.

What's keeping you from starting? *Begin now* to:

- pursue a goal
- realize a dream
- execute a plan
- start a project
- grab an opportunity
- work at an idea
- tackle a problem
- make a decision

Maybe there is a lesson for us in the classical story of Ulysses, who had to sail between Scylla (a sea monster) and Charybdis (a whirlpool). To go too close to either meant certain death. Ulysses did the only thing he could do – he steered as near the middle as he could. He risked losing everything, but he came through triumphantly. That is just what we must do in life – we must begin, we must take a risk. We may lose something in the process, but it will be worth it. We must always go forward! Begin today to:

- uncover new opportunities
- discover lovely solutions
- overcome serious hindrances
- unwrap the exciting surprises which God has in store for you
- roll back the dark clouds until you see the glorious sunshine

I once knew a couple who went through a very hard time indeed. Their only child died soon after his birth, and his mother became seriously ill afterwards. The father himself was shattered by his experiences in the Second World War, and returned home to find himself facing immense difficulties. Both he and his wife were nervous wrecks and they had barely enough to live on. The couple began to contemplate suicide. But it was at that point that a neighbour looked in on them and told them he had an old handcart they could use if they wanted to. He suggested they might try collecting and selling junk. The couple stared at him listlessly, but then a flame of hope flickered in their hearts. Doing something, even collecting junk, was better than doing nothing and wasting away. So they began a little junk business. Slowly but steadily it grew, and they won back their health. Eventually they even adopted two children. It is so important to *begin*, even if we cannot see where it will lead us.

We must begin, we must get going. Like many teenage boys, Peter was very slow to get going. He just wouldn't get up in the morning. Also, he often came in late at night. So Dad had a serious chat with him. 'And remember,' he said in conclusion, 'it's the early bird that catches the worm.'

Peter pretended to be puzzled. 'But Dad, if the stupid worm hadn't been up so early, it would never have been caught by the bird!'

'Not at all, son,' said Dad, rallying magnificently. 'That worm was on its way home!'

Sir James Young Simpson pioneered the use of chloroform as an anaesthetic. He was criticized by ignorant medical men who said chloroform was harmful, by those who contended that it was immoral, and by religious people who claimed that its use interfered with divine laws. But he fought on, and he won in the end. All the world owes a debt of gratitude to this man, who wore himself out in serving humanity. As he was dying he asked a friend at his bedside how old he was.

'You're 56,' replied the friend.

'Oh, well...' murmured Simpson. 'I just wish I'd been busier ... I wish I had begun sooner.'

The old verse goes:

Begin today and do what you can,
Being what you are.
Shine like the glow-worm if you cannot be a star,
Work like a pulley if you cannot be a crane,
Be a wheel-greaser if you cannot drive the train.
Use your brain, by beginning again.

Begin with God, for your life is far better with Him in it. In Bunyan's *Pilgrim's Progress* it says, 'Christian slept till the break of day, then he awoke and sang ... and *began*...' I love that sentence, and I try to live it every day.

'In the beginning was the Word...' (John 1:1). Jesus was there at the beginning. He is the Great Initiator. He never misses an opportunity to reach out and take our requests and make them His own. He is always 'on the ball'. He is 'the Beginning and the End' (Revelation 21:6).

STICK AT IT!

A grandmother was talking to her six-year-old grandson. He told her that he had been running that afternoon in his school's Sports Day. She knew he wasn't very athletic, so she didn't ask him how he had done in case he was feeling ashamed about it. But in fact he wasn't upset at all, and proudly told her, 'I was the only one to come in last!' That boy had the right attitude – a spirit of optimism and persistence!

It's so important to persist and stick at things. I like this poem, called 'The Man Who Sticks':

The man who sticks has the sense to see
He can make himself what he wants to be;
If he'll get off his coat and pitch right in –
Why, the man who sticks can't help but win!

Here is another poem which speaks about persistence:

They say that you just can't accomplish this thing,
No matter how often you try it.
You've blundered and failed, but you know in your
bones,
You've grit and you mean to apply it.
If tempted to give up the fight one dark day,
It's certain you'll very soon rue it.
You'd better keep on keeping on ... keeping on
Until with a grin you just do it!

The philanthropist Samuel Warren once remarked, 'There are two kinds of persons in the world – those who think first of difficulties, and those who think first of the importance of accomplishment in spite of difficulties.' David Shepherd, the famous wildlife artist, once gave a demonstration of his painting technique on television. As he completed his picture he said, 'Well that's it, I think. Not that I'm really satisfied with it. I'm never satisfied. When you're satisfied you make no progress.' That's true not only of painting but also of the whole of life.

One of the most notable of the historical characters who triumphed over difficulties was the famous Greek orator Demosthenes, who lived in the fourth century before Christ. As a young man he wanted to be a politician, but he had a dreadful stammer, a weak voice and diseased lungs. However, he was determined to succeed. He cured his stammer by talking with pebbles in his mouth. He gave his voice greater strength by going to the seashore every day and shouting at the waves. His determination swept away all obstacles and so he became one of the greatest orators of all time. Even Winston Churchill copied him in some ways.

We must aim high and persist until we achieve our goals. As the poet Robert Browning said,

> Ah, but a man's reach should exceed his grasp,
> Or what's a heaven for?

Although it is some years since I read Bunyan's *Pilgrim's Progress* in its entirety, I often turn to it and re-read passages which have helped me in the past. One passage which I read when I am feeling a bit discouraged is one of the incidents in Interpreter's house. Christian is shown a fire burning in the grate. A man is constantly throwing water on it, but the fire continues to burn. The mystery is explained when Christian is taken to the next room where, through a hole behind the fireplace, another man is pouring oil, so keeping the fire burning. There are circumstances which 'dampen' our spirits and there are people who are 'wet blankets'. Sometimes people 'pour cold water' on our ideas and suggestions. But there is an antidote to all this. If our determination is strong enough, it will be a fire which will withstand any amount of discouragement.

The late Dr William Barclay told the story of a trainee London taxi driver who had to study the maps of the city until he knew them by heart. In his examination he was asked the shortest route between two particular points in the city. Because of the answer he gave he failed the test. The route he had in mind would have been very short but would have meant taking his taxi down a long flight of steps and through a passage wide enough only for pedestrians! Short cuts are not always what they seem. We should always keep in mind that most of the things in life which are really worth having come to us only through patience and effort. Let's not be deluded by life's short cuts. It's persistence that wins in the end:

> One word won't tell folk who you are –
> You've got to keep on talking;
> One step won't take you very far –
> You've got to keep on walking;
> One inch won't make you very tall –
> You've got to keep on growing;
> One trip to church won't tell you all –
> You've got to keep on going.

As Paul advised, 'Praying always ... in the spirit, being watchful ... to this end *with all perseverance*' (Ephesians 6:18). I like this old Scottish proverb: 'Don't give up when the clouds surround you – it might be a sign that you're climbing higher!'

Paul Brickhill's book *Reach for the Sky* tells the inspiring story of the life of Group Captain Douglas Bader. He had lost both his legs in a plane crash and was hovering between life and death in a hospital bed. He happened to hear someone in the corridor outside his room telling someone else to be quiet. 'There's a boy dying in there,' the person said. The shock of those words awoke in him a fierce determination to live. From that moment he fought his way back to life. He went on fighting, and eventually became a distinguished RAF hero in the Battle of Britain. His story is a lesson to us all on the power of sheer determination.

In difficult times determination is all-important:

When everything is wrong as wrong,
And you yourself are wrong side out;
When folk or things just make you want
To weep alone, or loudly shout;
For goodness sake count up to ten,
Then grit your teeth and start again.

One must press through and turn disasters and difficulties into triumphs. Gideon did just that. In the power of the Spirit of God he took on a fierce, well-armed and numerous enemy with only 300 men and a few lamps and empty jars – and he overcame them and won the day!

One must press on and never quit. The old verse goes:

Something comes and hits you hard,
Knocks you flat as flat;
Makes you sorry for yourself –
Nasty business, that.

Will you keep on lying there,
Crushed by grief or pain?
Guess you'll stir yourself somehow
And get up again!

A well-known journalist wrote some years ago about an incident in his childhood:

When I was a schoolboy aged about nine, my home was about two miles from school. Cycling there on a bright sunny morning was easy as pie, because the road was downhill almost all the way. Coming home, however, was another story – pedalling uphill was a tiring job.

One winter's day I cycled home after darkness had fallen. Street lamps were very few and far between. I pedalled on and on till suddenly I stopped short. A street lamp at a corner lit up my house ... I had arrived sooner than expected, less tired than before. And then, very puzzled, I realized what had happened. I'd been pedalling into the darkness, seeing only a few square yards of what looked like a flat road picked out by the short, weak beam of my cycle lamp.

Even at the early age of nine I realized that if you don't keep looking up the hill, climbing it is easier.

This story shows that the way in which we look at our troubles and trials is of great importance. If we want to look at trouble we should use opera glasses, and use them the wrong way round. Then it will look very small indeed!

God has promised to help us in our 'downs', in our times of trouble: 'The Lord is a refuge for the oppressed, a stronghold in times of trouble' (Psalm 9:9). How good it is to be able to trust a higher power so completely with one's life!

It is important not only to begin well, but to overcome well! As the King in *Alice in Wonderland* said, 'Begin at the beginning ... and go on till you come to the end.'

Don't be an undergoer but an overcomer!
Don't cash in – cast out into the deep.
Not bitter but better,
not resisting but receiving,
not indifferent but decisive,
not lukewarm but burning with enthusiasm,
not destructive but a developer,
not give in – but get up!
Not scars but stars,
not outrage but c-ourage,
not disappointment but His-appointment,
not co-existing with evil – but opposing evil,
not if-I-can, but how-I-can,
not security but daring,
not dishonest but uncorrupted,
not the road of worry and stress but the life of peace
and rest,
not a mundane rat-race and dreary life-style –
but faith and a higher Christian mile!

Take to heart the following words – live them, practise
them, work at them, express them:

Whatever be your mood – don't be rude.
Whatever comes your way – please be brave.
Whatever cares you know – let them go.
Whatever path you choose – quit the blues.
Whatever be the test – do your best.
Whatever be the strain – don't complain.
To make life more worthwhile, whatever happens.
GET UP AND GO – AND STAY THROUGH TO
THE GOAL!

The poem tells us:

> If a trouble hits you hard
> You can weep all day,
> Moan and groan until you're ill –
> Sigh your soul away.
> Better far to battle on,
> Wear a gallant smile,
> Keep on somehow – God knows how –
> Mile on weary mile ...
> Till you come home to joy at last,
> All your worries long since past!

Yes, that's good advice. Keep soldiering on with God, and remember what His Word says, 'Do not be faint-hearted or afraid ... For the Lord your God is the one who goes with you' (Deuteronomy 20:3,4).

John Ruskin put it, 'The highest reward for a person's toil is not what they get for it, but what they become by it.' Dolly Parton's favourite saying is, 'The way I see it, if you want the rainbow, you gotta put up with the rain.'

The Chinese proverb says, 'The man who removes a mountain begins by carrying away small stones.' *Start where you are.* 'I never see God acting like this, this is the first time I've seen miracles ... why doesn't it happen in our church?' So often we hear such statements. But we have to start with moving the small hindrances, doing the tiny task, preparing ourselves to be used. Small words, tiny kind acts, sensitive conversation. Mother Teresa said, 'Kind words can be small and short and easy to speak, but their echoes are truly endless.'

Some people make excuses, or just think they are past it with their age. 'I'm too old, my day is done, I'm over the hill...' This is a trick of the mind, or our enemy Satan, or an idea given by the churches' over-emphasis on youth activities today. Some of the greatest revivals are happening among older people, are being led by elderly folk. Wigglesworth never started till he was 55 years old, and his most effective years were when he was 60–70 years old. Here is the golden opportunity.

Older people praying maturely, positive, earnestly, can lead the youth who know so little onto the road of awakening and power. 'In the last days I will pour out my spirit on all flesh ... the old men shall dream...' No matter what our age, God is calling us to go out and do! Franklin Roosevelt said, 'A radical man is one who has both feet planted firmly in the air.'

Turn from your problems. Nothing lasts forever – not even your troubles. Time is short, He is calling for your dedication. *Go and change things*. Let God act through you. Leo Kennedy said, 'The surest way to be late is to have plenty of time!' Know time is short – don't be late and miss it. Start small. Work little mira-cles, then go on to take mountains, nations, the whole world for Jesus. Milton Berle wrote, 'If opportunity doesn't knock, build a door.'

Success is more than aptitude, it's attitude!

START TODAY!

Sir William Osler put it: 'The best preparation for tomorrow is to do today's work superbly well.'

'Everything that is done in the world is done by hope,' said Martin Luther.

In a Bulgarian household where a Westerner was staying, the young daughter was sewing day and night. The visitor said, 'Don't you get tired of sewing, eternally sewing?'

She replied, 'No, I do it in love – it's my wedding dress!'

Before one of his long campaigns, Alexander the Great gave away everything that he possessed. One friend said, 'But you are keeping nothing for yourself!'

'Oh yes I am,' he said, 'I have kept my hopes!'

GET UP AND GO!

The secret of success is to start from scratch and keep on scratching. Don't let your 'going through' stop your 'going to'! Something in us is so impatient at times. Follow your vision, move forward, take time, but press on. See – seek – achieve. Your goal, your vision is your future. 'The steps of a good man are ordered by the Lord: and he delighteth in his way' (Proverbs 37:23).

Your persistency, your vision, gives you hope. A man who has no vision, no aim, no persistent goal, no dreams – has no wings! Persistent vision is personal, it makes you live a selective life. Break new ground. He who walks nowhere except where he sees others' footprints will make no discoveries. God will ask you in eternity, 'Did you follow my plan? Did you persist – get up and go?'

Enemies will oppose you, your friends will either stretch your vision or choke your dreams. Persist:

people can steal your coat of many colours, but no one can take your God-given dream away. Nothing can stop a man with the right attitude pursuing his goal. 'I will not be afraid of tens of thousands of people, that have set themselves against me round about' (Psalm 3:6).

It is not the man with a motive, but the one with a purpose who prevails. Go for that plan, that divine purpose. 'When my heart is overwhelmed, lead me to the rock that is higher than I' (Psalm 61:2).

FIND PURPOSE – FOLLOW IT – FULFIL IT

There is no mistake as great as not going on. Put your best foot forward. Nothing is built on good intentions. 'For as many as are led by the Spirit of God, they are the sons of God' (Romans 8:14).

Most men exchange their lives for much too little, because they have no plan. 'Friends, I forget what is behind me, I struggle for what is ahead, I run towards the goal, that I may win the prize of being called ... God will make it clear to you, we must keep going in the direction that we are now headed' (Philippians 3:14).

God's plan is for you to win in every facet of your life. Persistent vision will help you possess your tomorrow 'today'. Success is a journey not a destination. Plan, therefore – don't trust your future to the haphazard. The notion that whatever comes or turns up will do – 'whatever will be will be' – is fatalism. Leave it not to chance happenings. God will drop His plans, His goals, His inspiration, His ideas, His visions into your spirit – as you plan for Him, He will plan for you!

'Now thanks be to God who always causes us to triumph in Christ.' 'Listen to what the Spirit is saying to the churches, to everyone who wins the victory, I will give him some of the hidden food ... I will give each one a new name' (Revelation 2:7). Christ is never defeated, He never sponsors flops. With power and great glory He will overcome all things. Stay in the game: Christ is victorious, He is coming again.

In the third century Tertullian, the early Church Father, was arrested for being a Christian by the reigning emperor. They said, 'We will cut you into 1,000 pieces unless you deny that Jesus Christ is Lord!'

He responded, 'You may cut me into 10,000 pieces and throw me to the lions, and each piece will cry out "Jesus Christ is Lord!"'

May we persist with bringing this world the answer, the vision, the only hope, and that is the crucifixion and atonement of Jesus Christ. 'I will never brag about anything except the Cross of our Lord' (Galatians 6:14).

Take away the Cross and the Bible is a dark book. It would still be of great interest, curious and wonderful, but of no real use. Christ crucified is the foundation of the whole volume of Scripture. Christianity without a Cross, a resurrection, is not supernatural. All the works of God recorded in this book, and all His works since the foundation of the world, and ever to be yet performed, are centred in the precious Blood, wounds, suffering, atoning sacrifice of Christ. God wants you no longer tossed to and fro, and shoved about by every new idea or wind of doctrine. God puts no premium on ignorance. Rise to it, see the works of God in your life.

Exercise your God-given rights; do not pass through this life, unfruitful, traditional, seeing what ordinary men and women see: go the extra mile, see the acts of the apostles' power brought to the Church *today*!

Get up and go! Move on, work at it, pass on, 'They that wait upon the Lord shall renew their strength'. The original translation is, 'Those expecting God will pass on to power.' Only a person who hungers for a higher level can reach it.

One man said to me, 'My life is hit and miss.'

I said, 'That's why you are always missing it!'

Have direction, focus, purpose, drive – 'We look not at things which are seen but at things which we do not see' (2 Corinthians 4:18).

Once I pastored a church of nine people in a tiny country town in Lincolnshire. My attic was my office. God gave me a plan, and soon miracles began to flow. I went through the tiny villages preaching, healing the sick, holding revival meetings. Halls became crammed, new churches were born, God promoted me. Since then I have had an international crusade office, I have preached in nearly 50 countries of the world, been on TV and radio programmes worldwide, and taken the gospel to millions.

Wishers wish and wish and never do anything. *Complainers* always have somebody else to blame because they never make it. *Sleepwalkers* miss the train always by that one minute. But '*doers*' – come hail, snow, rain, storm or sunshine, they do not move away from God and His Word. They are always the winners – why? Because they get up and go!

God is in action. We are on our way, the deliverance

has come. Reach out and make your connection. Reach out and touch His hand; God is marching us to the sunset, not to the dawn!

Life is not a dress rehearsal. Every day is an opening night – a challenge to live, to possess your tomorrow today! Be diligent in work. Don't give up – 'No more forsaken and neither desolate ... but you shall be called "Beulah". For the Lord delighteth in you' (Isaiah 6:4). Daniel was able to declare, 'God has given me victory' (Daniel 6).

It's time to move on, time to move from where you are to where you want to be. 'The Lord our God spake unto us ... saying, 'You have dwelt long enough in this mount' (Deuteronomy 1:6).

'What your hands find to do – do with all your might.' Let the wisdom of God, the abilities of God, the giftings of God, and the power of God operate in you. Don't look back, many are always talking about the victories of the past. One pastor I was going to preach for in a large church in the north of Scotland introduced me by saying that all the preachers who come through to speak, either dwell on the future events – prophetic words – or the past – that is, history – then he declared, 'This preacher will tell you what God is doing *now*, at this time!'

God wants you to go forward now, to climb your mountains, cross your uncrossable seas, pass through your storms, leap over your hurdles. Stay on till you win.

God said, 'Your remembrance is before me.' God is divine action, God is new, God is fresh, God is real. Go and win.

The queen bee, an expert has told us, in its make-up and design should not be able to fly. It defies the rules of the bird family, the laws of aeronautics. According to all the theory and ideas it just cannot leave the ground. But the queen bee does not know the law of aeronautics – so she flies!

Get up and go! God in action is inspiring us to bring the world back to Him, back to the Ten Commandments, back to our Lord Jesus Christ, back to hope again!

I like the Apostle Paul's words: 'I can't impress this on you too strongly, God is looking over your shoulder ... He is about to break into the open with His rule, so proclaim the message with intensity; keep on your watch ... challenge ... urge your people, don't ever quit, keep it simple ... accept the hard times along with the good, *keep the message alive* ... do a thorough job ... this is the race worth running' (2 Timothy 4:1–9 *The Message*).

Rise up new creature! Stand tall for Jesus and look around you: you are in the kingdom of His dear Son. Assault the kingdom of Satan in Jesus' Name. Millions wait for the message of grace and mercy. Millions await the sound of your footsteps coming to their rescue with the gospel.

Now you know. You will never be the same again. Nothing can stop you. Time is flying and men are dying – the King's business requires haste!

GET UP AND GO – AND YOU WILL FIND THE GOD OF ACTION GOES WITH YOU!

Seeing 'God in Action' in the UK Today

Due to the overwhelming response of thousands to the present awakening in the United Kingdom, through the commitment to God's guidance of the Rev. Melvin Banks, his family and their team, he personally or one of his family would be happy to make themselves available to visit your town, city, suburb, church or fellowship, in order to share these amazing stories and testimonies. Please contact the address given below.

The Rev. Melvin Banks welcomes letters, invitations and prayer requests for you or your loved ones.

Also available are other books by Melvin Banks, published by HarperCollins, also videos, audio tapes and free literature. For the latest news of the Revival send a stamped addressed envelope to:

The Rev. Melvin Banks
International Crusade Office
44 Monks Way
Chippenham
Wiltshire
SN15 3TT
England
Telephone: (01249) 655712

OTHER BOOKS BY MELVIN BANKS

Healing Secrets
The Greatest Miracle of All
Power for Living
Is Anything Too Hard for God?
Wind of Fire
With God All Things are Possible
Expect a Miracle
Lay Hold of God's Power
Prayer Power